UNMASKING
THE
ADMINISTRATIVE
STATE

UNMASKING THE ADMINISTRATIVE STATE

The Crisis of American Politics in the Twenty-First Century

JOHN MARINI

Edited by Ken Masugi

New York • London

First American edition published in 2019 by Encounter Books,
an activity of Encounter for Culture and Education, Inc.,
a nonprofit, tax exempt corporation.
Encounter Books website address: www.encounterbooks.com

Manufactured in the United States and printed on
acid-free paper. The paper used in this publication meets
the minimum requirements of ANSI/NISO Z39.48-1992
(R 1997) (Permanence of Paper).

FIRST AMERICAN EDITION

LIBRARY OF CONGRESS CATALOGING-IN-PUBLICATION DATA
Names: Marini, John A., author. | Masugi, Ken, editor.
Title: Unmasking the administrative state : the crisis of
American politics in the twenty-first century / by John Marini ; edited By Ken Masugi.
Description: New York : Encounter Books, [2019] |
Includes bibliographical references and index.
Identifiers: LCCN 2018024187 (print) | LCCN 2018038056 (ebook) |
ISBN 9781641770248 (ebook) | ISBN 9781641770231 |
ISBN 9781641770231q(hardcover :qalk. paper)
Subjects: LCSH: Bureaucracy—United States. | Political culture—United
States. | United States—Politics and government.
Classification: LCC JK421 (ebook) | LCC JK421 .M3459 20189 (print) |
DDC 320.973—dc23
LC record available at https://lccn.loc.gov/2018024187
Interior page design and composition: BooksByBruce.com

For Nancy and Francesca

CONTENTS

PART ONE

THE TRIUMPH OF THE ADMINISTRATIVE STATE OVER THE CONSTITUTION

By Ken Masugi

In comments at the Heritage Foundation in October 2016, Justice Clarence Thomas twice mentioned what he termed his first "mentors" on the American Constitution, John Marini and me. We worked for him back in the late 1980s, when he was chairman of the Equal Employment Opportunity Commission. Given the occasion—a celebration of Justice Thomas's twenty-five years on the Supreme Court and his widespread (and deserved) recognition as its most steadfast and principled conservative—it might be useful for those concerned about constitutionalism and the court to better understand why Thomas might have emphasized two obscure academics, neither lawyers, as his first constitutional guides. In talks about his autobiography he explained that instead of speechwriters, he brought onto his staff political theorists who might discuss with him fundamental political principles of America and the West, such as liberty, natural law, and limited government, which support an originalist understanding of the Constitution.

Marini is the principal advocate of the notion that the "administrative state" has usurped Congress and the presidency and upset the separation of powers. In sum, the twentieth-century Congress, followed by its most recent successors, has surrendered its powers to the executive branch and been satisfied to pass hollow legislation that confers the real lawmaking powers on the unelected bureaucracy and judiciary. These institutions and, of course, ubiquitous lawyers have all come through the liberal academy—its law schools and political science and policy programs.

Marini, now a professor at the University of Nevada, Reno, first articulated this radical notion at Claremont Graduate School back in the 1970s and has continued to develop it, by expounding on the basic constitutional concepts of the separation of powers and federalism. He has also applied the notion of the administrative state to policy issues such as the budget, civil rights, and immigration. He has argued that frustration with the administrative state and the policies it encourages may explain the rise of Donald Trump. Marini's concept of the administrative state is far more radical, persuasive, and significant than similar notions favored by such profound commentators as Christopher DeMuth, Michael Greve, and Philip Hamburger. Another representative of this conservative viewpoint, columnist George Will, recently elaborated, in a 2015 op-ed for the *Washington Post*, how he believes that Thomas's objection to the administrative state lies in the issue of the delegation of congressional powers to the executive—an important issue, but in fact it is neither Thomas's nor Marini's ultimate concern. Neither Will nor others, such as Senator Ben Sasse, seem to accept that the administrative state represents a change of regime, an actual overthrow of the Constitution of 1787. Constitutional politics therefore requires a rethinking of politics, and thus requires a candidate on the order of Donald Trump, who comes from outside the system created by the administrative state.

Marini came to then-Chairman Thomas's attention when Thomas asked me to recommend some others who might also serve as special assistants. I forwarded him a copy of a Marini paper on the administrative state's overthrow of Congress's constitutional functions. He returned it to me with bold writing on top: "I must see Marini!!"

Never having worked in Washington, Marini deduced his notion of an unconstitutional counterstate from diverse intellectual sources, including Aristotle, *The Federalist*, Lincoln, and Tocqueville, as well as their interpreters, such as Leo Strauss and his students, principally Harry Jaffa. He took account of the radical assaults on constitutional government demanded by Rousseau and, above all, Hegel. The American Progressive progeny of the latter two includes primarily obscure Progressive Era political scientists and journalists; the most famous is President Woodrow Wilson. By working through their thinking, plus that of more recent political scientists, Marini concluded in theory what Thomas, who had once worked as an assistant in the Senate and in the Department of Education, learned through painful practice: republican government and the rule of law have succumbed to the current political arrangements, which have been devised by and for the benefit of Progressives. Marini has presented many of the foundational ideas for his arguments about the administrative state in three books: *The Politics of Budget Control*,[1] whose bland title masks the revolutionary argument it makes; a coedited book, *The Imperial Congress*,[2] and his coedited book on Progressivism, *The Progressive Revolution in Politics and Political Science*.[3] This book's selection includes other essays and papers written or delivered over the course of Marini's career, all of which advance arguments about the development, structure, and effects of the administrative state. The first three essays in the introductory section provide an overview of the book's major themes, in particular, Marini's explanation of the administrative state, his argument that appeals to the Constitution may no longer address the political crisis of our time, and his contention that Trump's 2016 presidential campaign illustrated the administrative state's effects on the American character.

In a 2016 speech included in this collection Marini defends a dying constitutionalism against Washington and global elites and notes Trump's plea for a more assertive citizenship:

In the modern administrative state, the power of government is unlimited, and the rights of citizens, and the rule of law, itself rests on a precarious ground. For if the government alone creates and confers rights, the constitution can no longer limit the power of government, nor can it protect the civil and religious liberty of its citizens.

Trump has established his candidacy on the basis of an implicit understanding that America is in the midst of a crisis. Those who oppose him deny the seriousness of the crisis and see Trump himself as the greatest danger.[4]

This makes sense of Trump's political strategy—his assault on the elites of both parties and the media, his disdain for experts and preference for successful practitioners, his mannerisms, and his appeal for a more comprehensive notion of the common good. And it puts his immigration, trade, and national security policies in a new light. A politics of citizenship may not yet be dead. But to see the challenges such a revolutionary endeavor would require points us to the need to understand the administrative state.

Marini's prescience on the administrative state illuminates an array of enduring, fundamental questions about America—on contemporary politics, the rise of Progressivism, the significance of Lincoln and the Civil War, and the meaning of the founding of America. The essays assembled here are a series of provocations on such topics and were selected by Marini and me; I have contributed the introductions to each section. We acknowledge the invaluable assistance of Bruno Cortes, Mickey Craig, and Douglas Jeffrey of Hillsdale College in the preparation of the manuscripts. For their abiding influence, John Marini and I thank our teachers, colleagues, and families. This book was made possible by the constant support of President Ryan Williams and the Claremont Institute, Ben Judge, Ben Weingarten, and, above all, Tom Klingenstein.

Hunting the Administrative State

I WANT TO THANK the Claremont Institute and Brian Kennedy for this award, the 2011 Salvatori Prize in the American Founding.... I finished my doctoral dissertation, "The Politics of Budget Control," at Claremont Graduate School the year before the Claremont Institute was established. You could say I have followed the progress of the Institute from its origin. As the Institute grew I began to participate in some of its regular programs. The Institute was committed to a serious study of statesmanship and political philosophy, thereby hoping to reestablish a theoretical ground for an understanding of the principles of the American Founding. I like to think that my scholarship was useful in elucidating some of the problems that had threatened, and even undermined, the principles of our founding, the principles of human equality and liberty.

My work, begun nearly forty years ago, focused on the problem and danger of centralized administration. At that time, the concept of the administrative state was not yet in common usage. My dissertation was subtitled "An Analysis of the Impact of Centralized Administration on the Separation of Powers." My research was animated by an awareness that the key institutions of the American government were not functioning in the way they were intended. It seemed as though the growth of the administrative functions of government had undermined the separation

5

of powers and prepared the way for unlimited power in the national institutions.

The political practice of modern centralized governments, therefore, seemed to tend almost inexorably in the direction of what Tocqueville had called centralized administration. He was convinced that this was the new form of despotism that threatened democratic societies. The obsessive concern with administrative detail would render democratic man incapable of self-government.

As Tocqueville noted,

> One forgets that it is above all in details that it is dangerous to enslave men. For myself, I would be brought to believe freedom less necessary in great things than in lesser ones if I thought that one could ever be assured of the one without possessing the other.... In vain you will charge these same citizens, whom you have rendered so dependent on the central power, with choosing the representatives of this power from time to time; that use of their free will, so important but so brief and so rare, will not prevent them from losing little by little the faculty of thinking, feeling, and acting by themselves, and thus from gradually falling below the level of humanity.... I add that they will soon become incapable of exercising the great, unique privilege that remains to them.... If one must conduct small affairs in which simple good sense can suffice, they determine that citizens are incapable of it; if it is a question of the government of the whole state, they entrust immense prerogatives to these citizens; they make them alternately the playthings of the sovereign and its masters, more than kings and less than men.... It is in fact difficult to conceive how men who have entirely renounced the habit of directing themselves could succeed at choosing well those who will lead them; and one will not make anyone believe that a liberal, energetic, and wise government can ever issue from the suffrage of a people of servants.[1]

Even before the middle of the twentieth century, it was becoming clear that the centralized administrative state led in principle to the universal and homogeneous state. The rational, or administrative, state and its social science, although incapable of recognizing tyranny, had opened up the prospect of the greatest tyranny of all. As Leo Strauss observed, "We are now brought face to face with a tyranny which holds out the threat of becoming, thanks to 'the conquest of nature' and in particular human nature, what no earlier tyranny ever became: perpetual and universal."[2]

It seemed that modern tyranny was linked to a rejection of nature and natural right. The political moderation of constitutional democracy was a consequence of a philosophy of government that was grounded in natural reason and the laws of nature. In his defense of constitutionalism, Leo Strauss noted, "it would not be difficult to show that... liberal or constitutional democracy comes closer to what the classics demanded than any alternative that is viable in our age."[3] As Strauss indicated, "According to the classics, the best constitution is a contrivance of reason, i.e., of conscious activity or of planning on the part of an individual or of a few individuals. It is in accordance with nature, or it is a natural order, since it fulfills to the highest degree the requirements of the perfection of human nature, or since its structure imitates the pattern of nature."[4] The most natural and reasonable political order or regime, in the classical sense of the term, is founded upon a political theory of constitutionalism or limited government. The American Constitution, understood in light of the principles of the Declaration of Independence, created such a regime based on modern principles of political thought.

In its American origins, administration was understood to be subordinate to a political theory of liberal constitutionalism. It had no constitutional authority in a regime that had established a limited government, one that distinguished the public and private sphere, the state and civil society. Moreover, politics and administration remained decentralized; the states and local governments were vibrant centers of political life. Most importantly, the practice of government was defined by its theory; the means were subordinate to the ends of republican government. See the Declaration of Independence. Consequently, administration was thought to be a function of practical reason or prudence, not, as it came to be in the post–Progressive Era, an objective or applied science, the instrumental rationality required in the service of the modern state. However, prudence as a political virtue required the capacity to take into account actual circumstances in light of an end. In political life, as James Madison insisted, the end is justice, or the best regime possible under the conditions that prevail. Constitutional regimes had circumscribed the powers of government, because the ends of politics were limited to the protection of the natural rights of man. That limitation was predicated upon recognition of the fact that the realm of the political does not encompass the whole range of human existence.

By attempting to understand the theoretical origins of the administrative state, it was necessary to examine the fundamental transformation in American politics brought about by the intellectual and political victory of Progressivism. It revealed a complete break with the American Founding and a total rejection of constitutionalism. It was based upon a philosophy of History. The political thought that laid the foundations of the modern administrative state—and legitimized its political practice—rested on the denial of a natural standard of political right. The understanding of nature, revealed by metaphysical reason, could not remain the ground of political right once the human mind had made the discovery of the rationality of the historical process. Thus, Hegel insisted that "the science of the state is to be nothing other than the endeavor to apprehend and portray the state as something inherently rational."[5] The Progressives in America accepted the Hegelian assumption that "the general dividing line between constitutions is between those that are based on nature and those based on freedom of the will."[6] Consequently, there could be no higher authority than the will of the sovereign people. In short, the modern administrative state was meant to establish the rational or technical means to carry out the will of the people. It required unlimited power in the state, and it was meant to replace constitutionalism or limited government.

The state, and modern social science, purports to have the capacity to institutionalize rationality in the service of will through utilization of a universal class, the bureaucracy. Paradoxically, this rationality is to be achieved through the efforts of that class of persons who are devoid of a personal passion for power. Their very disinterestedness would ensure the kind of independence and objectivity necessary to carry out the will of the people. Philosophy of History had distorted the relationship between theory and practice; practice had provided the basis for theory, and theory subsequently distorted the understanding of practice. There could be no principled or autonomous ground, in reason or nature, from which to make prudential judgments regarding politics. As a result, the practice of politics could not be moderated by any standard whatsoever. The twentieth century bore witness to the demise of moderation in politics and revealed the rise of those tyrannies spawned by the triumph of will.

The great thinkers of the nineteenth century, Strauss showed, had rejected nature as a standard of justice. They had all, in one form or another, embraced philosophy of History. Pointing specifically to the failures of Marx and Nietzsche, Strauss once again recognized the importance of prudence and moderation in political life: "But perhaps one can say that their grandiose failures make it easier for us who have experienced those failures to understand again the old saying that wisdom cannot be separated from moderation and hence to understand that wisdom requires unhesitating loyalty to a decent constitution and even to the cause of constitutionalism. Moderation will protect us against the twin dangers of visionary expectations from politics and unmanly contempt for politics."[7]

In the twentieth century, the rational administrative structures that have become dominant in the modern state are the product of "visionary expectations from politics." At the same time, they reflect in their neutral bureaucracies, an "unmanly contempt for politics," an indulgence that has accompanied the belief that partisanship has ended and rational rule has begun. Constitutional government does not induce visionary expectations from government, nor is it contemptuous of politics. It is limited government. It is moderated by a rootedness in nature, which requires a reasonable and realistic understanding of the relationship of theory and practice, of ends and means. Consequently, prudence, not science, is the virtue that is paramount in terms of understanding political practice. But prudence is necessarily concerned with means. It presupposes the possibility of moral virtue to direct men to the right, or good, ends.

Thus, the political theory of constitutionalism could not acquiesce in the view that good or even "rational" administration can replace the necessity for prudence in politics. This is so because man has not, and perhaps cannot, become fully wise concerning politics. Furthermore, technical rationality, or science, cannot replace the necessity of justice. Hence, not the most efficient nor enlightened bureaucracy could legitimately relieve the people of the responsibility of governing themselves. In a constitutional republic, unlike the theological regimes that preceded it, the title to rule could not be divine knowledge nor could it be the rational, or scientific, knowledge implicit in the idea of the modern state. Only limited government is compatible with moderation in politics.

This reminds us of the mission of the Claremont Institute: to "restore the principles of the American Founding to their rightful, preeminent authority in our national life." It has not been easy to restore an understanding of those principles, let alone reestablish their authority, in our national life. In our time, the likely defenders of constitutional government are those who love the country, mostly because it is their country. They recognize that the Constitution is responsible for the greatness of their country. However, there are those who think the country is fundamentally unjust. They believe the Constitution is responsible for its failure to achieve social justice. They believe that the purpose of the administrative state is the progressive transformation of society on behalf of will, or consciousness of what they understand as freedom. Unfortunately, neither its defenders nor its opponents understand the natural and rational foundation of constitutional government. Hence, the principles that establish the goodness, or justice, of limited government are without theoretical or political defense.

However, it is still possible to take political advantage of those who love the country. Although James Madison insisted in *Federalist* 49, "it is the reason alone, of the public that ought to control and regulate the government. The passions ought to be regulated by the government." He knew that "the most rational government will not find it a superfluous advantage to have the prejudices of the community on its side." The only exception would be in a nation of philosophers, where "a reverence for the laws would be sufficiently inculcated by the voice of an enlightened reason." He knew no such nation existed. But he would have insisted, nonetheless, that constitutionalism requires an enlightened or rational defense of free and limited government (*see Federalist* 49). Hence, he recognized the importance of a liberal education in terms of perpetuating an understanding of the principles of nature and reason. He was confident, as Washington had been, that the "foundation of our Empire was not laid in the gloomy age of Ignorance and Superstition, but at an Epocha when the rights of mankind were better understood and more clearly defined, than at any former period, the researches of the human mind, after social happiness, have been carried to a great extent, the Treasures of knowledge, acquired by the labours of Philosophers, Sages and Legislatures, through a long succession of years, are laid open for our use, and their collected wisdom may be happily applied in the Establishment of our forms of Government."[8]

Neither Washington nor Madison could have known that the so-called enlightened or learned in the academy and university would turn against "those treasures of knowledge" of which Washington had spoken. The self-destruction of reason was a product of a later Western philosophy of History itself. Indeed, modern education, influenced by that thought, has nearly succeeded in legitimizing the administrative state. In the process, it has helped to undermine the regime of civil and religious liberty. And the rights of man rest precariously in the hands of increasingly immoderate and unstable governments. We have learned in the twentieth century, contrary to the teaching of the Progressives, that tyranny is not a thing of the past.

Thus, I am certain the Claremont Institute will continue to fight to restore the principles of the founding. It will fight not merely because it wants to win, but because it deserves to win, and not for ourselves alone, but for our posterity. Even if it fails to persuade this generation of the goodness of the principles inherent in constitutionalism and is unable to convince the people of the potential danger of the tyranny inherent in the administrative state, perhaps, it can light the way for those in the future who in darker days can understand it because they will have experienced it. Then the work of the Institute might resonate with those who will, perhaps, once again be open to the restoration of the principles of the founding. In that time, it will be possible, once again, to restore their authority, because it will be easier to understand the goodness or justice of those principles.

2

Our Abandoned Constitution

AMERICA HAS A PROBLEM, not because of our Constitution but because constitutionalism as a theoretical doctrine is no longer meaningful in our politics.[1] A constitution is only meaningful if its principles, which authorize government, are understood to be permanent and unchangeable, in contrast to the statute laws made by government that alter with circumstances and changing political requirements of each generation. If a written constitution is to have any meaning, it must have a rational or theoretical ground that distinguishes it from government. When the principles that establish the legitimacy of the constitution are understood to be changeable, are forgotten, or are denied, the constitution can no longer impose limits on the power of government. In that case, government itself will determine the conditions of the social compact and become the arbiter of the rights of individuals. When that transformation occurred, as it did in the twentieth century, the sovereignty of the people, established by the Constitution, was replaced by the sovereignty of government, understood in terms of the modern concept of the rational or administrative state. It was a theoretical doctrine, the philosophy of History, that effected this transformation and established the intellectual and moral foundations of progressive politics.

Established on the foundation of natural rights, constitutionalism has been steadily undermined by the acceptance of the new doctrine of History. The Progressive movement, which is the political instrument of that theoretical revolution, had as its fundamental purpose the destruction of the political and moral authority of the US Constitution. Because of the success of the Progressive movement, contemporary American politics is animated by a political theory denying permanent principles of right derived from nature and reason. In exposing the theoretical roots of Progressivism and the liberalism it has spawned, it is possible to reveal the difference between a constitutional government and the modern state. That difference, both theoretical and practical, becomes apparent when comparing constitutionalism as it was understood by the American Founders and Thomas Paine and its transformation at the hands of the most successful Progressive politician of the twentieth century, Franklin Roosevelt.

Constitutionalism: Two Views

Thomas Paine spoke for nearly all the Founding Fathers when he wrote: "A Constitution is a thing *antecedent* to a Government; and a Government is only the creature of a Constitution. The Constitution of a country is not the act of its Government, but of the people constituting a Government."[2] Paine said he had to deny what had "been thought a considerable advance towards establishing the principles of Freedom … that Government is a compact between those who govern and those who are governed."[3] He knew that the defense of the sovereignty of the people and the protection of their individual rights required the firm establishment of the distinction between government and constitution, with the latter resting upon a social compact of the people themselves. The fact therefore must be, he insisted, "that the *individuals themselves*, each in his own personal and sovereign right, *entered into a compact with each other* to produce a Government: and this is the only mode in which Governments have a right to arise, and the only principle on which they have a right to exist."[4]

The social compact, therefore, must be understood in terms of a distinction between nature and convention. A constitution, unlike government, derives its authority from the laws of nature, or reason, which requires the protection of the natural rights of individuals as the chief purpose of government. It rests upon a political theory that established principles designed to serve that purpose. Consequently, it is possible to determine the powers and limitations of government precisely because its authority is derived from a more fundamental compact.

A constitution, therefore, Paine noted,

> is the body of elements... which contains the principles on which the Government shall be established, the manner in which it shall be organized, the powers it shall have, the mode of elections, the duration of parliaments... the powers which the executive part of the Government shall have... and the principles on which it shall act, and by which it shall be bound.[5]

Paine assumed that nature and reason, not government, established the ground from which those principles arose. The distinction between a constitution and government must rest upon the possibility of distinguishing nature from convention, reason from will (or passion), and natural (or fundamental) from positive law. The Founders, like Paine, had been unwilling to risk the defense of human freedom and the rights of individuals by reaffirming the age-old corrupt bargain between the rulers and the ruled. Consequently, the American Founders had insisted that the social compact is of the people themselves. It was not promulgated with the permission and consent of any actual governing body but rested on the eternal laws of nature and reason. Only upon the foundation of natural right had it become possible to establish the rational authority of an enlightened people to institute government on its own behalf.

A written constitution, therefore, is an attempt to spell out the conditions of just and reasonable government. It separates the law made by government (i.e., by legislative majorities) from the fundamental law, made by the people to protect their natural rights. The laws of legislative majorities are legitimate only insofar as they are consistent with the principles laid down in the fundamental law. A written constitution viewed merely as positive law would be wholly unintelligible theoretically. But in 1932, Franklin Roosevelt expressed a view, common among liberals, that the time had come to reinterpret the social contract in response to modern conditions. Animated by a progressive understanding of History, such a fundamental reappraisal was thought necessary because it was assumed that there could be no permanent principles of political right. In Roosevelt's creative interpretation, spelled out in his Commonwealth Club address in September 1932, he noted:

> The Declaration of Independence discusses the problem of Government in terms of a contract. Government is a relation of give and take, a contract, perforce, if we would follow the thinking out of which it grew. Under such a contract, rulers were accorded power, and the people consented to that power on consideration that they be accorded certain rights. The task of statesmanship has always been the redefinition of these rights in terms of a changing and growing social order. New conditions impose new requirements upon Government and those who conduct Government.[6]

Roosevelt assumed and simply asserted that the compact is between government and the people. But that is contrary to both the theoretical and practical meaning of the original social compact. The principles of the Declaration of Independence and the political theory of constitutionalism rested upon the defense of individual natural rights as the best ground to ensure the sovereignty and safety of the people.

Indeed, what established the link between the principles of the Declaration of Independence and the political science of the Constitution is the notion of the *people* as sovereign, with government as the people's creation and servant. It was on this ground that Jefferson could justify the revolution against Britain; it had become "necessary for one people to dissolve the political bands which have connected them with another and to assume among the powers of the earth, the separate and equal station to which the Laws of Nature and of Nature's God entitle them."[7] Therefore, it was with reference to the Laws of Nature that it had become possible to say on behalf of that people:

> We hold these truths to be self-evident, that all men are created equal, that they are endowed by their Creator with certain unalienable Rights, that among these are Life, Liberty and the pursuit of Happiness. That to secure these rights, Governments are instituted among Men, deriving their just powers from the consent of the governed. That whenever any Form of Government becomes destructive of these ends, it is the Right

of the People to alter or to abolish it, and to institute new Government, laying its foundation on such principles and organizing its powers in such form, as to them shall seem most likely to effect their Safety and Happiness.[8]

This is not a compact of government with the people. It is the *people* who assign government its role, which is the protection of their individual rights; when it fails to do so, it must be altered or abolished.

Similarly, the Constitution begins by institutionalizing the authority of the people as the foundation of the compact: "We the People of the United States, in Order to form a more perfect Union, establish Justice, insure domestic Tranquility, provide for the common defence, promote the general Welfare, and secure the Blessings of Liberty to ourselves and our Posterity, do ordain and establish this Constitution for the United States of America." It is the *people* who established a constitution. It was the Constitution, or the compact of the people, that instituted and limited the power of government, by subordinating governmental institutions to the authority of a written constitution (and separating the powers of the branches of government).

In Roosevelt's reinterpretation, government or the state determines the conditions of the social compact, thereby not only diminishing the authority of the Constitution but undermining the sovereignty of the people. By suggesting that the people accord government power on the condition that they are given rights, the concept of social or group rights (and subsequently entitlements), becomes the moral foundation of government. The purpose of government is therefore linked to the satisfaction of needs, economic and social. Consequently, Roosevelt would insist that "the issue of Government has always been whether individual men and women will have to serve some system of Government or economics, or whether a system of Government and economics exists to serve individual men and women."[9] Understood in this way, the economic (and social) system must come under the control of government before it can serve the people. And government must, of necessity, become the arbiter of rights, both economic and political. The will of the people must be established by government before it can be put into effect by the technical expertise of its bureaucracy. At that point, politics must give way to administration. In Roosevelt's view, the moral authority of government had come to replace the moral authority of the people's compact, and the sovereignty of the State would come to replace the sovereignty of the people. By undermining the attachment of individuals to the constitutional order as the best defense of their rights, Progressivism teaches them to believe that government is the only source and defender of their rights.

Will or Reason: "It is nearly impossible, theoretically or politically, to comprehend the distinction between the government and the Constitution"

America still has a written constitution, but it is nearly impossible, theoretically or politically, to comprehend the distinction between the government and the Constitution. Therefore, it is difficult to conceive of any rational limits on the power of government that can be derived from the Constitution. The theoretical foundations of social compact theory have been so undermined as to make constitutionalism obsolete as a political theory. The Progressives insisted that rights and freedom could not be understood as natural or individual, but social and dependent upon historical development. One important American Progressive thinker, Mary Parker Follett, who published *The New State* in 1918, outlined the new Progressive understanding of freedom and rights that is worth quoting at length for its clarity:

> Democracy has meant to many "natural" rights, "liberty" and "equality." The acceptance of the group principle defines for us in truer fashion those watchwords of the past. If my true self is the group-self, then my only rights are those which membership in a group gives me. The old idea of natural rights postulated the particularist individual; we know now that no such person exists. The group and the individual come into existence simultaneously: with this group-man appear group-rights. Thus man can have no rights apart from society or independent of society or against society. Particularist rights are ruled out as everything particularist is ruled out.... The truth of the whole matter is that our only concern with "rights" is not to protect them but to create them. Our efforts are to be bent not upon guarding the rights which Heaven has showered upon us, but in creating all the rights we shall ever have.... [As] the group process abolishes "individual rights," so it

gives us a true definition of liberty. We have seen that the free man is he who actualizes the will of the whole. I have no liberty except as an essential member of a group.... We see that to obey the group which we have helped to make and of which we are an integral part is to be free because we are then obeying ourself. Ideally the state is such a group.[10]

Progressives were confident that the replacement of natural right (philosophy) by History would make it possible to establish the conditions for the replacement of politics and religion by an uncoerced rational society. Political life and religion must vanish to enable the perfecting of economic and social conditions through the establishment of the new social sciences, thereby opening up the possibility of complete freedom, or individual self-fulfillment. The coming into being of the rational or administrative state is possible, and necessary, only at the end of History, when the rule of the philosopher or statesman can be replaced by the rule of organized intelligence, or bureaucracy.

The American Founders had derived the moral law from the laws of nature, or metaphysical reason. Nature and reason had established the theoretical and moral foundation of individual rights. Thus, freedom was necessarily subordinate to the moral law; rational limits on individual freedom were imposed by nature itself, by the natural human desire for happiness. As a result, the mind, human intelligence, and happiness were thought to be the possession of individual human beings. In his criticism of the liberalism of the Founders, John Dewey observed the problem posed by the doctrine of natural right:

> The earlier liberals lacked historic sense.... It blinded the eyes of liberals to the fact that their own special interpretations of liberty, individuality and intelligence were themselves historically conditioned, and were relevant only to their own time. They put forward their ideas as immutable truths good at all times and places; they had no idea of historic relativity, either in general or in its application to themselves.[11]

Dewey insisted that while earlier liberals recognized the "public function of free individual thought and speech," they persisted in "defending liberty of thought and expression as something *inhering in individuals* apart from and even in opposition to social claims" (emphasis mine). In Dewey's opinion, the new "liberalism has to assume the responsibility for making it clear that intelligence is a social asset and is clothed with a function as public as is its origin, in the concrete, in social cooperation."[12]

In the new social and scientific understanding, freedom cannot be thought of in terms of natural or rational limits on human behavior. Nor can it be understood in terms of "immutable truths" as the foundation of individual intelligence, rights, or happiness; but only in terms of "historic relativity" and the progress of social intelligence. It is *social mind*, not human nature, that established and revealed social reality as historically conditioned. Therefore, it is the progress of *social mind*, or social intelligence, derived from the ongoing consciousness of its freedom, that must reveal and establish merely relative, or historic, but nonetheless scientific truth as well. In the twentieth century, the new disciplines of the social sciences, the positivism that provided the scientific foundation for the study of law, would become the applied sciences of the rational or administrative state. These were founded on the historicist assumption that evolving consciousness of freedom, or will, would establish the intellectual and moral foundations of each historical epoch. As Roscoe Pound noted in his revealing theoretical work, *An Introduction to the Philosophy of Law* (1922),

> The limitations on human activity . . . got their warrant from the inherent moral qualities of men which made it right for them to have certain things and do certain things. These were their natural rights and the law existed simply to protect and give effect to these rights. There was to be no restraint for any other purpose. Except as they were to be compelled to respect the rights of others, which the natural man or ideal man would do without compulsion as a matter of reason, men were to be left free. In the nineteenth century, this mode of thought takes a metaphysical turn. The ultimate thing for juristic purposes is the individual consciousness. The social problem is to reconcile conflicting free wills of conscious individuals independently asserting their wills in the varying activities of life. The natural equality becomes an equality in freedom of will. Kant rationalized the law in these terms as a system of principles or universal rules, to be applied to human action, whereby the free will of the actor may co-exist along with the free will

of everyone else. Hegel rationalized the law in these terms as a system of principles wherein and whereby the idea of liberty was realized in human experience.[13]

Consequently, given the metaphysical turn after Kant and Hegel, the ground of political right, equality, and liberty must originate in freedom or will; not nature or reason. Once the Constitution came to be understood only in legal terms, and positivism established the foundation of law in legitimizing will, it became nearly impossible to make a rational defense of constitutionalism. As Harry V. Jaffa has written,

> For what is most important about left- and right-wing jurisprudence today, is not that they are of the Right or of the Left, but that they are "result oriented." Their so-called principles are not in their premises but in their conclusions. They differ in the particulars of their "value judgments," but not in the subjectivity of what they propose as the ground of constitutional law. Calling their subjective preferences "traditional morality" [or original intent] on the one hand, or "human dignity," in the other, does not make them less "value judgments," or less subjective. But if the basis of law is believed to be subjective, then the basis of law is believed to be will, not reason. The goal or perfection of the law, according to the whole tradition of Western civilization, is that it should be, in Aristotle's words, "reason unaffected by desire." This is what law means, according to the natural rights and natural law teaching of the Declaration of Independence. But law that rests upon nothing but "value judgments" is desire unaffected by reason.[14]

In denying the authority of reason, law itself, in the service of will, came to be understood in terms of social reconstruction. When coupled with the method of positive science, the state and its government provide the possibility of the ongoing transformation of society and man.

In 1914, Roscoe Pound, soon to be the influential dean of Harvard Law School, noted that law

> in its insistence upon abstract equality and security for the maximum of individual self-assertion it took no account of the moral worth of the concrete individual. Hence an infusion of ideas from without has

come to be necessary, as before, and such an infusion has been going on through the absorption of ideas developed in the social sciences.[15]

Consequently, Pound insisted upon a

philosophy of law stated in terms of can, not in terms of can't. It calls for a legal science which constructs as well as observes, for a legal science that observes in order that it may construct. It calls for a definite, deliberate, juristic program as part of an intelligent social program, and expects that program to take account of the maximum of human demands and to strive to secure the maximum of human wants.[16]

Pound insisted, therefore, that "the science of law is a science of social engineering having to do with that part of the whole field which may be achieved by the ordering of human relations through the action of politically organized society."[17]

Pound was well aware that intelligent social action must depend upon the scientific method and the technical knowledge generated in the graduate universities and law schools—institutions supported by the state. The social sciences and the scientific understanding of law were meant to replace the authority of theology and metaphysics—the authority that had established the foundations of constitutionalism. As the applied sciences of the state, the new sciences would provide the expertise necessary to carry out the will of the people. But for this to work, the people and their representatives would have to give up their reason so as to enable the social scientists to carry out their will. In short, they must give up the right to rule themselves.

Consolidating the Administrative State

America was among the last modern industrialized societies to rationalize politics by centralizing administration in the national government. It had become a great and powerful nation *before* it centralized administration in the national government. The consolidation of the administrative state was not the result of technological or historical necessity. It was an act of political will. The Constitution and its separation of powers as well as the politics of federalism had inhibited Washington from achieving such centralization. The progressive intellectuals had advanced the theoretical doctrine of the administrative state, and Roosevelt's New Deal attempted to expand and legitimize the administrative state. However, the administrative state was not institutionalized in any permanent way until the Great Society. When that task was accomplished politically, by the transformation of the central political branch of government, Congress, the constitutional separation of powers and the federal system were fundamentally altered.

At the beginning of the twentieth century, the Progressives looked to the presidency, through leadership of the political party, as the institutional means to overcome the constitutional separation of powers. Presidents of both parties had fought to aggrandize the administrative component of government, pushing Congress to expand the executive branch. Congress, representative of local interests and still tied to state power, was reluctant to do so. It remained a defender of decentralized administration. In 1965, Samuel Huntington noted that Congress could not function as a national institution because, administratively, it represented parochial and state interests. As a result, he insisted that the presidency had become the dominant force in American national politics. As Huntington observed, "today's 'aggressive spirit' is clearly the executive branch." The loss of power by Congress, he suggested,

> can be measured by the extent to which congressional assertion coincides with congressional obstruction. This paradox has been at the root of the "problem" of Congress since the early days of the New Deal. Vis-à-vis the Executive, Congress is an autonomous, legislative body. But apparently Congress can defend its autonomy only by refusing to legislate, and it can legislate only by surrendering its autonomy.... Congress can assert its power or it can pass laws; but it cannot do both.[18]

Apparently, Huntington assumed that administrative centralization was necessary and perhaps inevitable.

There was another option. Congress could adapt itself to the requirements of a centralized administrative state. But only if it gave up its power to *refuse to legislate*, which would require it to relinquish its primary function of deliberation, or public reasoning. Between 1968 and 1978, Congress passed more regulatory legislation in a decade than it had done in the whole prior history of the nation. It created new agencies, such as the Environmental Protection Agency, Occupational Safety and Health Administration, and the Consumer Product Safety Commission, to administer those laws. It required the wholesale delegation of lawmaking power to those newly created administrative and regulatory bodies, whose authority was dependent upon technical, or rational, knowledge. Congress could retain its autonomy as the central political body by establishing itself as the overseer of the executive branch and the regulatory bureaucracy. In the process, individual committees and members were empowered to oversee the various departments and independent agencies of the executive branch. They would soon become major players in the administrative policymaking process and would force the courts into the policymaking arena as well. Subsequently, Congress became, primarily, an administrative oversight body, which required greatly increasing its own technical staff. And it established itself as the keystone of the Washington establishment.

Until the mid-1960s, the American regime was centrally governed, but it was still administratively decentralized. Congress concerned itself primarily with the broad and general interests of the nation, and it functioned as a deliberative and representative lawmaking body. Private or specialized interests were brokered in the economic marketplace or administered at the state and local level of government. The general interests of government could be articulated, and partisan compromises could be accommodated within the political branches. This was so because the administrative functions of the national government were few, as were the organized constituencies allied to those functions. After the centralization of administration, the operation and interests of the executive and the legislative branches were fundamentally transformed. The role of the parties was also diminished because bureaucratic patronage would become more important than party patronage. In addition, the function of the judiciary had to be transformed. The bureaucracy has no constitutional authority, but it was given enormous power by the political branches. In the administrative state, the courts have been required to enter the policymaking process, as the final arbiters in the adjudication of cases arising in the administrative process. As a result, they have become fundamental players in the political and policymaking process.

By 1975, the characteristic activity of the federal government—and the legislature—had become the regulation or the administration of the details of the social, political, and economic life of the nation. Such a development could only strengthen the organized interests and their ties to the legislature, at the expense of executive control of the details of administration. Even the most sympathetic observers of congressional power did not fail to notice the change. James Sundquist of the Brookings Institution noted then:

> As members become managers of professional staffs, the chambers disintegrate as "deliberative bodies" in the traditional sense of legislators engaged in direct interchange of views leading to a group decision.... With each passing year, the House and Senate appear less as collective institutions and more as *collections of* institutions—individual member-staff groups organized as offices and subcommittees.[19]

To the extent that Congress is still tempted to make laws, it does so primarily on behalf of the expansion of the administrative state. For example, Congress passed what appeared to be a general law concerning health care reform, the Obama administration's Patient Protection and Affordable Care Act (Obamacare). But it is clear that this is not a law in the constitutional sense. It makes sense only within the context of an administrative state. The health reform bill was more than 2,500 pages long. But it was not a general law; rather, it established the legal requirements that would be necessary to ensure that the administrative apparatus would have the power to formulate the rules that would govern health care. As Charles Kesler wrote,

> When our founders thought about law, they often thought along the lines of John Locke, who described law as a community's "settled standing rules, indifferent, and the same to all parties," emphasizing that to be legitimate a statute must be "received and allowed by common consent to be the standard of right and wrong, and the common measure to decide all controversies" between citizens.[20]

As Kesler noted, you cannot "find any 'settled, standing rules' or a meaning that is 'indifferent, and the same to all parties.'" In fact, he suggests that is the point of such legislation:

> They operate not by setting up fences to protect each man's liberty. They start not from equal rights but from equal (and often unequal) privileges, the favors or benefits that government may bestow on or withhold from its clients. The whole point is to empower government officials, usually unelected and unaccountable bureaucrats, to bless or curse your petitions as they see fit, guided, of course, by their expertness in a law so vast, so intricate, and so capricious that it could justify a hundred different outcomes in the same case.[21]

As a result, Kesler insisted that

> a government of equal laws turns into a regime of arbitrary privileges. A "privilege" is literally a private law. When law ceases to be a common "standard of right and wrong" and a "common measure to decide all controversies," then the rule of law ceases to be republican and becomes despotic. Freedom itself ceases to be a right and becomes a gift, or the fruit of a corrupt bargain, because in such degraded regimes those who are close to and connected with the ruling class have special privileges.[22]

This extension of governmental power is compatible with the administrative state, but it cannot be understood to be within the letter or spirit of constitutional government.

Subverting Justice

The administrative state grew dramatically in the last third of the twentieth century, and it continues to expand. But despite its expansion under both parties, it has not attained legitimacy within the American constitutional order. The Constitution itself remains the source of legitimacy for those in and out of government who are opposed to the administrative state. Until the administrative state becomes legitimized, or constitutionalism delegitimized, an ongoing debate within the parties, and the electorate, concerning the desirability of expansion, limitation, or diminution of the size and scope of the federal government is almost inevitable.

Many years ago, I attempted to indicate the reasons for the failure of the administrative state to gain legitimacy within a constitutional regime of separated powers. I observed:

> In a constitutional system, the powers of government are thought to be limited; in the administrative state only resources are limited. In a constitutional regime, the most important political questions are those of principle or public right and how to achieve a common good (or justice); in the administrative state the most important questions revolve around money and finance (or entitlements). The constitutional system attempted to embody the principles of republican government into a structure of democratic institutions accountable to the people. Although the institutions were separated, and constituencies and perspectives differed, each branch participated in defining and pursuing the common good.[23]

The administrative state has undermined the capacity of our institutions to pursue the public interest. Congress has delegated political authority to unaccountable knowledge elites in the bureaucracy who are shielded from the popular control that might be exercised through elections. It has forced the unelected branch of government, the courts, to enter the policy arena to determine the legality of administrative decisions made by agencies that have no constitutional authority. In legitimizing the policies of agencies, the unelected courts have protected the political branches from responsibility for policies that are derived almost exclusively from the administrative process. Even when these policies are deeply unpopular, the electorate has no access to the centers of power in the administrative state that make the policies.

In short, the administrative state reflects a concern with administrative detail rather than principle, rulemaking rather than lawmaking, and the attempt to placate every private interest rather than the obligation to pursue a common good. In these ways, it subverts the aspiration for the fundamental ideal of government, that which makes human community possible: the desire for justice. As James Madison noted, "Justice is the end of government. It is the end of civil society. It ever has been, and ever will be pursued, until it be obtained, or until liberty be lost in the pursuit." When justice ceases to be the end of government, the natural rights guaranteed by the Constitution, and liberty itself, become ever more precarious. Nonetheless, all is not well within the administrative state. It seems that all modern bureaucratic governments are faced with the paradox of being less able to govern, the more completely they try to administer the social and economic details of life in society.

Donald Trump and the American Crisis

CHARLES KESLER'S ESSAY, "Trump and the Conservative Cause" (Spring 2016 *CRB*), is a model of conservative analysis. His moderate criticism of Donald Trump is surpassed only by his even more moderate defense of Trump. Kesler, of course, had little difficulty in deflating the most outlandish claims of Trump's critics. But he found it much harder to praise Trump. Like most contemporary political analysts, Kesler is well aware of the difficulty—if not the danger in some circles—of even defending Trump. Kesler is right to be wary. Trump has aroused more raw political passion than any candidate in recent memory.[1]

Since the end of the Cold War, American leaders have understood their offices in terms of global and administrative rule, rather than political rule on behalf of the American people and the sovereignty of the American nation. Yet those offices were established on the foundation of the moral authority of the people and their Constitution. Once elected or appointed, politicians and bureaucrats have utilized their will, in both domestic and foreign policy, in an unrestrained manner on behalf of bureaucratic rule. They govern on the implicit premise of elections as plebiscites, but it is no longer clear who confers the legitimacy of an electoral mandate. Bureaucratic rule has become so pervasive that it is no longer clear that government is legitimized by the consent of the governed. Rather it is the consent of the various national—and often international—social, economic, political, and cultural interest groups that determine the outcome of elections. True political rule requires, at a minimum, the participation of citizens in their own rule, even if not in government itself. But this is possible only when people understand themselves as citizens and when the regime recognizes them as citizens. This requires distinguishing American citizens from all others and identifying them as one people.

American elections have increasingly been framed by Washington professionals. Social scientists, media pundits, and policy professionals may tilt liberal or conservative and may differ in their party preferences, but they are united in their dependence upon intellectual authority, derived from empirical science and its methodology, in their understanding of politics and economics. At the same time, historicism or (critical theory) has established itself as the closest thing to a public philosophy when it comes to understanding history, society, and culture. Applied to elections, the empirical method required that politics be understood in terms of measurable and quantifiable aggregates. This proved compatible with the positivist understanding of law and interest-group liberalism.

Critical postmodern theory established personal autonomy and group diversity as central to what is morally defensible in terms of public policy. As a result, political partisanship and analysis has focused on race, class, gender, and other such demographics, to provide the kind of information that has become central to the shaping and predicting of elections and to legitimize dividing the electorate into categories that came to be understood in moral terms. Consequently, political campaigns have made a science of dividing the electorate into groups and reassembling them as voting blocs committed to specific policies and issues denominated by the demographic categories themselves. This strategy requires the systematic mobilization of animosity to ensure participation by identifying and magnifying what it is that must be opposed. Appeals to the electorate are strategically controlled by the experts. Which issues are allowed to be raised seems to be more important than the manner in which they are packaged and sold to the electorate.

Understood in this way, what is central to politics and elections is the elevation of the status of personal and group identity to something approaching a new kind of civil religion. Individual social behavior, once dependent on traditional morality and understood in terms of traditional virtues and vices, has become almost indefensible when judged in light of the authority established by positivism and historicism. Public figures have come to be judged not as morally culpable individuals, but by the moral standing established by their group identity. Character is almost unrecognizable and no longer serves as the means by which the people can determine the qualifications for public office of those they do not know personally. As a result, it is difficult to establish the kind of public trust that made it possible to connect public and private behavior, or civil society and government. When coupled with the politicization of civil society and its institutions, the distinction between the public and the private or the personal and the political has almost disappeared. Anything and everything can become politicized, but things can only be understood and made intelligible—or made politically meaningful— when viewed through the lens of social science and postmodern cultural theory. In short, the public and private character of American politics has been placed in the hands of the academic intellectuals.

Kesler focuses his defense of Trump on the observation that Trump alone has succeeded in making political correctness a political issue. Kesler knows that political correctness poses a problem not only for politics, but for intellectual life as well—that it is a problem for the university as well as for civil society. Regardless of his motives, therefore, Trump has gone to the heart of the matter and made a political issue of these intellectual and social crises. Trump has not attempted a theoretical justification for doing so. That remains to be made by the thinkers. Such a justification begins by recognizing that when Progressivism was confident of itself, it understood the past as rational and as providing light for the way to a glorious future. When progressive intellectuals lost confidence in the idea of progress and Enlightenment reason, they abandoned the hope of a future good and began to revise the meaning of the past. When Nietzsche analyzed the malady posed by historicism's abandonment of its rationality, he came to realize that "the excess of history has attacked the plastic powers of life; it no longer understands how to avail itself of the past as hearty nourishment."[2] The politics of our time is dependent upon how we avail ourselves of the past—whether as "hearty nourishment" or as a life-threatening poison.

Postmodern intellectuals have pronounced their historical judgment on America's past, finding it to be morally indefensible. Every great human achievement of the past—whether in philosophy, religion, literature, or the humanities—came to be understood as a kind of exploitation of the powerless. Rather than allowing the past to be viewed in terms of its aspirations and accomplishments, it has been judged by its failures. The living part of the past is understood in terms of slavery, racism, and identity politics. Political correctness arose as the practical and necessary means of enforcing this historical judgment. No public defense of past greatness could be allowed to live in the present. Public morality and public policy would come to be understood in terms of the formerly oppressed.

In this light, it is not surprising that Trump is seen not only as the enemy of political correctness, but as the enemy of those whose intellectual lives have been shaped by positivism and historicism. Trump is not an academic or an intellectual. He seems to understand politics in an old-fashioned way. He appeals to the people as citizens and Americans, on the assumption that the people establish the legitimacy of parties and elections. He rejects the authority of the professionals and insists that he is interested in unifying the country. He claims to do so by appealing to a common good. Of course, it is not easy to appeal to a common good when so much of the country has come to understand itself in terms of its diversity. In such a time, an appeal to American citizenship is itself almost a revolutionary act, because it requires making a distinction between citizens and all others. Along the same lines, Trump has appealed to the rule of law and has attacked bureaucratic rule as the rule of privilege and patronage on behalf of social, economic, foreign policy, and political elites. This appeal is made difficult by the fact that the administrative state has fragmented, isolated, and infantilized the people by undermining or destroying the institutions of civil society. In these terms, the success of Trump's campaign will depend upon the American people's ability to still recognize the existence of a common or public good.

■   ■   ■

Since local politics and administration came to be centralized within the administrative state, elections have provided the people their only possibility of participation in public life. Politics at the state and local level, along with the private institutions of civil society, took on a new face after administration was centralized. It wasn't long before the brightest and most ambitious college faculty and graduates began gravitating to Washington, DC—the new center of economic, social, and political decision-making. In turn, the federal government and bureaucratic apparatus became dependent upon the intellectual elites to provide expertise. But what to do with the people who participate in politics only as citizens? In terms of elections, the old partisans of both parties—the party pros who had devoted their life to trying to understand politics in terms of mobilizing the people—were no longer needed once partisan appeals could be marketed like any other commodity. Both political parties have benefited from the kind of predictability made possible by the incorporation of scientific professionalism in the organizing and shaping of campaigns and elections.

In addition, both parties have participated in recognizing the legitimacy of the cultural narrative established by postmodern theory—and enforced by political correctness—as the ground of understanding civil society, public policy, law, and bureaucracy itself. Before the end of the twentieth century, contemporary politics had created an equilibrium agreed on by both parties and underwritten by the intellectual authority of positivism and historicism. This equilibrium has functioned as a new kind of iron law of politics: there are Red States and there are Blue States and there are a handful of Purple (or battleground) States. Political conflict could be contained by focusing on the latter. Elections were understood in terms of division rather than unification, and it became almost impossible for any candidate to appeal to the electorate on behalf of a common good. That is not surprising, because positivism and historicism had rejected any understanding of the meaning of a common good. Modern American politics had become intelligible only from the perspective of positivist social science and postmodern historicism or Progressivism, both of which begin and end with interest-group diversity and individual autonomy.

Trump appears to have understood that the political parties no longer establish a meaningful link between the people and the government. Party patronage has been replaced by bureaucratic patronage, and a professional elite has established itself as the vital center between the people and the government. The authority of that elite cannot be understood simply in terms of social, economic, or even political power. What unites the vital center—what establishes its prominence and legitimizes its public authority—is knowledge. Members of the vital center understand the world through their attachment to their professions: academia, science, economics, business, media, entertainment, and even religion. They often lack political consciousness of themselves as a class. Many of them do not even think of themselves as political. Their interest and loyalty are to what it is they profess to study and what they think they know, and what establishes their intellectual and political authority is their production of what is seen as useful knowledge in the administrative state. Indeed, it could be said that without the policy sciences, the administrative state would be almost impossible to operate. It is the technical requirements of the modern administrative state that have made it possible to politicize the elites in a manner that disguises their political role. When nearly every social, economic, scientific, religious, and political problem is decided in a bureaucratic or legal way—and always from a central authority, usually Washington, but sometimes New York or one or two other places—the professional elites are given a stake in the political and bureaucratic world. Trump has apparently refused to acknowledge the authority of this policymaking establishment and in doing so has perplexed nearly all of the public intellectuals, both liberal and conservative. In refusing to allow the established vital center to mediate the political debate, he has gone directly to the people. And so doing, he has made it nearly impossible for the vital center to condone or even attempt to understand—let alone praise—his candidacy.

In a popular election, a rousing rhetorical defense of a political candidate is nearly impossible when those who have held political offices and attained social respectability are unable to praise the candidate. In the attempt to evaluate Trump, liberals have judged him from the perspective of postmodern culture, labeling him a reactionary racist, a nationalist, and a xenophobe. Conservatives have not objected to this postmodern characterization of Trump; they have simply tried to add a conservative twist by seeking to revive the old language of character, virtues, and vices—as though this language still has a public or political meaning! Unable to politicize a language that no longer resonates even with the libertarian or economic conservatives, their moral judgments could only be interpreted in terms of self-interest—a concept still relevant in contemporary discourse.

This was not always the case in American politics. A political discourse once existed that understood itself in terms of principles of public right, and the stewards of public office were once judged by nonpartisan standards that presupposed virtues such as honesty, integrity, character, and honor. It was an agreement on the need for such virtues that made it possible to entrust those offices to political partisans and to distinguish theoretical and practical reason or prudence. While it was possible to agree on abstract principles, it was also possible to disagree on the practical way those principles were to be accommodated with respect to contemporary circumstances. Policymaking was not understood in terms of expertise, nor had technical knowledge replaced the prudential judgment of the politician. Moreover, a public language still existed that made it possible to agree on what kind of public and private behavior was praiseworthy or blameworthy. But that old language was dependent upon a reasonable and objective understanding of virtue and vice. Such language eludes us in an age when subjective values have replaced public and private virtue, and when principles are merely subjective policy preferences that are defined and defended simply by being nonnegotiable.

Although it is easy to blame Trump for politicizing the personal—by ridiculing those who seek and hold public office—this was his way of connecting with people who had become mere spectators, not citizens, when it comes to Washington politics. Perhaps he did so because there had been no honest evaluation of Washington that originated in Washington: no policy ever really fails, private corruption never rises to the level of public corruption (let alone is punished), no officeholder of significance has been held personally responsible for their behavior since Watergate. Ironically, it has taken a reality television star—one who knows the difference between the real and the imagined—to make reality a political issue with respect to Washington.

Indeed, in recent years, Washington has presented itself as a kind of reality show. It is difficult to distinguish what is real from the way it is spun. Benghazi was just one example of the unwillingness of the Washington establishment to denounce deception in a political matter. Trump was willing to denounce the deception by passing personal judgment on those policies, personalities, and issues, and he was willing to judge them as personally accountable. Moreover, Trump is understood personally and not politically, because he has never held political office.

He is primarily vulnerable to criticism on the ground of his personal behavior, one leading aspect of which is a lack of respect for office seekers and officeholders and their policies. As a result, it has become difficult to judge Trump politically or in terms of the past. In short, Trump cannot be properly evaluated in political terms.

It is not surprising, therefore, that few are willing or able to praise Trump in an unqualified manner. Insofar as Trump has refused to "walk on paths beaten by others," as Machiavelli would say, "he has all those who benefit from the old orders as enemies, and he has lukewarm defenders in all those who might benefit from the new orders." But it is not "fear of adversaries" alone that makes it difficult to bring about change, Machiavelli writes, but "the incredulity of men, who do not truly believe in new things unless they come to have a firm experience of them." In our post-Machiavellian age, which is open to every kind of novelty, we are faced with a new kind of incredulity—one that prevents men from believing in the old things of which they no longer have any experience. It has become far easier for modern man to accept change as something normal, almost natural. What has become difficult to understand, let alone preserve, are things that are unchanging or eternal. History, understood in terms of the idea of progress in politics, economics, science, and technology, has made change, or the new, seem almost inevitable. As a result, the desire for the newest has become almost irresistible.

When Lincoln was faced with the dilemma of understanding what must be preserved and what can be changed, he had to come to grips with the meaning of conservatism. He did so at a time when not only the understanding of the unchangeable—that is to say, self-evident truth—but also its political meaning had been denied. And Lincoln, who was charged by his enemies with being a revolutionary, did not defend himself as a conservative. As he noted in his Cooper Union speech, "You say you are conservative—eminently conservative—while we are revolutionary, destructive, or something of the sort. What is conservatism? Is it not adherence to the old and tried, against the new and untried? We stick to, contend for, the identical old policy on the point in controversy which was adopted by our fathers who framed the Government under which we live; while you with one accord reject, and scout, and spit upon that old policy, and insist upon substituting something new." Lincoln noted that his opponents were unanimous in their defense of the new, despite their disagreement concerning what the new policies should be. "True, you disagree among yourselves as to what that substitute shall be," he said. "You are divided on new propositions and plans, *but you are unanimous in rejecting and denouncing the old policy of the fathers.*" Is not the contemporary understanding of politics, as made intelligible only in terms of historicism, the modern confirmation of the fact that there is general agreement between liberals and conservatives because both have rejected "the old policy of the fathers"—that is, natural right itself?

In contemporary politics, both liberals and conservatives are necessarily open to the new. But in many of the most important ways, they have rejected the old policy of the fathers. True, conservatives have not yet seen fit to denounce the fathers. But how much of the legacy of the fathers do they still find defensible? Lincoln was aware that the only proper defense of the tried and the true—of tradition—was a defense of the unchanging principles of political right understood in terms of an unchanging human nature. This presupposed a distinction between theoretical and practical reason, which made it possible to distinguish unchanging principles from policies that must change according to circumstances. This understanding assumed the benevolence of nature and nature's God, as well as the capacity of human reason to comprehend and impose those rational limits on human freedom that are necessary to ensure human happiness. It is only if the old can also be defended as the good that conservatism, or the tried and the true, can remain a living thing. The historicist understanding of freedom purports to reveal that nature itself is tyrannical and has attempted the self-destruction of philosophic reason by liberating the creative individual from the chains imposed by nature and reason. Identity is something that must be freely chosen and self-created by the individual alone, and it must be defended by government and law in civil society. Social institutions dependent upon the old morality have become intellectually indefensible. In terms of contemporary social and political thought, it is the good understood as the old that is no longer defensible, and its political defense has therefore become untenable. This alone makes the defense of reasonable conservatism—and constitutionalism itself—something akin to the defense of a dream that masquerades itself as reality in the minds of its votaries.

The public good, once thought to be a legacy of the best that had been inherited from the past—including the American Founding, the

Declaration of Independence, and the Constitution—is not easily defended politically because it has been undermined intellectually. The most
controversial aspect of Trump's campaign, his slogan to "Make America
Great Again," goes to the heart of the problem. Trump's view presupposes that the old America was good and established the conditions for
its greatness. Is this true? Or is America something to be ashamed of, as
the protesters against Trump have insisted, having accepted the teaching
of postmodern cultural intellectuals? Trump's defense of the old America
goes unrecognized by conservatives, either because they have succumbed
to the postmodern narrative or because Trump is unable to make the
intellectual case for the old America. Thus, the intellectuals stand almost
to a man against him.

It is possible that the Trump phenomenon cannot be understood
merely by trying to make sense of Trump himself. Rather, it is the seriousness of the need for Trump that must be understood in order to
make sense of his candidacy. Those most likely to be receptive of Trump
are those who believe America is in the midst of a great crisis in terms
of its economy, its chaotic civil society, its political corruption, and its
inability to defend any kind of tradition—or way of life derived from
that tradition—because of the transformation of its culture by the intellectual elites. This sweeping cultural transformation occurred almost
completely outside the political process of mobilizing public opinion and
political majorities. The American people themselves did not participate
or consent to the wholesale undermining of their way of life, which government and the bureaucracy helped to facilitate by undermining those
institutions of civil society that were dependent upon a public defense
of the old morality. This great crisis has created the need for a Trump, or
someone like Trump, and only those who recognize it as a crisis can be
receptive to his candidacy. To be clear, the seriousness of the need does
not mean that the need can be satisfied, perhaps even by a Lincoln, let
alone a Trump. Nonetheless, Trump has established his candidacy on the
basis of an implicit understanding that America is in the midst of a crisis.
Those who oppose him deny the seriousness of the crisis and see Trump
himself as the greatest danger. And here again, Trump's success will likely
depend upon his ability to articulate the ground of a common good that
is still rooted in the past—a common good established by a government
that protects the rights of its citizens in a constitutional manner and

establishes limits on the authority of government by demanding that the rule of law replace that of bureaucratic privilege and status.

Trump may or may not succeed in becoming president of the United States. All of those who have a stake in preserving Washington as it now exists are his enemies, and the public that is drawn to him is fickle. Much will depend upon the ability of the established order, which has authority and respectability on its side, to erode the trust that Trump has built with the constituency he has created. In any case, the need that brought Trump to the fore will not disappear with Trump's demise. Few serious policy analysts took Trump seriously. Like the Soviet experts who did not foresee the collapse of the Soviet Union, policy experts have failed to anticipate, or even detect, the crisis of America. Trump's success has revealed that one of our fundamental tasks—a task he has addressed when no else would—is the need for political rule to be reanimated in a way that allows public opinion, understood to arise in the creation of constitutional majorities, to establish the legitimacy of politics, policy, and law, in a manner compatible with the rule of law and the common good. That requires revitalizing the meaning of citizenship and reaffirming the sovereignty of the people and the nation. It also requires the restoration of the link between the people and the political branches of the government, so that both can become the defenders of the Constitution and the country.

PART TWO

THE ADMINISTRATIVE STATE IN PRACTICE: CONGRESS AS THE ENABLER

By Ken Masugi

As we saw in Part 1, Marini's case for the deconstruction of the adminis-trative state rests on arguments based on political philosophy, constitu-tional development, and, above all, commonsense judgment about the politics of free men and women and its requirements. In Part 2, "The Administrative State in Practice: Congress as the Enabler," Marini's essays describe how Congress legislated away its constitutional function to the administrative state: President Woodrow Wilson devised the rationale for the change from separation of powers to government by experts. Political science thus replaced political judgment. Then came the Great Society's constitutional transformation. Congress lost the will to legislate and became facilitators of the administrative state. We know the result as the phenomenon of bureaucratic government, and everyone knows about its growth, power, inefficiencies, and capture by constituencies that were supposed to be regulated. The latter are well-studied and are not Marini's themes.

Marini's interest is in the administrative state as a separate form of government that calls into question the foundations of constitutional gov-ernment. He also examines how even the judiciary, advocated by many as a check on bureaucratic excesses, takes on certain traits of the administra-tive state in its willfulness and distance from popular restraints. As for the interests of the two major parties, both agree that in some respects the power of the national government is unlimited. As Marini writes, "The

Republicans deny any limitations on the power of government in terms of national security and foreign policy. The Democrats believe that government has unlimited power as regards domestic policy. Taken together, it becomes impossible to establish the ground of constitutionalism when there is no consensus between the parties on how to limit the power of government."

Marini further demonstrates the growth of the administrative-state mentality on key issues such as the budget, which establishes priorities for the government. His essay on immigration reflects on the significance of the loss of a robust notion of citizenship in a country that holds to Progressive notions of the state. His discussion of the decline of constitutional government culminates in a bold treatment of Watergate, arguing that it ought to be understood as a war between the defenders of the administrative state and its constitutionalist critic, President Richard Nixon. The lessons for today are staggering.

4

Congress: Reluctant Defender of the Administrative State

THE QUESTIONS POSED for this panel[1] are the following: First, what role did Congress play in building and expanding the administrative state? Second, how significant is the problem that has resulted from the transformation of Congress? Third, what can Congress do to change the administrative state? To the first question: Throughout much of the first half of the twentieth century, it was primarily progressive presidents of both political parties who fought to aggrandize the administrative component of government, relentlessly pushing Congress to expand the executive branch. Congress, representative of local interests and still tied to state power, was reluctant to do so. It remained a defender of decentralized administration because it insisted upon maintaining its deliberative, representative, and lawmaking functions. After LBJ's Great Society was launched, Congress faced a dilemma: whether to continue its constitutional function or adapt to its new function as guardian of the administrative state. It gladly acquiesced to the latter, easier course.[2]

Once the centralization of administration had become institutionalized, the operation and interests of the executive and the legislative branches were fundamentally transformed. The representative role of the parties was diminished, because bureaucratic patronage became more important than party patronage. In addition, the function of the judiciary was transformed. In the administrative state, the bureaucracy has no constitutional authority. But, it is given enormous power by the political branches. Consequently, the courts have been required to enter the policymaking arena, as the final arbiters in the adjudication of cases arising in the administrative process. As a result, they have become fundamental players in the political and policymaking process. In legitimizing policies of the agencies, the unelected courts have protected the political branches from responsibility for policies that are derived almost exclusively from the administrative process. Thus, the electorate has no access to the centers of power in the administrative process, even when they are deeply unpopular. Congress, or the president, controls the administrative details of politics through the bureaucracy, and the judiciary reigns supreme in the realm of political principles. The Supreme Court determines what passes for the moral will of society by construing what passes for the contemporary meaning of the law as well as the Constitution.

Insofar as Congress is still tempted to make general laws on behalf of a perceived public good, it does so primarily on behalf of the expansion of the administrative state. For example, Congress passed what appeared to be a general law concerning health care reform, the Obama administration's Patient Protection and Affordable Care Act. But it is clear that this is not a law in the constitutional sense. It makes sense only within the context of an administrative state. The health reform bill was more than 2,500 pages long. But it was not a general law; rather, it established the legal requirements necessary to provide the administrative apparatus with the legal authority to formulate the rules that would govern health care nationwide. Like the creation of the gigantic, bureaucratic Department of Homeland Security, or the Dodd-Frank legislation that regulates the banking industry, this was a congressional action on behalf of the expansion of administrative power. This kind of extension of legislative power is compatible with the government as part of the administrative state, but it cannot be understood to be within the letter, let alone the spirit, of constitutional government. The constitutional arrangement of power no longer establishes the political conditions out of which a common good can be articulated.

How significant is the problem that has resulted from the transformation of Congress? Of course, the Constitution still structures the institutions of American government, but the separation of powers no longer operates effectively on behalf of the principle of limited-government constitutionalism. Nor do any of the respective political branches of government seem to understand the importance of defending their institutional prerogatives in a manner that is compatible with their constitutional purpose. In short, it seems that political conflict in America has been transformed, in a practical way, by the growth of the administrative state. The political institutions of the national government no longer understand their political power as subordinate to the Constitution; rather, the Constitution has been subordinated to the requirements of the administrative state. As a result, the political institutions cannot pursue a common good that must be established by defending the institutional prerogatives that make it possible for the constitutional separation of powers to work on behalf of the American people. Constitutionally, both political branches of government must participate in defining the public good, in terms of their institutional purpose. In this way, ambition can be made to counteract ambition.

Since the consolidation of the administrative state, neither party, nor political branch, in the absence of extraordinary events such as extreme crisis or war, can begin to articulate a conception of a common good that would enable it to establish a governing consensus on behalf of a national public purpose. Nor is there a common ground of policy agreement between the branches of government that can be established by, and on behalf of, a national political electorate. Under these conditions, it is nearly impossible to legitimize the actions of government politically by appealing to the electorate and getting the *consent of the governed*. Unlike constitutional rule, administrative rule is the rule of organized intelligence on behalf of organized interests.

In other words, it seems that the constitutional arrangement of power no longer establishes the political conditions out of which a common good can be articulated, let alone achieved, by the political branches of government. As a result, it has become more difficult to prevent the domination of a single *will* as that which establishes the ground of legitimacy and establishes what passes for public morality in American politics and society. Whether a unified will is understood in terms of presidential plebiscite, judicial fiat, or a public opinion that purports to establish the majority, or minorities, as the embodiment of moral will; the triumph of will has served to undermine rather than encourage genuine political conflict and debate. In the absence of such political conflict, there is no need of public deliberation, or accommodation of differences of political *opinion*. Unless it is in response to elections, it becomes unnecessary to even attempt to formulate, articulate, or defend a conception of a public good. Rather, the only necessity of government is that of mobilizing and accommodating the various organized, political, economic, demographic, or social *interests*. As a result, the administrative process has become more important than the political, or formal, lawmaking process that had once been established in order to make the separation of powers work in practice. In addition, it has diminished the institutional power inherent in each of the respective political branches of government and has replaced political rule with bureaucratic patronage and interest-group privilege, thereby undermining the rule of law.

The actual practice of the political branches of the American government is driven increasingly by the ongoing necessity of accommodating the various interests and constituencies that have coalesced around the administrative state. In other words, it is an element of government itself—the bureaucracy—that has established the purpose, unity, and the rational authority of the political branches. And the courts, too, have sanctioned that transformation by allowing Congress to delegate authority to administrative bodies through the use of vague and unfinished or incomplete mandates that cannot be characterized as legislation, and in no way resemble general law. In short, after nearly a half century of its growth, the bureaucracy has revealed itself to be the *conservative* defender of liberalism, the keystone of the rational state. Once established, the bureaucracy, and the political, economic, and social forces beholden to it, have sought to progressively replace politics by substituting administrative rulemaking for general lawmaking, and rule by expert in place of that of elected official. In practice, this means that the political rule of law must increasingly give way to executive or administrative discretion.

The Democratic Party has been far more effective in establishing political and legal control of the bureaucracy and has understood itself as the defender of the administrative state. It has supported bureaucratic expansion when in control of the legislative branch and defended or expanded its prerogatives when in control of the presidency. It was the primary force behind the bureaucracy's establishment, and it has been perceived by the bureaucracy as its ongoing defender. On the other hand, since 1968, the presidency has, at various times, posed the greatest threat to its expansion. Only after 1994, when the Republican Party took control of the House and Senate for the first time in forty years, did that party attempt to use its control of the legislature as the means by which to rein in the power of the bureaucracy. By that time, however, the presidency had become more than a mere defender of bureaucratic power; every president since Clinton has seized the opportunity to enhance executive power through more detailed control of the administration. The administrative presidency of the past two decades has replaced the administrative Congress of the 1970s and 1980s as the branch of government that has come to dominate politics, by defending and expanding administrative and regulatory power on behalf of bureaucratic rule. As regards the administrative state itself, although it is more powerful than ever, what still remains in doubt is its legitimacy. Although the political institutions have abandoned their constitutional roles, the people still look to the Constitution, not government, as the source of legitimacy. This, not political or policy differences, is at the heart of the quarrel that has come to establish the ground of partisanship in America.

The bureaucracy has itself become a political faction on behalf of administrative rule. What, then, can Congress do to change the administrative state? There is little incentive within the Washington establishment to change the way it does business. Any real change will likely come only if a president can mobilize an ongoing political constituency that can begin to effectively oppose the entrenched interests and their supporters in government. The administrative state has established tremendous power in Washington, but it has engendered considerable opposition in the country at large. That hostility to bureaucracy is often understood in terms of support or opposition to big government. Since Reagan, the Republican Party has been identified as the greatest threat to the expansion of the administrative state. The Democratic Party, on the other hand (and elements of the Republican Party, too), has embraced the administrative state as the embodiment of the moral and political good. As a result, both the Democratic Party and the bureaucratic establishment are more likely to believe in the essential justice of the administrative state. Consequently, both are more likely to defend the use of administrative power against political opponents who appear to deny its legitimacy.

Moreover, it has become clear that the *neutrality* of the bureaucracy, once thought to be the fundamental requirement of its legitimacy, and the condition of its acceptance by all partisans, is no longer understood to be the necessary ground of its bipartisan support. Bureaucratic rule is defended as essential to solving, in a nonpolitical way, the problems of modern technical, or rational, government and society. *Moreover, the bureaucracy has itself become a political faction on behalf of administrative rule.* When allied with control of the presidency, or one branch of Congress, it is now nearly impossible, institutionally, to prevent that part of the government committed to the perpetuation of the administrative state from preserving the political conditions of unlimited bureaucratic rule. More importantly, the defenders of administrative government are increasingly unable to understand, let alone tolerate, those who fail to recognize or accept the legitimacy of the administrative state. Consequently, both the Democratic and Republican Party defenders, and their defenders within the political institutions and the bureaucracy, are more likely to believe that the practical requirements of the administrative state confer legitimacy on administrative rule, which becomes for them the contemporary equivalent of constitutional authority.

The growth and consolidation of the administrative state has made it more difficult to control the apparatus of government by political means alone. It is no longer clear that the bureaucracy understands itself as the willing servant of its political masters, once the "masters" came to be perceived as a threat to the administrative state. This reality soon becomes apparent to all who hold elective or appointive office; the bureaucracy is much more hospitable to the interests of the defenders rather than the political opponents of the administrative state. Moreover, the necessity of operating within a framework dominated by the administrative process has made it difficult for members of Congress to understand the importance of defending the prerogatives, let alone the constitutional purpose, of the legislative body itself. As a result, political partisanship on behalf of—or in opposition to—the administrative state has replaced institutional loyalty and threatens to undermine the political conditions of constitutional government itself. The growth of the administrative state has established such expansive powers within the national government that those powers cannot be circumscribed in a manner that is compatible with constitutional limitations. Nor can each of the political institutions, established as separate powers, function amicably in a constitutional manner; that is, one that requires each branch to pursue public policies on behalf of a common good.

The administrative state, with the blessing of Congress, the presidency, and the Supreme Court, grew dramatically in the last third of the twentieth century, and it continues to expand in the twenty-first. Despite its expansion under both parties, it has not attained legitimacy within the American constitutional order. The Constitution itself remains the source of legitimacy for those in and out of government who are opposed to the administrative state. Until the administrative state becomes legitimized, or constitutionalism delegitimized, the ongoing contentiousness between the political branches of government, the parties, and within the electorate, concerning the desirability of expansion, limitation, or diminution of the size and scope of the federal government, seems almost inevitable.

State or Constitution? The Political Conditions of Bureaucratic Rule: The Executive, Congress, and the Courts under the Administrative State

THE CONSTITUTION STILL DETERMINES the institutional structure of the American government, but it no longer appears to animate its politics. Constitutionalism as a theoretical political doctrine is no longer meaningful in our intellectual discourse concerning public policy and the moral foundations of politics. Contemporary politics is animated by a modern theory of the state that denies the power of government can be limited. A constitution is meaningful only if its principles, which authorize government, are understood to be permanent and unchangeable, in contrast to the statute laws made by government that alter with the circumstances and changing political requirements of each generation. If a written constitution is to have any meaning, it must have a rational or theoretical ground that distinguishes it from government.

When the principles that establish the legitimacy of the Constitution are understood to be changeable, are forgotten, or are denied, the Constitution can no longer impose limits on the power of government. In that case, government itself will determine the conditions of the social compact and become the arbiter of the rights of individuals. When that transformation occurred, as it did in the twentieth century, the sovereignty of the people, established by the Constitution, was replaced by the sovereignty of government, understood in terms of the modern concept of the rational or administrative state. The modern state is predicated on the assumption that the power of government cannot be limited; its purpose is to solve not only every political problem, but every economic, social, cultural, and religious problem as well. It was a theoretical doctrine, the philosophy of History, that effected this transformation and established the intellectual and moral foundations of progressive politics. Established on the theoretical foundation of natural rights, constitutionalism has been steadily undermined by the acceptance of the new doctrine of History. The Progressive movement, which is the political instrument of that theoretical revolution, had as its fundamental purpose the destruction of the political and moral authority of the US Constitution. Because of the success of the Progressive movement, contemporary American politics is animated by a political theory denying permanent principles of right derived from nature and reason. In exposing the theoretical roots of Progressivism and the liberalism it has spawned, it is possible to reveal the difference between a constitutional government and the modern rational state. That difference, both theoretical and practical, becomes apparent when comparing constitutionalism as it was understood by the American Founders and the modern administrative state as envisioned in theory by Hegel and the American Progressives in practice.

A peculiar kind of administrative state, distinctively American, was consolidated within the constitutional order during the past century. It did not appear to violate, in any procedural way, the letter of the Constitution. The political branches voted for its establishment, and the courts upheld most of its provisions. Nonetheless, it has contributed to undermining the political conditions of limited government and self-rule. In attempting to provide administrative solutions to social, economic, and political problems, it undercut or destroyed those institutions within civil society that had established the foundations of self-government, including the family and the church. Consequently, political opposition to the administrative state arose when it became clear that the administrative state had undercut political rule and undermined political consent by depriving contemporary majorities of the ability to control public policymaking.

The legality of the administrative state remains unquestioned, but legality can only authorize the laws or rules that allow the exercise of power. Legitimacy, however, derives from the reason, or principle, that underlies and justifies law itself. In America, the principle that made it possible to establish a consensus authorizing and legitimizing the use of power was constitutionalism itself. The Constitution is a political document dependent upon a political theory that justifies its claim to legitimacy. It was based on a social compact designed to secure those natural rights (equality and liberty) that exist prior to government, and it establishes government's purpose in terms of their defense. That theory derived from a reasonable, or philosophic, understanding of nature and human nature, or natural right. Its political or practical success is dependent upon a separation of the powers of government. Human nature and the nature of power itself required such inventions of prudence. The power of government must be limited because political conflict, or factionalism, is sown into the nature of man. Those limits are best ensured by making ambition counteract ambition.

No particular branch, or individual, can establish the political meaning of the Constitution. All of the respective branches, and their members, derive their legal authority from the Constitution. And, they must exercise those powers on behalf of a common good, the meaning of which is established in the political or institutional rivalry created by the structure and moral authority of the social compact, or constitutionalism itself. The ongoing process of politics, responsive to coalitions capable of becoming majorities, must engender a governing consensus; no branch of government can, by law or judicial decision, establish itself, or government, as the ground of legitimacy. The Constitution seeks to regulate political conflict and control passion or will, but no human enterprise can end such conflict or transcend it. At best, as James Madison noted, in a government dominated by passion or will, "The *passions*, not the *reason*, of the public would sit in judgment. But it is the reason, alone, of the public that ought to control and regulate the government. The passions ought to be controlled and regulated by the government" (*Federalist* 49). In other words, prior to government, it is the reason of the public, or the principle of constitutionalism, that authorizes government and legitimizes the regulation of passion. It is the Constitution, therefore, that establishes the ground of political right by protecting individual liberty and by preserving political conflict in civil society. It does so by promoting differing views of the public good within the government itself, by separating its powers, and by providing independent constituencies in support of each branch. In short, government cannot easily establish, or justify, unified will as the ground of political right.

However, the modern administrative state becomes intelligible only in light of a philosophy of History that establishes passion as the driving force of History and will as the foundation of morality and ground of legitimacy.[1] The *state* is revealed as a rational and ethical organization. Its government's legitimacy is established through the promulgation of law, which is a reflection of its sovereign or moral will. Only when will establishes the ground of morality does it become possible to end quarrels over the fundamental principles that give rise to political conflict. When law, in the service of moral will, establishes right, its implementation is no longer understood in political terms. Politics is replaced by administration. Consequently, administrative rule must be derived from knowledge or organized intelligence. The problems of economy and society come to be understood in technical or scientific terms, not as political dilemmas. In short, the rational *state* presupposed the end of politics and religion and its replacement by an uncoerced rational society, one freed from factionalism and superstition. It also presupposes the end of the necessity of constitutional, or limited, government. Furthermore, it looked forward to a time when the social sciences would become the applied sciences of the rational state.

The administrative state's power rests upon its legality, but its legitimacy remains in doubt as long as public sentiment remains wedded to the principle that established and justified constitutionalism. Moreover, it has not succeeded politically in establishing the *rational* state as the ground of legitimacy. It is difficult to do so, because it has become increasingly clear that the growth of the administrative state has eroded the sovereignty of the people. As the power and authority of administrative rule has come to dominate civil society it has also alienated the affections of the people with respect to its government. That disaffection has resulted in divided government. The political branches have reorganized themselves in such a manner as to be most attentive to the special economic, social, cultural, scientific, and environmental interests, which are regulated by the rulemaking power of the administrative apparatus. The political branches appear to oversee, intervene, or referee the process by which the private organized interests engage in an ongoing way with the rulemaking administrative apparatus. However, the price of such accommodation of private interests is the inability of the elected government to pursue a common good. As a result, the political parties find it increasingly difficult to mobilize majorities capable of creating the kind of political consensus that could establish stable governing coalitions that have public support.

Under these conditions, only the courts seem to be required to take the Constitution, or the common good, seriously. But even the highest legal—ostensibly nonpolitical—branch of the national government, the Supreme Court, can justify the use of power only in terms of its status as a coequal branch of government, whose authority is also derived from the Constitution. It purports to discern the authoritative meaning of the Constitution by interpreting its provisions in light of contemporary conditions. It is able to do so without political interference only because the two branches (Congress and executive) have acquiesced in allowing the court this power on the condition that the court sanction, or legitimate in law, their role within the administrative state. Although one branch of government, itself established by the Constitution, can exercise its will as the justification for the authority of the other two political branches, it cannot do so without compromising the political principle of constitutionalism. Nonetheless, the courts have become fundamental players in the political and policymaking process. In legitimizing the policies of the agencies, the unelected courts have protected the political branches from responsibility for policies that are derived almost exclusively from the administrative process. Even when they are deeply unpopular, the electorate has no access to the centers of power in the administrative state. Congress, or executive branch officials, mandate and ratify the administrative details of policies that are formulated by the bureaucracy, allowing the judiciary to reign supreme in the realm of political principles and public morality. The Supreme Court determines what passes for the moral will of society by construing what passes for the contemporary meaning of the Constitution.

The separation of powers makes it difficult for a single branch to establish the legitimacy of the use of power by legal argument alone; all of the respective branches must exercise their own powers on behalf of a defense of their institutional and constitutional purpose. Only in that way can the politics of governing support the principle of constitutionalism. The purpose of the separation of powers is to inhibit the ordinary, if sometime necessary, acceptance of will (however understood) as the ground of political right. In short, not all of the branches acting in concert can establish constitutional legitimacy in the long run if power is used in violation of the principle of limited government. The legitimate powers of government are those whose purposes are compatible with the defense of the sovereignty of the people, the protection of their rights, and the maintenance of the rule of law. Of course, such political, or constitutional, rule presupposes the sovereignty of an *enlightened* people as the authority of the compact. It requires that legitimate government be established on the foundation of the consent of the governed. It almost goes without saying that when a people cease to be enlightened concerning the protection of their rights or are insufficiently vigilant concerning the use of power by government, they cannot retain the form of constitutionalism regardless of its structure. They have already lost its spirit by failing to understand or by denying its principle.

In other words, contrary to the view that the unlimited power of government is a necessary and inherent attribute of the rational state, it is *government* itself that must be limited by the principle of constitutionalism. When the Constitution comes to be understood historically or as a progressive document, whether by the court or the political branches, it can no longer provide a principle of legitimacy on behalf of limited government or in defense of natural right. Moreover, the government of the state becomes increasingly indifferent to the necessity of justifying its legitimacy in terms of the sovereignty of the people. Consequently, it becomes impossible in practice to ensure that the consent of the governed can remain a necessary condition of political right. When legitimacy is thought to be derived from *moral will* embodied in the concept of the rational state, however established, the state itself must come to be understood as sovereign. At that point, it is clear that rights are a product of the state and must be conferred only by its government. In the final analysis, it is rationality alone that establishes legitimacy within the state.

The ongoing political and intellectual battles of the twentieth century have revolved around the difference between limited-government constitutionalism and the unlimited power required by the modern rational state. Beneath the surface of the partisan battles over the size and scope of the national government, however, there is a deeper, more fundamental quarrel over the justice or injustice of constitutionalism itself. The modern rational, or administrative, state was established on the assumption of its theoretical and practical superiority over every earlier form of government. It rested on the view that constitutionalism was an historical anachronism. The legitimacy of the modern administrative state, and its inherent rationality, is derived from a philosophy of History that has presupposed the end of political conflict. Only then is it possible to replace politics by establishing technical, rational, or bureaucratic rule.

Throughout much of the twentieth century, the practical defense of the administrative state—the only one apparently agreeable to all political parties—rested upon its alleged nonpartisanship, or neutrality. Although it was clear from the start that bureaucracy was in fact a partisan on behalf of the administrative state, the inability to comprehend the purpose, or theoretical character, of the administrative state had obscured its political dimension. By the beginning of the twenty-first century, with the institutionalization of the administrative state, political partisanship in defense of the administrative state has almost replaced the ongoing necessity of defending the political and constitutional powers of the legislative and executive branches of government. Thus, it has become easier to see that the practical domination of government by administration threatens to undermine political or constitutional rule. It has also forced a reappraisal of the theoretical origins of the rational state, which has made it necessary to reveal historicism in its political dimension, thereby making Progressivism a part of the political debate.

In the last two decades, it has become clear that the bureaucracy can no longer be understood, or justified, in terms of its neutrality. The bureaucracy has become a partisan defender of the rational state, and it has allied itself with political partisans of both parties in defense of its interest. However, bureaucratic rule has become controversial and will remain a contentious issue in American politics as long as it lacks legitimacy. Moreover, it cannot establish its legitimacy in a regime structured by the constitutional device of separation of powers, which legitimizes only political power. The bureaucracy has no constitutional authority whatsoever. Its power must be derived from legislative authority delegated to it or judicial authority that upholds its rulemaking power. Nonetheless, the wholesale delegation of power to the administrative apparatus has transformed the operation of the political branches and undercut their ability to function amicably in pursuit of a constitutional, or common, good. In short, administrative centralization has produced a disjunction between the theoretical and practical or political dimensions of constitutionalism, and between the principles that legitimize action and the practice of the institutions of government derived from those principles. It has undermined the most important practical safeguard of constitutionalism: the political cooperation necessary for the separation of powers to work.

The proponents of the administrative state have viewed separation of powers as an antiquated relic guaranteed to ensure deadlock. In their view, the fundamental distinctions in society cannot be understood in terms of politics or limitations on the powers of government. Economic and social conditions determine what must be done. Nor is there a fundamental distinction between government and civil society or the public and private sphere, which must be preserved as a condition of self-rule. Rather, the crucial practical distinction, one elaborated by the early Progressives, is that between the political institutions and parties that authorize policies and legitimize them in the form of moral will and the administrative apparatus that rationalizes them and makes them practicable or real. Nonetheless, the progressive theorists and politicians, who had established the administrative apparatus as a means of overcoming limitations on the power of government imposed by the Constitution, have not yet succeeded in undermining attachment to the principle of constitutionalism. Insofar as the people understand the Constitution as the ground of their sovereignty, they have become increasingly aware of the necessity of imposing limits on bureaucratic power and have sought to restrict the scope of administrative rule. It is not surprising, therefore, that in recent years, the Constitution itself has become a partisan tool utilized by those who seek to retain, or reanimate, political rule in opposition to the encroachments of the administrative state. In doing so, they have demanded that the Constitution remain the primary source of legitimacy and the standard by which to measure rightful authority in the American regime.

The American administrative state cannot be judged on the basis of political theories that already presuppose the legitimacy of the modern state.[2] Nor can it be assumed that administrative centralization is the inevitable consequence of the necessity to adapt to changes in society brought about by industrialization and urbanization or by progress in science and technology. The American administrative state was put in place *after* the major transformations of society had occurred. It was the result of conscious political choice. Consequently, the American administrative state must be judged by its impact upon the practical politics of the constitutional system. How does it affect the conditions of pre-bureaucratic rule: of limited government, separation of powers, and American federalism? Has it undercut political freedom and undermined the conditions of self-government? To the extent the administrative state is a problem in American politics, it is the result of the manner in which the institutions of government, and the constituencies allied to them, have adapted to the presence of a centralized bureaucracy.

Politics or Administration

Nearly every American political or constitutional crisis has revolved around the conflict generated by the differences arising from the separation of powers. The practical operation of that separation is nowhere better revealed than in the federal budgetary process. It is the one place in which the political branches have been forced to interact by the authority of the Constitution itself. Taxing and spending, revenues and expenditures—all are required for all governmental activity, noble or ignoble, of great or little purpose. Both branches of government have been given significant power dealing with taxing and spending. Partisan political rhetoric, and utopian expectations, often make it difficult to measure the success or failure of government actions. Of course, high hopes cannot be measured in dollars alone, but they require dollars to make them real. In observing the opinions that animate politics, or attempting to justify the policies and programs, assessing its personnel and management; nothing provides a better focus into the uses of power than control of the purse. That power, and its purpose, is spelled out in concrete ways by attaching dollars to what is to be done. It is not surprising that both political branches of government have sought to guard their powers with regard to the purse. And, throughout much of American history, both branches have attempted to understand their own monetary powers in terms of their institutional and constitutional purpose. There was, however, a fundamental transformation in American politics that began to reveal itself by the end of the twentieth century. Although the Constitution

still structured the institutions of American government, the separation of powers seemed no longer to operate on behalf of the principle
of constitutionalism. Nor did any of the respective political branches
of government seem to understand the importance of defending their
institutional prerogatives in terms of a constitutional purpose. In short,
it appeared that American political conflict had been transformed in a
practical way by the growth of the administrative state. Neither party nor
political branch, in the absence of extraordinary events such as 9/11, could
begin to articulate a conception of a common good that could establish
a governing consensus on behalf of the electorate or provide a common
ground of agreement between the branches of government.

In other words, it seemed that the constitutional arrangement of
power no longer established the political conditions out of which a
common good could be articulated let alone achieved by the political
branches of government. As a result, it has become more difficult to prevent the domination of a single *will*, however understood, as that which
establishes the ground of morality and creates legitimacy in American
politics. Whether will is understood in terms of presidential plebiscite,
judicial fiat, or public opinion that purports to establish the majority, or
intellectual minorities, as the embodiment of moral will, the triumph of
will tends to undermine rather than encourage genuine political conflict
and debate. In the absence of such conflict, there is no need for public
deliberation or accommodation for differences of political *opinion*. Unless
it is in response to elections, it becomes unnecessary to formulate, articulate, or defend a conception of a public good. Rather, the only necessity
of government is that of mobilizing and accommodating the various
economic or social *interests*. As a result, the administrative process has
become more important than the political, or formal, lawmaking process
established in order to make the separation of powers work in practice.
Consequently, it has diminished the institutional power inherent in each
of the respective political branches of government and has undermined
the rule of law by replacing political rule with bureaucratic rule.

The actual practice of the political branches of the American government is driven increasingly by the ongoing necessity of accommodating
the various interests and constituencies that have coalesced around the
administrative state. In other words, it is an element of government
itself—the bureaucracy—that has established the purpose, unity, and

rational authority of the political branches. And, the courts, too, have sanctioned that transformation by allowing Congress to delegate authority to administrative bodies by passing unfinished or incomplete laws. In short, after nearly a half century of its growth, the bureaucracy has revealed itself to be the *conservative* defender of the liberal or rational state. Once established, the bureaucracy, and the political, economic, and social forces beholden to it, have sought to progressively replace politics by substituting administrative rulemaking for general lawmaking and to rule by expert in place of that of elected official. In practice, the political rule of law must increasingly give way to executive or administrative discretion.

The various crises that have occurred between the branches, whether the more recent government shutdowns or the potential showdown over the debt limit, are only the latest in a long series of such crises in Washington. In fact, with few exceptions, the budgetary process has formed the battleground between the parties and the political branches of the government—the executive and the legislative—in every administration since LBJ's Great Society. That starting point is not a coincidence: the Great Society marked the beginning of an expansion of the political power of the federal government and a centralization of administrative authority in Washington that had long been the domain of local and state governments. In addition to destroying the fabric of federalism, this centralization had the effect of undermining the separation of powers, making it difficult if not impossible for Congress, the president, and the bureaucracy to function amicably in pursuit of a national interest. What we have seen in subsequent decades is the steady expansion of a modern administrative state that is distinctively American in that it coexists with a limited-government constitution.

In America, the administrative state traces its origins to the Progressive movement. Inspired by the theories of German political philosophers, Progressives like Woodrow Wilson believed that the erection of the modern state marked an "end of History," a point at which there is no longer any need for conflict over fundamental principles. Politics at this point would give way to administration, and administration becomes the domain not of partisans but of neutral and highly trained experts. America's Founders shared a radically different understanding, an understanding based not on History but on nature. James Madison wrote in *The*

Federalist Papers that factionalism is "sown in the nature of man"; thus, there will always be political conflict—which at its starkest is a conflict between justice (the highest human aspiration concerning politics) and its opposite, tyranny. This conflict between justice and tyranny occurs in every political order, the Founders believed, because it occurs in every human soul. It is human nature itself, therefore, that makes it necessary to place limits on the power of government.

Progressive leaders were openly hostile to the Constitution not only because it placed limits on the powers of government, but because it provided almost no role for the federal government in the area of administration. The separation of powers of government into three branches—the executive, the legislative, and the judicial—inhibited the creation of a unified will and made it impossible to establish a technical administrative apparatus to carry out that will. Determined to overcome this separation, one of the chief reforms promoted by early Progressives was an executive budget system—a budget that would allow Progressive presidents to pursue the will of a national majority and establish a non-partisan bureaucracy to carry it out. Congress was initially reluctant to give presidents the authority to formulate budgets, partly because it infringed on Congress's constitutional prerogative—but also because it was still understood at the time that the separation of powers stood as a barrier to tyranny and as a protection of individual freedom. Eventually, however, Congress's resistance weakened.

For several decades after a federal budget process was put in place, a consensus concerning the size and purposes of the federal government limited the conflict over control of public finances. Administrative functions at the national level were few, in keeping with a system of decentralized administration, an autonomous civil society, and a constitutional system that underscored the limited character of government. This would change in the 1970s, during the Nixon administration, when Congress reorganized itself to become a major player in the administrative process that had risen with the Great Society. The public consensus in support of limited government and balanced budgets began to break down. Moreover, Republican presidents, at times representing national majorities opposed to the expansion of government, and Democratic Congresses organized around private interests in support of democratic expansion became rival forces to an extent incompatible with the pursuit of a long-term public interest.[3]

In looking at the changing expectation and perceptions of Congress over the last half century, it is not hard to see that a fundamental transformation of the institution has taken place. Not too long ago, it was the conservatives who were the heartiest defenders of Congress. Recently, John Samples, of the Cato Institute, revisited an old political controversy concerning the status and purpose of the legislative branch within the American regime. In doing so, he engaged the arguments of an older generation of conservative defenders of Congress, those who had been troubled by the waning influence of that institution since the New Deal. Samples looked primarily to James Burnham, whose book *Congress and the American Tradition*, published in 1959, raised the question whether Congress as an institution could long survive in the age of executive dominance. Burnham was not sanguine about the prospects of its survival. He was persuaded "that the political death of Congress would mean plebiscitary despotism for the United States in place of constitutional government, and thus the end of political liberty." Burnham, like Willmoore Kendall, believed that "to keep their political liberty, Americans must keep and cherish their Congress." Burnham traced the decline of the legislative body to the rise of the bureaucratic state. He insisted that "Congress has let major policy decisions go by default to the unchecked will of the executive and the bureaucracy."[4]

In order to retain its status of first among equals, Burnham insisted, "Congress must find a way to concentrate on essentials. If it is to continue to be a partner and peer within the central government, then its principal energies must go to deciding major issues of policy, not to the critique of details." He assumed that "the assemblies, by their very nature, cannot be bureaucratized in the modern mode. Among the giant institutions into which society is currently for the most part arranged, the assemblies are undoubtedly anomalous, a breach in the pattern; and if all modern institutions have got to conform to the managerial-bureaucratic norms, then the assemblies are on an irreversible way out." Burnham foresaw the growth of the bureaucratic state, but he did not foresee a role for the legislative branch within that state. Was Burnham right in his assumption that legislative assemblies could not be bureaucratized?

However, after more than fifty years, John Samples was not persuaded that Burnham was right in his diagnosis of Congress. He insists that Congress has reasserted its power in many areas and has proved to be more than a match in terms of exercising that power in its defense against encroachment by the other branches of government. He does not deny that the "New Deal and its echoes did set Congress on a declining path toward obsolescence, and in 1959, the administrative/welfare state seemed triumphant." However, Samples insisted that "had the fifteen years after World War II continued for the next fifty, Burnham's bold prediction might well have been confirmed, including the demise of Congress. But the administrative-welfare state lost, and never quite regained, public confidence, and if those athwart History did not quite stop its progress, they also did not wholly fall under its wheels. The question remains whether, when historians look back at the beginning of the post–New Deal era, they will note with surprise the revival of the United States Congress."[5] It is hard to deny that Congress, when united, has ample power in terms of defending itself against the other branches. However, is Samples right in his assumption that not Congress but "the administrative-welfare state lost" the confidence of the American public? Or, is it the case that Congress has become an integral part of the "administrative-welfare state"?

Perhaps, Burnham was only partly right in his insistence that Congress holds the key to the preservation of political liberty in America. He assumed that "legislative supremacy" was the fundamental condition of the maintenance of republican government. However, the American Founders did not believe that Congress as an institution would or could be the primary defender of liberty. Nor did they depend upon the presidency or the Supreme Court exclusively to fulfill that role. The American Founders established the Constitution, and the separation of powers, as the surest defender of freedom. This purpose could only be achieved by subordinating the power of all the branches to their constitutional purpose. It was the result of an abandonment of their constitutional role that both of the political branches of government were enabled to participate in the establishment and consolidation of the modern administrative state.

It seems that Burnham was wrong in his assumption that *assemblies cannot* be "bureaucratized in the modern mode." It is only a constitutional assembly that cannot be legitimately bureaucratized, precisely because deliberation and general lawmaking remain its fundamental constitutional purpose. In denying Burnham's claim that Congress would cease to be a major player in modern government, Samples has shown that the revival of Congress indicated that it had been possible for Congress to give up its *lawmaking power* without relinquishing its *authority* over those administrative bodies to which it had delegated that power. In other words, it had become possible for Congress to establish itself as a major player in the politics of the bureaucratic state.

Burnham's book was written before Congress reorganized itself to accommodate its transformation from primarily a legislative body to an administrative oversight body. Throughout much of the twentieth century, presidents of both political parties had fought to aggrandize the administrative component of government, pushing Congress to expand the executive branch. Congress, representative of local interests and still tied to state power, was reluctant to do so. It remained a defender of decentralized administration because it insisted upon maintaining its deliberative and lawmaking function. There was another option for the legislative branch. Congress could adapt itself to the requirements of a centralized administrative state. However, it could do so only if it gave up its power to *refuse* to legislate on behalf of the administrative state. It was necessary to relinquish its primary constitutional function of deliberation and lawmaking in the national interest in order to use its legislative power in the service of the administrative state. It did so by the wholesale delegation of power to newly created administrative and regulatory bodies, whose *ostensible* authority was dependent upon technical, or rational, knowledge. Congress could retain its autonomy, and *political* authority, by establishing itself as the overseer of the executive branch. In the process, individual committees and members were empowered to oversee the various departments and agencies of the executive branch. They would soon become major players in the administrative policymaking process. Subsequently, Congress would become, primarily, an administrative oversight body, the "keystone of the Washington establishment," in Morris Fiorina's phrase, but of a new establishment.

The Bipartisan Support for the Administrative State: Democratic Force, Republican Fraud

Political scientists John H. Aldrich, Brittany N. Perry, and David W. Rohde have noted:

Prior to the 1990s, the House Appropriations Committee was understood to be one of the least partisan committees in Congress. Within the committee, interparty bargaining and compromise were commonplace and subcommittees were primarily in charge of making decisions on the details of bills in their jurisdiction (Fenno 1965; Smith and Deering 1984; White 1989)... After the election of 1994 however, perspectives on the Appropriation Committee changed considerably... Members of the Republican Party empowered their party leadership to make significant institutional modifications. The new speaker of the House... centralized power and worked to ensure the committee system would achieve the interests of the party. On the Appropriations Committee in particular, the old order of bipartisan unity and committee autonomy were swept away as Gingrich took control, sidestepping seniority norms, to appoint loyal partisans to serve or chair the committee. The leadership began to monitor actions within the Appropriations Committee's more closely and to exert pressure on its members' behavior when necessary.[6]

The problem with such a strategy is that it had the effect of transforming the legislative body into something approximating a parliamentary system, with the Speaker attempting to lead the government from the House in the manner of a prime minister. By establishing unity within the leadership of the most powerful committees, the Speaker sought to steer politics and control administration from the legislative branch. However, the Constitution had already provided for a unified executive. In the ensuing political battles during the Clinton administration, it was not the power of the legislature that was enhanced. The presidency is the focal point of national politics, the only office with a national constituency. In the attempt to shape public opinion, the unity of the executive prevailed over the diversity of the legislature. Moreover, the Gingrich reforms had the effect of undercutting the political virtues that are only possible in a legislative body: deliberation, representation, and the accommodation of interests that culminate in lawmaking on behalf of a public good. Still, in subsequent years, as Aldrich has noted: "Every Speaker of the House, Hastert, Pelosi, and Boehner, Republican and Democrat, has continued to be granted power to shape House Rules and they continued to use these Rules to control operations within the Appropriations Committee over time."[7]

Indeed, after September 11, 2001, the Bush presidency succeeded in further undermining any attempt to reestablish regular order in the House. With the creation of the Homeland Security Department, justified as necessary in the war on terror, the bureaucracy was enabled to treat domestic security in the same way as national security, dramatically expanding executive power in a manner that could have been done only as part of its war-making powers. Consequently, it became more difficult to draw the line between the domestic and foreign policymaking powers of the president. Congress empowered the executive branch by nationalizing its police powers in the name of national security. It also created the opportunity for increased centralization of power in the congressional leadership through its use of emergency powers. As a result, unlike earlier wars, nearly all of the money for the Afghanistan and Iraq wars during the Bush administration, and Obama's as well, was funded outside of the regular budget process through annual emergency spending provisions. Furthermore, the last two presidents have assumed broad powers in domestic affairs, such as no-bid contracts, that had been defensible only in times of war. Although Bush used that power primarily in terms of defense contracts to fight the war on terror, Obama has done so on behalf of a domestic agenda in support of environmental and other partisan interests of the Democratic Party.

George W. Bush's sinking popularity by the end of his second term had approached the levels of disapproval of Richard Nixon after Watergate, and the loss of both houses of Congress dramatically weakened his presidency and his party. Nonetheless, the powers of the presidency and the executive branch were hardly touched. Congress did not reassert its authority after his presidency. When Barack Obama took office, unlike Gerald Ford, he inherited all of the executive powers that had been claimed by Bush and more. Unlike Bush, Obama was more interested in using those powers on behalf of consolidating his domestic policy agenda, rather than pursuing a vigorous foreign policy. Whatever their differences, it has become more difficult to determine the limits on the legitimate power of government when one party denies any limitations in terms of domestic or national security and the other party believes government has unlimited power with regard to domestic policy. Taken together, it is politically difficult to defend the principle of constitutionalism when there is no consensus on the necessity of limiting the power of government under any circumstances as so described. Of course, political conditions may require the use of unlimited power in extraordinary circumstances, but it is incumbent upon the political branches to draw the line between normal and abnormal conditions.

The American Founders were well aware of the fact that government must have all of the powers that are necessary in times of war. However, they insisted that Congress and the president must establish a meaningful distinction between war and peace. Each branch must participate in clearly establishing the conditions of war, identifying the enemy, and determining what constitutes the end of hostilities. Only in that way is it possible to reestablish the conditions of normal government. Peace, not war, must determine the manner in which the institutions of government must operate in normal times. Under the conditions established by the ongoing requirements of the war on terror, it is almost impossible to distinguish war and peace or to determine when the emergency measures can be dispensed with. If the necessity of preparation for war is a constant and ongoing condition of civic life, no limitations can be imposed on government. This condition is compatible with bureaucratic rule, but not political or constitutional rule. In light of this transformation of the governing institutions, it was not surprising that after the 2010 midterm elections, the new Republican majority in the House did little in terms of reinvigorating congressional prerogatives on behalf of political rule. Indeed, they further eroded the powers of the rank-and-file membership. As former Senate Parliamentarian Robert Dove noted not long ago: "What you have in Congress right now is a situation in which things are simply bucked up to the top level—the two leaders in the Senate, the Speaker in the House. They frankly ignore the regular order and go on their merry way." Although it is true, it is also the case that the president and the executive branch bureaucracy now play a major role in establishing and driving the agenda of Congress. That transfer of power to the administrative apparatus has facilitated centralizing decision-making in the leadership of the two branches. In the absence of ongoing oversight of the executive branch through the committee structure of Congress, the bureaucracy will establish its own priorities. Any attempt to remedy this situation would require something like a return to regular order. That would make it possible for rank-and-file members to influence legislation and administration at the committee level.

In the past, members devoted their career to those policy areas in which their committee had jurisdiction. It was in the ongoing process of subcommittee hearings, bill markups, floor amendments, and conference reports that a congressional consensus could be established that all could live with even if they didn't like it. It enabled Congress as an institution to participate not only in legislation but also in administration by controlling the budgets of the agencies. In futile gestures, such as getting rid of earmarks, the Republican leadership has forced rank-and-file members to petition the Office of Management and Budget (OMB) in order to influence the administration in their own districts. Those reforms were meant to remedy features of Democratic Party majority control that Republicans did not like. But, like it or not, they are effective ways of establishing political control of administration. Unfortunately, in the absence of member participation, the considerable expertise and control that came with longevity on a committee has been nearly lost. Furthermore, when the committee and subcommittee members no longer participate, you get speedy, ill-considered legislation cobbled together by the Senate and House majority leadership staff, which is heavily influenced by interested stakeholders in the private sector. All of these things together cannot help but strengthen the interests of the administrative state.

With a divided legislature and the majority party, or a minority party in one chamber, whose members become surrogates on behalf of the executive branch (or the administrative state), it is difficult to establish a distinctively legislative perspective on policymaking. As a result, no policy that is representative of the interests of Congress as a legislative body is likely to emerge; rather, the administrative process becomes the center of all politics. That process undermines the power of the electorate within the states. They have little way of participating in national politics, because their representatives in Congress are far less able to influence policy and are often powerless even to influence administration except by petitioning the executive branch. Even those in leadership positions must be more attentive to the powerful and centralized, well-organized national interests than they are to their national or constitutional duty or to the interests of the constituencies that elected them.

In short, the leaders of both branches of government have ceded power to the bureaucracy and enabled it to rule on behalf of the national, economic, sub-political (states and local governments), social, scientific, educational, religious, and cultural elites. It is those elites who have obtained a privileged position in terms of lobbying the national political branches and the regulatory bodies. The political branches have, in turn, allowed those interests the ability to bargain and negotiate with the departments and agencies that promulgate the rules by which they are governed. It is difficult to say that this process has produced a regime in which the rule of law must establish the conditions of equal treatment of all citizens. Rather, it sanctions unequal privilege for those who have a seat at the table and allows them to participate in negotiating the rules that govern everyone.

Is it possible for the separation of powers to work properly once the administrative state has been put in place? Or, have we reached a point in which it is no longer possible to understand American politics in terms of constitutionalism? Although the Constitution structures the political institutions and establishes the powers and the conditions of office for all of the branches of government, those powers are no longer used on behalf of a constitutional purpose. At best, in recent years, the branches have defended their institutional powers only when it was necessary to defend the bureaucracy against threats to its existence. In any case, the separation of powers no longer works as it was intended, on behalf of establishing limits to the powers of government by preventing the domination of *will* in any one (or all) of the branches of government. The reason of the Constitution, as Madison noted in *Federalist* 49, should control the passions and regulate the conditions of politics on behalf of the people, not the government. In the administrative state, the passions of the people are used on behalf of government for the purpose of undermining the political conditions of self-rule.

Constitutionalism and the Challenge of the Administrative State

It is not an exaggeration to say that separation of powers epitomized the political science of *The Federalist*. In fact, it was this institutional arrangement that was thought to be most vital to the science of politics that derived from those "inventions of prudence" of which James Madison spoke. Although prudence, or *practical reason*, was necessary in terms of establishing the practical or political science of free government,

Madison's "new science of politics" also had a theoretical foundation. Madison assumed that the principles of the new regime were derived from a philosophical understanding of human nature; they were the product of *theoretical reason.*

The attempt to approximate those abstract theoretical principles within an actual regime required a government of separated powers because of the *practical necessities* of politics.[8] There are limits on human action imposed by nature itself. The Founders did not simply choose to structure the institutions of government and society in the manner prescribed in *The Federalist*; they were forced to acknowledge a fundamental political reality: factionalism, or conflict, is sown into the nature of man. Therefore, politics is an enduring part of the human condition. That perspective was undermined by the political thought that established the theoretical ground of Progressivism. The leaders of the Progressive movement in politics sought to destroy the separation of powers on the assumption that politics would give way to administration and expertise could replace partisanship.

The modern rational, or administrative, state is established on the foundation that government must be the embodiment of a unified will. That will is developed in the process of mobilizing majorities through political parties animated by the leadership of the political branches of government. When the will is established in law by the political powers of government, the task of carrying out that will is essentially a technical, or administrative, task. For that reason, Woodrow Wilson would insist that the separation of powers inhibited a unified will; the proper separation is not one that separates the branches of government, but one that creates a distinction between *politics and administration.* Politics establishes the moral will of a people in the form of its laws; the purpose of administration is to carry out that law, or will, in a technically rational manner, one that transcends political partisanship.

In this Progressive understanding, when the rational, or historical, process has advanced sufficiently to produce a democratic society, limited-government constitutionalism is no longer necessary. In the modern state, Wilson believed, government cannot be a threat to the liberties of the people. Indeed, the purpose of government is to establish the rights, and relieve the necessities, of the people. Moreover, the political questions, and disputes over principles, would have been resolved by the historical process itself. The emergence of the rational state has revealed and reconciled all of the fundamental political contradictions of the past. As a result, it becomes possible to transcend politics in the realm of practice. Consequently, just as the theoretical problems are no longer understood in terms of theoretical reason, the practical problems of government are no longer understood in terms of practical reason or political prudence. Rather, the "inventions of prudence" that had established the political science of *The Federalist* were consigned to the ash heap of History. Morality itself, Kant had argued, could only be derived from practical reason, or will, not theoretical reason as Madison had supposed.[9] Once morality is made intelligible as will, all of politics is reduced to a technical task—that of carrying out or *administering* the will.

In America, the administrative state was not institutionalized until well into the twentieth century. Only after Congress reorganized itself in such a way as to augment its administrative authority at the expense of its political power did it become difficult for the political branches to understand, let alone utilize, their powers in terms of their constitutional purpose. As a result, the separation of powers could no longer serve as a defense of the political on behalf of the people, rather than government. The power and authority of the administrative state cannot be limited; its establishment could not but undermine the principle of limited government, or constitutionalism. Consequently, the political institutions found it necessary to reorganize themselves so as to be able to operate in the service of the modern administrative state. Insofar as the Constitution is still meaningful, it is only in the realm of law. And, it is therefore understood primarily as a legal document. All of the branches of government now seem to agree that only the Supreme Court has the obligation to take it seriously. Constitutionalism, as a theoretical and political doctrine, is no longer able to establish and defend the conditions of limited government and democratic self-rule. No legal doctrine can preserve the conditions of political freedom; it can only attempt to legitimize will.

The importance of the administrative state has not been lost on those constitutional law professors who specialize in administrative law, scholars such as Cass Sunstein, Peter Strauss, and Jerry Mashaw. As Harvard Law Professor Adrian Vermeule has observed:

> The administrative state is the central and unavoidable topic of modern
> constitutional theorizing. The single most striking difference between

the constitutional arrangements of the late 18th century and today—
"constitutional" in the sense of the actually obtaining structures and
practices of government—is that the modern state is, by any conceivable
measure, largely an administrative state. In the institutional landscape
of the late 18th century and well into the 19th, one may see precursors
of the administrative state, but one simply does not observe the massive
and elaborately reticulated bureaucracy that structures and constitutes
the experience of government for almost all citizens.[10]

It is difficult for any observer to deny the reality or the pervasiveness
of the administrative state. However, it is questionable whether those
observers, who view politics from the perspective of the administrative
state, have not already been shaped by the theory and practice of the
modern rational state. Their views, derived from a philosophy of History,
all presuppose the obsolescence of the political theory that established
the principle of constitutionalism. They are shaped by, and their scholarship is dependent upon, the social sciences that were created to generate
knowledge on behalf of the administrative state. In short, the scholars
who study administrative law, and the lawyers and social scientists who
analyze its laws, economics, and society, do so as part of the apparatus of
the administrative state. Their status, and authority, is dependent upon
the technical and rational sciences that were intended to be the applied
sciences of the administrative state. Indeed, they are its handmaidens.
Thus, it would seem that the only reason for taking the Constitution
seriously is not for reasons of its intellectual or theoretical authority, but
because of political necessity. It is a tacit admission of the fact that the
bureaucratic state cannot establish political legitimacy apart from the
Constitution.

The difficulty of analyzing the Constitution in a manner that is not
prejudicial to the political principle of constitutionalism arises from the
very fact that the disciplines of the social sciences, and the positivism of
the law schools, have been structured on the foundations of the theoretical primacy of the rational state, based on a philosophy of History. The
Progressive theorists themselves were the *founding fathers* of the social
science disciplines. They established science, or positivism, as the authority not only for law, but for all meaningful human knowledge. From
the beginning, they were well aware of the necessity of undermining
the political theory of the American Founding. They did so in order to

destroy the legitimacy and authority of the Constitution. They rejected the Constitution because it had limited the powers of government and subordinated administrative authority to political control.

The American Founders, however, established a political theory of constitutionalism that had denied the autonomy of administration. They did not think it possible to separate administration from politics nor did they think that practical reason could be promulgated as the ground of morality. The inability to reconcile theoretical and practical reason had resulted in the inevitability of politics and factionalism. Consequently, they had affirmed the practical and political necessity of separating the powers of government, so as to allow "ambition to counter ambition." They were well aware, as Alexander Hamilton noted in *Federalist* 72, "[that] the administration of government, it its largest sense, comprehends all the operations of the body politic, whether, legislative, executive, or judiciary." But they were persuaded that the concentration of all of those powers in the same hands "may justly be pronounced the very definition of tyranny" (Madison, *Federalist* 47). They were convinced that all men are self-interested by nature. Therefore, all politics, including administration, must be understood in terms of partisanship, or political conflict.

Unlike Hegel or Woodrow Wilson, the Founders would have denied the possibility of a class of men, civil servants, who would seek only knowledge, not power. Thus, they would have denied that any institution or person could be safely entrusted with all of the powers of government. Nor could any institution of government (Congress or president) delegate its power to an administrative body in which all of those powers are reunited. In undercutting the authority of theoretical reason as well as prudence, the Progressive theorists established technical expertise as decisive in producing and legitimizing social, political, and economic knowledge. In addition, *positivism*, or the scientific method embodied in the social sciences and law, has created the condition in which the disciplines themselves have become the arbiters of the legitimacy of politics and law.

Therefore, as the heirs of the legacy of Progressivism, modern scholars cannot in any meaningful way adapt the administrative state to the Constitution, even assuming that to be possible. Rather, given their training as well as their perspective and status within the administrative state, they can do *no more* than attempt to adapt the Constitution to the administrative state. However, the candid scholars of administrative law are already well aware that the Constitution does not animate our politics. One cannot help wondering why it is that they are not led to conclude that the Constitution is meaningless and obsolete as a political document. They could forthrightly condemn it precisely because it is a defense of limited government in a world incapable of such limitation.[11]

The tacit premise of the rational state, and the defense of the administrative state, rests upon the assumption that the power of government cannot be limited. That is so because it is the *conditions of society and economy* (History) that determine what must be done. It is precisely the amelioration of those conditions that brings about the need of the social sciences. Therefore, it is the purpose of government to solve every political, economic, and social problem. Indeed, the rational state was meant to be the vehicle for the administration of *progress*. As a result, the very complexity of modern conditions makes it necessary to empower those with knowledge or expertise to rule. It is not surprising, as William J. Novak has observed, that "the very origins of modern social-scientific inquiry in the United States were wholly coincident with and participatory in the construction of the new state-centered socioeconomic policies of the Progressive era."[12]

Indeed, it was not only constitutional politics that was an impediment to radical reform; the rule of law itself came to be seen as an impediment. As Novak noted:

> Overwhelmingly, and with few exceptions, the rule of law is portrayed throughout the synthetic literature as something of an obstruction, a brake, an inertial force, a structural impediment, an ideological hindrance, an exceptionalist constitutional barrier to the development of a modern regulatory and administrative welfare state in the United States. From the first treatises of progressive social science to the newest institutional studies, law, courts, and judges are represented continuously as the great bogeyman of liberal reform—the agents of an exceptionalist and backward-looking American jurisprudential tradition that regularly frustrated modern welfare-state-building efforts.[13]

Once the administrative state was established, however, it did not take long for the legal establishment, like the bureaucracy itself, to become the conservative defenders of the liberal or rational state. Although Novak was right about the initial reaction of the Progressives to "law, courts, and judges," the courts, the judges, and the law itself, with the help of its new intellectual defenders, would soon come to be incorporated as major players within the nexus of policymaking established within the administrative state.[14]

In the course of the twentieth century, each of the branches has participated, in one way or the other, in legitimizing the administrative state. The courts, too, by deferring to the legislature in terms of sanctioning the delegation of power to the administration, have found it difficult to exercise their constitutionally mandated judicial judgment in an independent manner. This is particularly so when those cases or controversies arise out of the administrative process. Once the court entered, or was forced to enter, the policymaking process, it was natural that it would defer to the political branches, especially Congress.[15]

It is difficult for the court to maintain its independent judicial judgment in individual cases when it must defer to the authority of the legislature, which amounts to privileging those players within the policy arenas established by Congress. In the many cases decided since the *Block* case, the courts have implicitly taken the side of government against any individual harmed by agency-made rules, depriving them of access to an independent judiciary. The courts are unable to perform their judicial function in a constitutional manner, because they have deferred to the legislature's delegation of power to the agencies. They have done so without holding the legislature responsible for the use of that power in terms of clarity of language or purpose. In allowing Congress, through such delegation of power, to pass purposely unfinished laws, which are not really laws, they facilitate an arrangement that allows the bureaucracy and the special interests a bargaining arena for establishing the rules that govern society.

It is hard to imagine that this process, which subordinates the public interest to the demands of organized private interests (by legitimizing and accommodating those interests as equal partners within the administrative realm), can establish anything approximating the rule of law. Moreover, the courts have simply acquiesced in legitimizing the authority of the governing apparatus—legislative, executive, and administrative— within the administrative state. As a consequence, the political standard of Congress is no longer one of public lawmaking on behalf of a national or public good, but the accommodation of all of those private interests capable of lobbying Washington. It appears that the satisfaction of *every* interest replaces the necessity of establishing the rule of law as essential to a common good. At the same time, it is not clear that every citizen can have his day in court.

All that Congress seems to demand is the ability to intervene in this policy nexus for the purpose of satisfying its own special interests as individual members and on behalf of the national political, economic, and social elites. In doing so, the constitutional and institutional power of the legislature is undermined and the practical operation of separation of powers is endangered. When Congress delegated its power in broad grants of authority to the bureaucracy, it could not but empower the president and the executive branch officials, because it must allow nearly absolute discretion in the promulgation and enforcement of most rules and regulations. The political branches and the national political parties, organized around the private interests of national elites, have created a centralized administrative structure that encompasses every national political, economic, social, religious, educational, scientific, and entertainment-media elite. The organized interests are all well served by the federal government. The electorate, however, has access to the national government only through the parties. And, the political parties no longer serve as a link between people and the government.

Consequently, once administrative centralization occurred, the connection between the parties, the electorate, and government was severed, and the electorate's access to government was severely constrained. Because bureaucratic patronage has replaced party patronage, money flows to the states and localities from the center. However, nationally organized interests, and their lobbyists, co-opt and organize those political, economic, and social interests at the state and local level by bringing all political bargaining to the center. The member of Congress's political fate is no longer decided by his own electoral constituency. As a result, officeholders have need of their constituents only when it is necessary to get their votes at elections. Because much of their money is provided by the centrally organized interests at the national, state, and local levels—and the policies of the administrative state have provided subsidies for large numbers of their constituents—incumbents have a tremendous advantage. But that advantage depends upon the maintenance of the status quo—in other words, continued support and defense of the administrative state. This kind of administrative centralization has also empowered the leadership of both houses at the expense of the members, because the organized interests now deal directly with the leadership and their staffs and the executive bureaucracy. It is the leadership, therefore, that determines the kind of resources given or withheld from the membership. Under these circumstances, the notion of a common good cannot arise within the legislature.[16]

Moreover, the Supreme Court is protected in its role as the sole interpreter of the Constitution by the ongoing necessity of legitimizing the policies of the administrative state through constitutional construction. Only in that way is it possible to operate the administrative state on behalf of organized interests while at the same time placating a population that still thinks of its rights in terms of the Constitution. The reality of contemporary politics makes it clear that the practical operation of the separation of powers is no longer animated by the principle or spirit of constitutionalism, not in form or in substance. Contemporary politics, in all of the institutions of government, is organized and energized by the necessities imposed by the primacy of administration and is animated by its theory. It may be the case that modern government requires a centralized administrative state, although that is not self-evident. But, if that is the case, then the operation of the separation of powers, understood in terms of constitutional government, is no longer possible in a meaningful way.

It was precisely such a transformation from a constitutional regime to an administrative state that occurred in the twentieth century. It was the result of the triumph of progressive principles based upon a theory of government that mandated a fundamental alteration of the practice of politics, one animated by unlimited power on behalf of a moral or political will. However, in America, that moral will must still be established within the political branches of government, but its practical implementation has been placed in the hands of technically trained administrators. Consequently, the sovereignty of the people—made practicable in the protection of individual natural rights and the defense of the political as the primary necessity of constitutionalism—had to be replaced by the sovereignty of government, a creature of the fundamental moral entity, the ethical, or *rational state*. Rights are then a product of the government of the state. They are allocated to various groups in the form of political privilege, which when established by will is made moral in the form of rights. The primacy of administration derives from the necessity of technical expertise, but it is put in the service of a theoretical and moral doctrine. That doctrine, the philosophy of *History*, had effected this transformation and established the intellectual and moral foundations of Progressivism, which culminated in the modern administrative state. As a result, the theoretical and practical ground of constitutionalism, understood in terms of nature or reason, and political prudence, was so undermined as to become almost meaningless.

The administrative state, with the blessing of Congress, the presidency, and the Supreme Court, grew dramatically in the last third of the twentieth century, and it continues to expand in the twenty-first. Despite its expansion under both parties, it has not attained legitimacy within the American constitutional order. The Constitution itself remains the source of legitimacy for those in and out of government who are opposed to the administrative state. Until the administrative state becomes legitimized, or constitutionalism delegitimized, the ongoing contentiousness between the political branches of government, within the parties, and in the electorate, concerning the desirability of expansion, limitation, or diminution of the size and scope of the federal government seems almost inevitable.[17]

6

Budgets, Separation of Powers, and the Rise of the Administrative State

THE TITLE OF THIS PANEL, "Separation of Powers and Today's Budget Process," appears to rest on the assumption that the budget process can reveal both the practical and theoretical dimensions of the political problems that have arisen in American government in the past half century. Of course, budgets reveal only part of the deeper problem that arises from the difficulty of accommodating the administrative state within the structure of a constitutional regime. But, in looking at the practice of contemporary government, and attempting to understand the modern character of separation of powers, a good vantage point is provided by observing the budget process. It provides a political focus, which can help illuminate the theoretical doctrine of the separation of powers. Moreover, it remains a good practical way of seeing how the political branches relate to each other at a point at which they must necessarily interact.

Nearly every political crisis revolves around the functioning of the separation of powers. And the federal budget provides a lens that can focus on the way money shapes the debate over policies and the purposes of government. In addition, those partisan quarrels help to reveal what lies behind the preconceptions of politicians and parties concerning their view of the public good. If the modern budget stands at the heart of

American politics, was it the rise of the administrative state that brought it to the fore and changed its character and purpose? Has that change affected the operation of the separation of powers, making it more difficult for the political branches to function well on behalf of a national interest?

The various contemporary crises between the branches, such as the recent government shutdown or the showdown over the debt limit, are only the latest in a long series of such crises in Washington. In fact, with few exceptions, the budget has formed the battleground between the parties and the political branches of the government—the executive and the legislative—in every administration since LBJ's Great Society. That starting point is not a coincidence: The Great Society marked the beginning of an expansion of the political power of the federal government and a centralization of administrative authority in Washington that had long been the domain of local and state governments. In addition to destroying the fabric of federalism, this centralization had the effect of undermining the separation of powers, making it difficult if not impossible for Congress, the president, and the bureaucracy to function amicably in pursuit of a national interest. What we have seen in subsequent decades is the steady expansion of a modern administrative state that is distinctively American in that it coexists with a limited-government Constitution.

For several decades after a federal budget process was put in place, a consensus concerning the size and purposes of the federal government limited the conflict over control of public finances. Administrative functions at the national level were few, in keeping with a system of decentralized administration, an autonomous civil society, and a constitutional system that underscored the limited character of government. This would change in the 1970s, during the Nixon administration, when Congress reorganized itself to become a major player in the administrative process that had risen with the Great Society. The public consensus in support of limited government and balanced budgets began to break down. Moreover, Republican presidents, at times representing national majorities opposed to the expansion of government, and Democratic Congresses organized around private interests in support of its expansion, became rival forces to an extent incompatible with the pursuit of a long-term public interest.

It is no longer easy to understand the powers of government in terms of their use on behalf of a constitutional purpose. So, it has become difficult to assess, let alone defend, the various uses of the powers of government, whether in the executive, legislative, or judicial branches, in terms of their constitutional purpose. Instead, we are forced to judge the politics of the administrative state in terms of a defense of Congress, the presidency, or the Supreme Court, based primarily upon the policy preferences of the observer. Once the legitimacy of the administrative state is granted, it is nearly impossible to establish an objective ground outside of politics or will as the only justification for the use of power. If the constitutional structure is to become meaningful in terms of understanding contemporary partisanship, it is necessary to see how the branches were intended to operate on behalf of constitutional government. In short, it is necessary to reestablish the theoretical ground of constitutionalism in order to recreate an objective ground of judgment in terms of justifying the uses of powers within each of the branches of government.

The American Founders considered the legislative branch to be the first branch of government. It was thought to be the one with the most power, and therefore most difficult to rein in. They armed the other two branches with significant powers but assumed that the legislative branch had ample power to defend itself. It was assumed that each branch would exercise its power from an institutional perspective, but on behalf of a constitutional purpose. Although the institutional perspective was fundamental, that was only the starting point. It was also necessary to recognize the constitutional purpose of its power within a regime of separated powers; that is, each branch must pursue a public good from the perspective of its own branch. It is thinking about the whole, from the perspective of the parts, that would allow each of the branches to participate in defining a public good.

Understood in this way, it is in the interest of each branch to cooperate with the others in terms of pursuing the national or common good. But that cooperation should also encourage sound public policymaking that is attentive to the interests of a diverse public. Only when each branch represents its institutional perspective in a constitutional way is it possible to reconcile, in a political manner, the various interests of a diverse public and also retain and defend the administrative powers of state and local governments. In observing Congress over the last fifty years, it becomes clear that its power to deliberate and legislate—in other words, its lawmaking power—is no longer the source of its primary authority, as was intended by the Constitution. Rather, to retain its status as the first branch of government, its lawmaking power was subordinated to its administrative oversight power. As a result, the political and legal standard by which to judge Congress is no longer its constitutional power, but rather its fundamental role in organizing and consolidating the administrative state.

So, it is no longer clear that the bureaucracy is the willing servant of its political masters, once these elected "masters" came to be perceived as a threat to the administrative state. This reality soon becomes apparent to all who hold elective or appointive office; the bureaucracy is much more hospitable to the interests of the defenders rather than the political opponents of the administrative state. Moreover, the necessity to operate within a framework dominated by the administrative process has made it difficult for members of Congress to understand the importance of defending the prerogatives of the institution itself, not to mention its constitutional purpose. As a result, political partisanship on behalf of—or in opposition to—the administrative state has replaced institutional loyalty and threatens to undermine constitutional government itself.

Indeed, after September 11, 2001, the Bush presidency succeeded in further undermining any attempt to reestablish regular order in the House. With the creation of the Department of Homeland Security, justified as necessary in the war on terror, the bureaucracy was enabled to treat domestic security in the same way as national security, dramatically expanding executive power in a manner that it would normally have only as part of its war-making powers. Consequently, it became more difficult to draw the line between the domestic and foreign policy powers of the president. Congress empowered the executive branch by nationalizing its police powers in the name of national security and also created the opportunity for increased centralization of power in the congressional leadership through its use of emergency powers. As a result, unlike earlier wars, nearly all of the money for the Afghanistan and Iraq wars during the Bush administration was funded outside of the regular budget process through annual emergency spending provisions. The president assumed powers in domestic affairs, such as no-bid contracts, that were defensible only in times of war.

Although Bush's popularity by the end of his second term approached the levels of disapproval of Nixon after Watergate, the powers of the presidency and the executive branch were hardly touched. Congress did not reassert its authority after his presidency. When Obama took office, unlike Gerald Ford's succession of Nixon, he inherited all of the executive powers that had been claimed by Bush. Unlike Bush, Obama was more interested in using those powers on behalf of consolidating his domestic policy agenda, rather than pursuing a vigorous foreign policy. It seems that both parties are in agreement insofar as they believe that the powers of the national government are unlimited. *The Republicans deny any limitations on the power of government in terms of national security and foreign policy. The Democrats believe that government has unlimited power as regards domestic policy. Taken together, it becomes impossible to establish the ground of constitutionalism when there is no consensus between the parties on how to limit the power of government.* The American Founders knew that government must have all of the power that is necessary in times of war. But that means that Congress and the president must establish a distinction between war and peace; they must clearly identify the enemy and determine what constitutes victory, so that it is possible to reestablish the ground of normal government. Peace, not war, must determine how the institutions operate in normal times. Under the conditions established by the war on terror, it is impossible to distinguish war and peace, or know when victory has been achieved. If the necessity of preparation for war is a constant and ongoing condition of civic life, no limitations can be imposed on government. This condition is compatible with bureaucratic rule, but not political or constitutional rule, as we have previously argued about the Progressive revolution.

A written Constitution is meaningful only if its principles, those which authorize and legitimize governmental authority, are understood to be permanent and unchangeable, in contrast to the statute laws made by legislatures and governments that alter with changing circumstances and the political requirements of each generation. In other words, such a regime must have a theoretical or reasonable ground that distinguishes it from government. When the principles that establish the legitimacy of the Constitution are understood to be changeable, are forgotten, or are denied, the Constitution can no longer impose limits on the power of government. In that case, government itself will determine the conditions of the social compact and become the arbiter of the rights of individuals, as well as every other interest in society.[1]

Progressivism, Immigration, and the Transformation of American Citizenship

AMERICA HAS OFTEN BEEN CALLED a nation of immigrants, as if that is what has distinguished it among the nations of the earth. But every human society that did not spring full-blown from the soil with a common identity is a nation of strangers, or immigrants, who were somehow united in civic friendship. Some nations with long histories have forgotten their origins, or what it was that made it possible to distinguish themselves from others. The problem of immigration, therefore, is unintelligible in the absence of an understanding of what it is that constitutes the ground of unity or common identity. Any human association that considers itself as separate or distinct from other political societies—or, in modern times, one which considers itself sovereign—must make distinctions between those who are citizens and those who are not.

America established the ground of political citizenship in the equal natural rights of man. It required a social compact and consent to authorize the power of government. The social compact made it the primary purpose of government to protect the rights of individuals. By limiting the power of government, the compact assured the autonomy of civil society, making it unnecessary for religion to utilize the authority of government. Once equality is understood in terms of the equal protection of equal rights, considerations of religion, ethnicity, race, or culture cannot be decisive as the ground of citizenship, although they might have some prudential bearing on who might become citizens.

The philosophy of History and the new idea of the rational state, which was at the core of the Progressive movement, undermined the natural right foundation of the American regime. This resulted in the repudiation of the social contract and the principle of equality. The social compact and the natural right theory upon which it was based represented a philosophic way—through nature and reason—of understanding political and moral phenomena. That tradition was fundamentally undermined by the acceptance of a philosophy of History. Joseph Cropsey characterized this transformation in human thought by observing "that the replacement of philosophy by History was the condition of the replacement of politics and religion by society and economics."[1]

In the rational state, the authority of science—and the new disciplines of the social sciences—would provide the theoretical and practical knowledge necessary to transform society and administer progress.[2] The Hegelian idea of the state was meant to reestablish a political whole that would reunite the social and economic, the public and private, and make citizenship the ground of freedom and public virtue.[3] The Progressive thinkers, intoxicated by the new philosophy of History, looked to society and economics as fundamental to an understanding of the historical process. They gravitated, subsequently, to the concepts of race and class, and eventually, culture, as tangible factors in their attempts to elucidate that process. In their view, there are no permanent human problems. Consequently, every problem can be solved by the transformation of society and economics. That transformation required the rule of organized intelligence in the form of a rational bureaucracy within the state. The state itself becomes the embodiment of the whole and as such is an ethical organization. In denying the natural right foundation of philosophy, the truth of equality as the foundation of equal citizenship was also undermined.

The American Founders insisted that the abstract principle of natural equality spelled out the way in which all men are the same: in terms of their natural rights. But the diversity in the faculties of men, and the factionalism which is derived from those differences, is also sown into the nature of man. This is recognition of the way in which men differ. Thus, social inequality, which grows out of the differences inherent in the faculties of men, is a necessary outcome of a free society. The defense of freedom therefore required a defense of property, understood in terms of the protection of the fundamental individual rights of conscience, opinion, interest, and labor. In separating church and state, government and civil society, and the public and private sphere, equality and liberty is reconciled in a reasonable way that is compatible with the nature of man.

Progressive thought, on the other hand, established a new ground of citizenship, which rested on a denial of the doctrine of natural right and the older understanding of the principle of equality as an abstract truth. In addition, it denied the traditional view that freedom is subordinate to the moral law. It is the new historical understanding of freedom and equality that would provide the foundation of equal citizenship in Progressivism. In the modern state, rationalization, or centralization, then would require the imposition of a governmental uniformity upon civil society, without regard to individual rights or natural differences.

The philosophy of History, therefore, established a new ground by which to determine the common good. That new understanding provided the foundation upon which citizenship would depend—the creation of a rational, or organic, will. By the end of the nineteenth century, the two tangible forces most descriptive of economy and society, *class* and *race*, had gained ascendancy over every other category of knowledge providing the ideological foundation for the understanding and exercise of will. Both forces would be discredited in the twentieth century, but long before race theory was discredited politically by Hitler and the Nazis, it had gained intellectual respectability in the natural and social sciences. Indeed, race theory had become so pervasive during the first part of twentieth century that Hannah Arendt, writing during World War II, noted,

Few ideologies have won enough prominence to survive the hard competitive struggle of persuasion, and only two have come out on top and essentially defeated all others: the ideology which interprets history as an economic struggle of classes, and the other that interprets History as a natural fight of races. The appeal of both to large masses was so strong that they were able to enlist state support and establish themselves as official national doctrines. But far beyond the boundaries within which race-thinking and class-thinking have developed into obligatory patterns of thought, free public opinion has adopted them to such an extent that not only intellectuals but great masses of people will no longer accept any presentation of past or present facts that is not in agreement with either of these views.[4]

Although the notion of racial superiority was repudiated in the aftermath of World War II, the understanding of History, which made racial theory credible, retained its authority. Perhaps in the twenty-first century it still holds sway. As Arendt surmised before the middle of the last century, any objective understanding of the historical past or present outside of the categories of race and class has had little resonance among intellectuals or the mass public. There is little doubt that class, understood in an historicist manner, however discredited by the political demise of Communism, is still the most useful way in which to evaluate economics and politics in the disciplines of the social sciences. Race has been thoroughly discredited in politics and theory. It has, however, attained a new status as a moral phenomenon, primarily as a symbol of exploitation that would become the ground of group solidarity.

In its origins, race was an important element in the philosophic understanding of History; but it was not the decisive element. While the very real historical events of the twentieth century discredited the political theory of racial superiority, the difficulty of separating the category of race from History has remained. Even when the natural and social sciences began to doubt the authority of race as an explanation for legitimizing political power, it remained a fundamental category in the understanding of identity and citizenship. In his attempt to make sense of that term, *race*, at the beginning of the twentieth century, Henry Adams noted in *The Education of Henry Adams*, "History offered a feeble and delusive smile at the sound of the word; evolutionists and ethnologists disputed its very existence; no one knew what to make of it; yet, without the clue, history was a nursery tale."[5]

The great tragedies spawned by the Nazi and Communist parties, although defeated as political movements, did not result in a rejection of the ideological ground that engendered them. By the end of the twentieth century, it was clear that mass and elite opinion had not gone beyond the categories of race and class. Despite the fact that political rhetoric in America had proclaimed equality as the fundamental goal, the theoretical ground of the principle of equality had been undermined by the philosophy of History. It has never been restored. Consequently, the leading intellectual movements of our time provide seemingly endless variations on the historical categories of race and class. The postmodern movements—political, social, or cultural—which have looked to establish identity in the categories of race, sexual orientation, or gender, are themselves offshoots of the evolution of historical consciousness.

Despite the civil rights movements of the last half century, ostensibly based on the principle of equality, nearly every political and administrative solution to the problem of equal rights has required an unequal treatment of individual citizens. In practice, therefore, the public policies of the administrative state have not been based upon any understanding of the social compact. The principle of equality, understood in terms of the natural rights of individuals, could no longer serve as the foundation of citizenship. Rather, the new notion of citizenship presupposed the necessity of subordinating individual rights to the fundamental requirements of the administrative state. Consequently, the notion of citizenship as a tangible or meaningful thing has resonance only within the framework of the historical categories of race, class, or culture. Thus, it is not surprising that within the policymaking apparatus of the administrative state, group rights provide the best—perhaps the only—way to establish identity as a member of the state.

As a result, it has become nearly impossible in the administrative state to execute public policies in any way other than the unequal treatment of individual citizens. The undermining of the principle of equality, and the regime of civil and religious liberty after the Civil War, transformed the meaning of citizenship. It was inevitable that this transformed meaning would have a profound effect upon the problem of immigration. Consequently, it was not merely the influx of aliens that could change a nation; ideas have transformed the meaning of citizenship for the native born as well. Moreover, immigrants, too, are shaped by the regime which accepts them. They typically adapt to whatever they perceive as the expectations and aspirations of that regime. Not surprisingly, the expectations and aspirations of citizenship in a regime of civil and religious liberty (for natives and immigrants alike) are far different from those expectations that have been created within the administrative, or welfare, state. It is necessary, therefore, to elucidate the relationship between the idea of regime and the notion of citizenship as it developed in America.

The American Founders established a foundation of citizenship unlike any that the world had ever seen. It was not based on religion, nationality, race, or any previous category of citizenship. It was based on the acceptance of an idea, the natural equality of all men. Although nearly all immigrants would come from countries shaped by those previous categories of citizenship, none of them could be fundamental as the foundation of American citizenship. Therefore, immigration policy would have to be decided on a prudential basis, which would allow exclusion on numerous practical grounds. The understanding of equality as the foundation of citizenship is necessary but not sufficient in itself. It is also essential to take into account the problem of the character of prospective citizens, or their capacity for self-government. This, too, poses a practical problem in a regime in which there is no historical antecedent.

It is not altogether apparent what kind of regime—or categories of citizenship, religion, nationality, color—has established the proper kind of character to merit inclusion in a regime in which equality and liberty constitutes the basis of citizenship. At the time of the American Founding, religious belief was thought to be fundamental in determining the capacity for citizenship. It was necessary, therefore, to understand equality as a principle in order to see that it was possible, within a social compact, to have different religious beliefs and yet be fellow citizens. What are the differences among human beings that can be reconciled within the social compact, and what are those that cannot be reconciled? An understanding of human nature is helpful, but most differences of citizenship—like those of the regimes that produced them—are conventional.

However, no matter what the answer to the question of the differences of character, the American regime had to establish whatever prudential considerations were thought necessary in terms of restricting immigration to those who could best be assimilated into the social compact. Still, no older category of citizenship, even though it might have established the character of decent citizens in previous regimes, could serve as the exclusive ground of citizenship, especially if it undermined the principles of the social compact. Yet, in the period after the Civil War, that is precisely what happened. Progressive intellectuals, animated by a new understanding of History that resulted in a rejection of natural right, denied that the idea of equality could establish the foundation of citizenship in the modern state. Armed with the authority of science, they came to believe that capacity for citizenship was dependent upon race, class, or subsequently, culture.

The twentieth century has made it clear that the problems of immigration and citizenship have become almost impossible to understand on prudential or practical grounds. Thus, any considerations of means or moral capacity—the things necessary for understanding character— are no longer thought to be relevant to the discussion of citizenship. The category of race, established as the ground of morality in the state because it is the embodiment of the will of a people, had become an end in itself. Thus the notion of race had replaced the principle of equality as the ground of the meaning of citizenship. As a result, every prudential argument is quickly condemned as racist by the intellectuals and increasingly the politicians and public as well. It has not been easy to reestablish the idea of equality as the foundation of the regime. Consequently, even those principled pieces of legislation, such as the Civil Rights Act of 1964, have not been interpreted on the basis of an understanding of the principle of equality but in terms of the historical categories of race or class. It is important, therefore, to understand the meaning of citizenship in a regime of civil and religious liberty before it becomes possible to see how and why it differs from the notion of citizenship in the administrative state.

Citizenship in a Regime of Civil and Religious Liberty

American statesmen from Washington to Lincoln understood America as a regime of civil and religious liberty.[6] The uniqueness of America, they thought, was to be seen in the manner in which it was able to reconcile politics and religion, civil and religious liberty, or freedom and morality.[7] They understood man and citizenship—and man's capacity for self-rule and the desire for freedom—in the light of human nature.

In most European nations a common morality and religion, or faith, was the ground of citizenship. However, after the Protestant Reformation, religion itself was a source of division among Christians.[8] Religion could no longer serve as the authority for political life and citizenship. A common religion, in which *individuals* shared a common faith, had established a means for determining the moral basis of self-government. But religious differences among the various Protestant and Catholic sects had only provided the occasion for bloody warfare.

Although the religious doctrines of certain Christian sects appeared to be compatible with freedom and self-government, others seemed to foster a dependency that perpetuated despotic rule. The European nations shared a common religion, but Christianity itself had not established the conditions for a common citizenship. "For when pressed into political service," Charles Kesler has observed,

> Christianity—a religion centered around belief in Christ rather than obedience to a revealed code of laws (e.g., Torah or *sharia*)—had the distressing if somewhat paradoxical tendency both to deflate civil laws' significance and to inflate their pretensions. That is, the pursuit of true Christianity tempted some believers to desert the earthly for the heavenly city, but tempted others to commandeer temporal laws in order to enforce the faith. The one tendency sapped the foundations of citizenship; the other turned citizenship into fanaticism.[9]

The solution to the problem of citizenship, therefore, required a solution to the problem of religion. Kesler suggests that

> by building government on the basis of natural rights and the social contract, the American Founders showed how, for the first time since the days of the Holy Roman Empire, men could be good citizens of the City of God and good citizens of their earthly city without injury or insult to either.... The key to the solution was the insistence that questions of revealed truth be excluded from determination by the political sovereign or by political majorities. Indeed, majority rule and minority rights could be made consistent only on this basis. Under modern conditions, limited government thus becomes essential to the rule of law.[10]

The structure of republican government and its democratic processes are made possible only upon recognition of the fact that moral authority does not emanate from government or from majorities. It was the new understanding of natural right, and the political doctrine of equality, that had established a foundation for individual rights. The social compact, therefore, provided the theoretical and moral basis for majority rule. At the same time, it was necessary to limit the power of a numerical majority to the protection of the rights of each on behalf of the rights of all. It was for this reason that it was possible for George Washington to celebrate the fact that America had extended the rights of citizenship to Jews, probably for the first time in the modern history of a Western nation. In his letter to the Hebrew congregation in Newport, in 1790, Washington stated the reason why this was so:

> The citizens of the United States of America have the right to applaud themselves for having given to mankind examples of an enlarged and liberal policy worthy of imitation. All possess alike liberty of conscience and immunities of citizenship. It is now no more that toleration is spoken of as if it were by the indulgence of one class of citizens that another enjoyed the exercise of their inherent natural rights, for happily the Government of the United States, which gives to bigotry no sanction, to persecution no assistance, requires only that they who live under its protection should demean themselves as good citizens in giving it on all occasions their effectual support.[11]

The great achievement of the American Founders was to establish a solution to the problem of political obligation that had eluded Western man since the collapse of the Roman Empire. As Kesler has observed,

> Civil liberty meant finding a new ground for law and citizenship that would protect decent politics from arbitrary claims of divine right. Religious liberty meant separating church membership from citizenship in order to protect the conscientious pursuit of true religion from civil or ecclesiastical tyranny. Civil liberty and religious liberty have the same root, a theoretical or philosophical insight: the doctrine of natural rights.[12]

In practice, that philosophic doctrine required the separation of church and state, which made it necessary to separate politics or government from civil society, thereby distinguishing the public and private sphere. It was this doctrine that established the ground of modern constitutionalism. The view of America as a regime of civil and religious liberty lasted only so long as the tradition of natural right remained viable.

The American Founding, through toleration of religion, showed that it was no longer necessary to share a common faith as a fundamental requirement of citizenship. Furthermore, the ground of citizenship would no longer rest upon color or a common blood. The acceptance of the principles of the American Founding made it necessary to establish the foundation of equal citizenship on the natural rights of man. As Abraham Lincoln noted prior to the Civil War, immigrants who had come to America, although unrelated to the Founders by blood, found that they had something in common that was more important than ties of blood. Lincoln observed that

> if they look back through this history to trace their connection with those days by blood, they have none, but when they look through that old Declaration of Independence they find that those old men say that "We hold these truths to be self-evident, that all men are created equal," and then they feel that that moral sentiment taught in that day evidences their relation to those men, that it is the father of all moral principle in them, and that they have a right to claim it as though they were blood of the blood, and flesh of the flesh, of the men who wrote that Declaration—and so they are.[13]

What was to become indispensable as the ground of citizenship, therefore, was recognition of an abstract truth—that all men are created equal.

The new understanding of citizenship, which had important ramifications for the problem of immigration, required an almost philosophic defense of the principle of equality. Furthermore, knowledge of the meaning of equality is only the necessary, but not the sufficient, condition for establishing the social compact. It is also important that prospective citizens have the capacity for self-government, or the right kind of character—one compatible with the exercise of freedom and its defense—in order to perpetuate the regime. But in such a regime, there is no tangible factor, in terms of religion, race, or nationality, by which to determine the basis of citizenship. Practically speaking, immigration into America would, of necessity, be understood in a prudential manner. But the question arises: What determines the proper kind of character for a regime in which equality and liberty constitute the foundation of the compact? Religion, nationality, race, or the kind of regime—despotic or not—are all things that will be taken into consideration.

Interestingly, the Immigration Act of 1790 is often cited as support for the view that the American Founders understood immigration and citizenship in terms of race. That act was an attempt to facilitate the quick naturalization—in only two years—of immigrants. European whites, of course, would be those best equipped to become citizens so quickly. The act, then, was based on excluding those—particularly Indians and blacks—who were, or had been, slaves. It was not color or race but civilization that was the standard for their judgment. The former slaves and savages were not sufficiently civilized to have developed the kind of education, manners, and especially the deliberative capacity necessary to participate in the social compact. The problem of immigration was understood in a prudential way that was compatible with an understanding of nature and reason. The idea that race—as a biological category, understood through history and science—could be more fundamental in terms of understanding man's humanity than reflection upon human nature or reason was not intelligible to the Founders. It was not until the end of the nineteenth century that such an historicist understanding of man would become legitimized in the science of biology. The Founders did not understand man, or race, in terms of history, science, or biology. Rather, they understood man in terms of nature and the cultivation of reason—or lack thereof.

The American Founders were not oblivious to the fact that there would be immigrants from particular regimes who could not be easily assimilated. As a result, prudence would require the necessity of extending residency requirements for such immigrants. When the Federalists passed the Alien and Sedition Act, they extended the number of years necessary for naturalization to fourteen (as opposed to two in the old act). They were concerned that the increase of immigrants from Europe, many of whom had fled the French Revolution and were thought to have the kind of habits of character that could be modified by association with free citizens, would require a longer period of naturalization. Of course, those prudential arguments could not be separated from the political problems of the time, and therefore they can be sound or unsound in terms of policy. However, no policy based on prudence, which is concerned with means, should have the effect of undermining the end or principle of the regime.

Citizenship in a free society could encompass many differences based on religious, ethnic, or racial grounds. It would be necessary, of course, that those who established the compact consent to the fact that all of those differences can be accommodated on the ground of equality. But immigration policy could not be indifferent to the moral character of its prospective citizens. Therefore, prudence would dictate that those immigrants would be best suited who were most capable of grasping and appreciating the principles of equality and liberty. It would be those who were self-reliant and most interested in self-government who would be encouraged to become citizens. Most importantly, there could be no expectation that government should extend privileges to any group or deny the rights of any individual. Immigration could in no way undermine the principles of the social compact, which provided the foundations of citizenship for those who had established it.

In 1819, John Quincy Adams illustrated the importance of this fundamental necessity. He gave the following reply to a German immigrant who wondered why America had not adopted measures to encourage immigrants from Europe by extending favors on their behalf. Adams noted that Americans were not "in any manner insensible to the great benefits" of immigration,

> but there is one principle which pervades all the institutions of this country, and which must always operate as an obstacle to the granting of favors to new comers. This is a land, not of *privileges*, but of *equal rights*. Privileges are granted by European sovereigns to particular classes of individuals, for purposes of general policy; but the general impression here is that *privileges* granted to one denomination of people, can very seldom be discriminated from erosions of the rights of others. But hence it is that no government in the world possesses so few means of bestowing favors, as the governments of the United States. If the powers, however, of the government to do good are restricted, those of doing harm are still more limited.[14]

Immigration policies, understood in light of the social compact, could offer no more than freedom and opportunity to prospective citizens. A government or society that offered incentives and privileges to newcomers could do so only at the expense of the equal rights of all citizens.

The American Founders established a new ground of citizenship compatible with an understanding that equality and freedom was subordinate to the moral law. That view required the protection of the freedom of the mind and conscience, which meant the free exercise of religion. Thus the Founders for the first time solved the problem of political obligation in a democratic manner. This had become possible because of the rediscovery of the doctrine of natural right. The social compact, based on the principle of equality, would give rise to a free society. A free society would in turn require the necessity of distinguishing the sacred and secular, the political and social, and the public and private sphere.

The new Progressive political thought, on the other hand, denied natural right and the social compact. Through the idea of the state, Progressivism hoped to establish a new conception of government and citizenship, one that would empower government to reorder the economy and society with the purpose of resolving the tension between the individual and society, or between freedom and necessity. With the establishment of the modern administrative state, the role of government could not be understood to be the protection of the individual natural rights of citizens. Consequently, the social compact would become meaningless.

History, Science, and Race

The ideas of natural right and the social compact had animated the early American understanding of citizenship and immigration. With the acceptance of historicist—or Progressive—thought in the period after the Civil War, the foundation and meaning of citizenship was fundamentally altered. That transformation had a profound effect on the problem of immigration as well. The political meaning of equality had rested upon an understanding of man as a rational and moral being. As long as nature provided the standard by which to judge political right, freedom and equality were understood to be subordinate to the moral law. In the modern state, a new understanding of freedom would become the foundation of morality and citizenship.

Rousseau's denial of the view that rationality constituted the distinction between man and the animals led him to conclude that man has no nature, only a capacity for self-perfection.[15] He argued, "Therefore it is not so much understanding which constitutes the distinction of man among the animals as it is his being a free agent.... It is above all in the consciousness of this freedom that the spirituality of his soul is shown."[16] After Rousseau, freedom would no longer be understood in terms of the nature of man, nor could it be subordinate to the moral law. Rather, freedom, or will, would become the foundation of morality. The political problem was then one of creating a general, or moral, will.

It is difficult to overstate the importance of consciousness of freedom and the idea of perfectibility in the minds of the Progressive intellectuals. Thus Herbert Croly, one of the most important Progressive intellectuals of the early twentieth century, insisted that "democracy must stand or fall on a platform of possible human perfectibility."[17] Croly measured the progress of man in terms of his willingness to serve his fellow man. "If it be true that democracy is based upon the assumption that every man shall serve his fellow-men, the organization of democracy should be gradually adapted to that assumption."[18] Nonetheless, Croly was well aware that

> the majority of men cannot be made disinterested for life by exhortation, by religious services, by any expenditure of subsidized words, or even by grave and manifest public need. They can be made permanently unselfish only by being helped to become disinterested in their individual purposes... In the complete democracy a man must in some way be made to serve the nation in the very act of contributing to his own individual fulfillment. Not until his personal action is dictated by disinterested motives can there be any such harmony between private and public interests.[19]

The bureaucracy, by creating the occupations to be established within the administrative state, would become the means of reconciling private and public interests, or the particular and general will.

It was the German theorists, primarily Kant and Hegel, who established the ground of humanity—and subsequently citizenship in the state—upon the new understanding of freedom and the cultivation of moral will. Because man was now understood to have made himself human through his own efforts, or in the course of his history, it was no longer possible to understand nature and reason as the fundamental attributes of man's humanity. Rather, it is the capacity for, and consciousness of, freedom that distinguished man among the animals. The process by which man had made himself human through the use of his freedom, or will, was a result of his ability to adapt and transform his environment in the course of history.

Subsequently, the tangible ingredients by which to identify the evolution of social and economic man would come to be understood through the concepts of race, class, or variations of those categories—concrete factors such as geography, climate, and language. These things taken together with art and civil religion would, after the influence of Hegel, come to be understood as culture. In looking at the historical differences in the progress of the evolution of man, it was not long before it was thought possible to measure the superiority of different peoples and classes or groups. In undermining the natural right foundation of individual citizenship, moral will, based on the new understanding of freedom, was legitimized within the concept of the state.

One important American Progressive, Mary Parker Follett, in *The New State*, written early in the twentieth century, outlined the new Progressive understanding of freedom and rights. She noted,

> Democracy has meant to many "natural" rights, "liberty" and "equality."
> The acceptance of the group principle defines for us in truer fashion
> those watchwords of the past. If my true self is the group-self, then my
> only rights are those which membership in a group gives me. The old
> idea of natural rights postulated the particularist individual; we know
> now that no such person exists. The group and the individual come into
> existence simultaneously: with this group-man appear group-rights.
> Thus man can have no rights apart from society or independent of
> society or against society. Particularist rights are ruled out as everything
> particularist is ruled out.... The truth of the whole matter is that our
> only concern with "rights" is not to protect them but to create them.
> Our efforts are to be bent not upon guarding the rights which Heaven
> has showered upon us, but in creating all the rights we shall ever have.[20]

In Follett's view, those rights had to be understood in terms of the group and not the individual. Thus she noted,

> As an understanding of the group process abolishes "individual rights,"
> so it gives us a true definition of liberty. We have seen that the free man
> is he who actualizes the will of the whole. I have no liberty except as
> an essential member of a group.... But liberty is not measured by the
> number of restraints we do not have, but by the number of spontaneous

activities we do have.... We see that to obey the group which we have helped to make and of which we are an integral part is to be free because we are then obeying ourself. Ideally the state is such a group, actually it is not, but it depends upon us to make it more and more so. The state must be no external authority which restrains and regulates me, but it must be myself acting as the state in every smallest detail of life. Expression, not restraint, is always the motive of the ideal state.[21]

The Progressive understanding of freedom and citizenship necessitated the rejection of the notion of individual private rights because individuals would become free as citizens only when they exercised their will on behalf of the group, or ultimately participated as members of the ethical state, understood as the embodiment of the organic will of a people. John Dewey had expressed much of this same view a generation before Mary Parker Follett. In an early essay, "The Ethics of Democracy," published in 1888, Dewey observed:

The essence of the "Social Contract" theory is not the idea of the formulation of a contract; it is the idea that men are mere individuals, without any social relations *until* they form a contract.... Society, as a real whole, is the normal order, and the mass as an aggregate of isolated units is the fiction. If this be the case, and if democracy be a form of society, it not only does have, but must have, a common will; for it is this unity of will which makes it an organism. A State represents men so far as they have become organically related to one another, or are possessed of unity of purpose and interest.... But human society represents a more perfect organism. The whole lives truly in every member, and there is no longer the appearance of physical aggregation, or continuity. The organism manifests itself as what it truly is, an ideal or spiritual life, a unity of *will*. If, then, society and the individual are really organic to each other, then the individual is society concentrated.... In conception, at least, democracy approaches most nearly the ideal of all social organization; that in which the individual and society are organic to each other.... The organism must have its spiritual organs; having a common will, it must express it.[22]

Mary Parker Follett had contended that "as the collective idea and the collective will, right and purpose, are born within the all-sufficing social process, so here too the individual finds the wellspring of his life."[23] The individual will and collective purpose is reconciled within the social process of the group, which taken as a whole becomes the moral will within the modern state. Therefore, the group process and social—or organized—intelligence becomes institutionalized in the regulatory apparatus of the administrative state. Thus, the state, because it encompasses an organic social and ethical whole, produces within itself the technical or rational means—the bureaucracy—which can enable it to establish policies for carrying out the will of the people. With the establishment of the scientific method, Charles Merriam observed, "Politics as the art of the traditional advances to politics as the science of constructive intelligent social control."[24] Thus, the modern state would require centralized control of the political, social, and economic sphere. Subsequently, the Progressives would argue that the unity of the citizenry would necessitate a commonality of race or common blood.[25]

Equality and Citizenship

Modern science and philosophy of History had not only transformed the meaning of freedom, but the understanding of equality and citizenship as well. The categories of race and class had become central to the elucidation of man as an historical being. Interestingly, the most important battleground in the Progressives' attempts to undermine the natural right foundation of the social compact came to revolve around the interpretation of the meaning of the American Civil War. The Progressives hoped to replace the old view of the social compact with the new Hegelian understanding of the modern state. During the Civil War, Lincoln had defended America as a regime of civil and religious liberty. In his view, the social compact had established the political conditions of equality and liberty. Slavery was incompatible with both equality and liberty when understood in light of nature and philosophic reason.

The Civil War, as Abraham Lincoln always insisted, was about the issue of slavery and was fought over the principle of equality. With the victory of the Union armies, it seemed likely that Lincoln's understanding of the meaning of equality would prevail. In that case, equality would have remained the indispensable ground of national citizenship. But such was not to be the case. The Progressive intellectuals, and the new social science disciplines then being developed in the new research universities, denied the natural right foundation of the regime. They also rejected the social compact and the abstract principle of equality itself. Charles Merriam, a celebrated political theorist of the time, explained the reason for the rejection. He noted, "the influence of the German school is most obvious in relation to the contract theory of the origin of the state and the idea of the function of the state. The theory that the state originates in an agreement between men was assailed by the German thinkers and the historical, organic, evolutionary idea substituted for it."[26] Merriam was well aware that

> considering the question as one of principle, it is evident that much depends on one's political theory. If we believe that government has no jurisdiction over men unless they have consented to it, and that every man is entitled to equal civil and political rights, regardless of his fitness for them, then it follows that to deprive any man of the suffrage for any cause, or any people of self-government for any cause, is a departure from democratic principles. . . . If, on the other hand, it is believed that liberty and rights are necessarily conditioned upon political capacity, and that the consent of the governed is a principle which, in the present state of affairs, cannot be perfectly realized, then the situation is altered.[27]

Nor was Merriam alone in his defense of Southern principles. Herbert Croly, the great Progressive reformer, agreed with Merriam and the slave owners. The slaveholders were correct in their view, Croly insisted, because "negroes were a race possessed of moral and intellectual qualities inferior to those of white men."[28] In the view of the Progressive intellectuals, man is an historical being, and History, not nature, had determined what it means to be a human being. The struggle among the races in history determined the race that deserved to be on top. The superiority of the white race and the inferiority of the black race is the scientific proof of the inequality of men. This proof had become evident as a result of the evolutionary theory of human development. Furthermore, they insisted that, if individual rights cannot be derived from the principle of equality, the source of legitimacy, or right, is derived from the state and its laws, not nature.

Abraham Lincoln was admired, and even revered, by many of the

Progressive intellectuals. But it was not because he had anchored the moral authority of the regime in the principle of equality. That view would have made it impossible to defend political inequality on any ground whatsoever. Moreover, the Progressives denied what Lincoln affirmed: that the foundation of the social compact rested upon an understanding of natural right. The Progressive intellectual and political movements, whether animated by social Darwinism, socialism, anarchism, or communism, were united in rejecting the natural rights foundation of the social compact. Rather, they came to embrace the modern idea of the state. Charles Merriam was typical of the Progressive intellectuals. He noted, "The present tendency, then, is to disregard the once dominant ideas of natural rights and the social contract.... The origin of the state is regarded, not as the result of a deliberate agreement among men, but as the result of historical development, instinctive rather than conscious; and rights are considered to have their source not in nature, but in law."[29]

Merriam was not unique in his view that the American Founders had misunderstood the meaning of liberty. He was well aware that the Southern opinion had differed from the view of the Founders. Furthermore, in looking at recent trends in scholarship, Merriam observed,

> The modern school has, indeed, formulated a new idea of liberty, widely different from that taught in the early years of the Republic. The "Fathers" believed that in the original state of nature all men enjoy perfect liberty, that they surrender a part of this liberty in order that a government may be organized, and that therefore the stronger the government, the less the liberty remaining to the individual. Liberty is, in short, the natural and inherent right of all men; government the necessary limitation of this liberty. Calhoun and his school, as it has been shown, repudiated this idea, and maintained that liberty is not the natural right of all men, but only the reward of the races or individuals properly qualified for its possession. Upon this basis, slavery was defended against the charge that it was inconsistent with human freedom, and in this sense and so applied; the theory was not accepted outside the South. The mistaken application of the idea had the effect of delaying recognition of the truth in what had been said until the controversy over slavery was at an end.[30]

The remarkable assertion that slavery had obscured the truth of the historical and scientific fact that race established the ground of liberty and political right was not uncommon among the Progressives. Merriam, consequently, agreed with Calhoun: "Not only are men created unequal...but this very inequality must be regarded as one of the essential conditions of human progress.... This fundamental fact that individuals or races are unequal, is not an argument against, but rather in favor of, social and political advancement."[31]

It is not surprising that the new disciplines of the social sciences, including political science, were almost unanimous in their rejection of the doctrine of natural right, the principle of equality, and the social compact. The social sciences rejected slavery, but the rejection was on the ground that slavery was an historical anachronism. This view was confirmed by the events of history, as evidenced in the victory of the Union armies. It made it possible, subsequently, to defend the new scientific understanding that political capacity, or the suitability for self-government and freedom, was dependent upon the progress of the races. As Merriam had noted in his defense of Calhoun, it was the "mistaken application of the idea" of racial superiority in the defense of slavery that "had the effect of delaying recognition of the truth in what had been said until the controversy over slavery was at an end."[32] In Merriam's view, Calhoun's theory had been vindicated only after the institution of slavery had been destroyed. With the end of slavery, it had become possible to see the historical and scientific truth that only certain races were capable of self-government.

The historians' admiration of Lincoln rested upon what they considered an historic achievement, the establishment of the modern state or nation. Lincoln's own understanding of his actions in defense of constitutionalism was dependent upon the necessity of upholding the conditions of the social compact, which required a reaffirmation of the founding principles of the regime. Yet, the Progressives interpreted his role as an historical vindication of the idea of the state and the denial of the social compact as the foundation of constitutionalism. Charles Merriam, commenting on what he perceived to be the fundamental accomplishment of Lincoln, observed, "In the new national school, the tendency was to disregard the doctrine of the social contract, and to emphasize strongly the instinctive forces, whose action and interaction produces a state. This distinction was developed by Lieber, who held that the great difference between 'people' and 'nation' lies in the fact that the latter possess organic unity....In general, the new school thought of the Union as organic rather than contractual in nature." As Merriam noted, "The contract philosophy was in general disrepute, and...the overwhelming tendency was to look upon the nation as an organic product, the result of an evolutionary process."[33]

Merriam concluded that it had become necessary to recognize the fact that the concept of the *nation* was dependent upon a theoretical understanding of the state. The notion of a *people*, on the other hand, can only be understood with reference to the theory of a social compact made by individuals. Thus, Merriam insisted that the "[N]ation carried with it the idea of an ethnic and geographic unity, constituted without the consent of any one in particular; 'people' was understood to be a body formed by a contract between certain individuals. The very fact that the Union was 'pinned together with bayonets' was enough to show that the doctrine of voluntary consent had faded into the background."[34] In the modern state, it was no longer necessary to establish the legitimacy of government by securing the consent of the governed. Merriam assumed that because the Southern states had not been allowed to secede from the Union, the social compact—like slavery—had become an historical anachronism.

For Merriam, the Civil War itself had destroyed the conditions of the social compact. He concluded:

> [T]he general idea was that the United States, by virtue of the community of race, interests, and geographical location, *ought to be* and is a nation; and ought to be held together by force, if no other means would avail. This was the feeling that underlay the great national movement of 1861–1865, and it could not fail to be reflected in the philosophy of that time and in the succeeding interpretations of that event.[35]

History itself had provided the ground of the new theory. Like evolution, success in the struggle had proved the rightness of the cause. Lincoln, who had tried to preserve a regime of civil and religious liberty based on the principles of the American Founding, was celebrated by Progressive social scientists and historians for having established a modern state.

The Southern intellectuals had rejected Lincoln's understanding of the meaning of equality as an abstract truth, which was the way it had been understood by the American Founders. But the Northern intellectuals had also rejected Lincoln's defense of the principle of equality. They insisted that the idea of equality had been undermined by the discoveries of the new biological and social sciences. Thus Charles Merriam insisted, "From the standpoint of modern political science the slaveholders were right in declaring that liberty can be given only to those who have political capacity enough to use it, and they were also right in maintaining that two greatly unequal races cannot exist side by side on terms of perfect equality."[36] Furthermore, Merriam agreed with the Southerners that "rights do not belong to men simply as men, but because of the superior qualities, physical, intellectual, moral or political, which are characteristic of certain individuals or races."[37] The denial that the principle of natural human equality was a standard for political right made it impossible to defend equality as the fundamental ground of citizenship. The new sciences had established race and class as the necessary foundation of political and social life. As a result, equal citizenship based on an understanding of individual natural rights was no longer intelligible as a practical matter.

Nearly all of the scholarly opinion following the Civil War was critical of the North's attempt to establish the former slaves as equal citizens. The North was condemned for extending the franchise, and the South was praised for obstructing black voting. The leading political scientist of the day, Columbia's John W. Burgess, observed that "it is the white man's mission, his duty and his right, to hold the reins of political power in his own hands."[38] He further wrote, "The claim that there is nothing in the color of the skin from the point of view of political ethics is a great sophism. A black skin means membership in a race of men which has never of itself succeeded . . . to reason, has never, therefore, created any civilization of any kind."[39] By the end of the nineteenth century the authority of science had come to buttress the claims of historicism. It was as though the theories of Darwin and Hegel had been merged.

It is instructive to see how the historians of the time had come to understand Reconstruction. James Ford Rhodes,

who wrote the first detailed study of the Reconstruction period, fully subscribed to the idea that Negroes were innately inferior and incapable of citizenship . . . Rhodes thought it a great pity that the North had been unwilling to listen to such men of science as Louis Agassiz who could have told them that the Negroes were unqualified for citizenship. "What the whole country has only learned through years of costly and bitter experience," declared Rhodes, "was known to this leader of scientific thought before we ventured on the policy of trying to make negroes intelligent by legislative acts: and this knowledge was to be had for the asking by the men who were shaping the policy of the nation."[40]

The learned opinion of the time was summed up in a single sentence by William A. Dunning of Columbia University. He noted that the whole difficulty of Reconstruction stemmed from the fact that the "antithesis and antipathy of race and color were crucial and ineradicable."[41] In looking back on that period, nearly every historian has considered Reconstruction to be a political failure. But, given the intellectual opinion of the time, it is hard to see how it could have succeeded.

Immigration Law and Citizenship

The importance of race or class for an understanding of immigration and citizenship in the last part of the nineteenth century cannot be overstated. As I have shown above, the concept of race was first understood within the framework of a philosophy of History. In the nineteenth century it came to be understood as a category of science. It was Robert Knox in 1850 who "reintroduced the notion of race into biology,"[42] and the newly formed social sciences were quick to adopt the science of race and eugenics. But with the development of the modern university, the idea of the state also came to be understood on the basis of culture as derivative of the discovery of the historical sense. In the new discipline of political science, John Burgess argued, "the State is the national community, and the government is the agent of the State." According to Burgess, "The American state, however, had a longer genealogy and a 'transcendent mission.' It was rooted historically in a 'predominant Teutonic nationality,' and it was destined to be 'the perfection of the Aryan genius for political civilization.' This meant that it was essential neither to 'sectionalize' it into states nor to 'pollute' it with non-Aryan elements."[43]

It was not long before the idea that race was the ground of American citizenship came to dominate the debate concerning immigration. As

Daniel Tichenor has observed, Francis Walker, president of MIT and former chief of the national census, "was among the first prominent intellectuals to apply Darwinian and Spencerian theories of racial hierarchy to the new European immigration."[44] Walker was concerned that immigration "was increasingly drawn from the nations of southern and eastern Europe—peoples which have got no great good for themselves out of the race wars of centuries, and out of the unceasing struggle with the hard conditions of nature…and that have thus far remained hopelessly upon the lowest plane of life."[45] In Walker's view, Darwinian evolutionary theory had provided the best means for determining character and the capacity for citizenship.

In the early 1890s, Walker had "embraced Teutonic theory to justify excluding newer European immigrants. 'They have none of the *inherited instincts and tendencies* which made it comparatively easy to deal with immigration of olden time.… They are beaten men from *beaten races*; representing the worst failures in the struggle for existence."[46] Walker is not wrong in suggesting that immigration policy must take into account the distinctions between nations in terms of judging the character of prospective citizens. Of course, the American social compact would benefit most from citizens who are likely to value freedom, and presumably they would come from non-despotic and well-governed stable regimes. However, it was not clear that the historical notion of *race*, a new scientific construct in Walker's time, which denied that the principle of equality must be understood in terms of nature and natural right, had been responsible for the success of any particular regime.

The new understanding of race was not merely a descriptive account of the differences that exist among men, the result of the variety of regimes, languages, religions, and colors. That kind of knowledge had always been understood in terms of common sense and politics—as friends and enemies, or citizens and strangers. The category of race when linked to science came to be used as a means of distinguishing superior and inferior humans solely by consideration of what had been a new construct—race. Indeed, the new science of eugenics, founded in the 1880s by Francis Galton, cousin of Charles Darwin, had gained popularity as a means of promoting or discouraging population growth by distinguishing between the superior races that ought to produce more offspring and the inferior races that ought to produce less.

As Jay Varma has observed, it was not long before "the concept that ethnic groups were biologically distinct races entered popular discourse with the institutionalization of the science of eugenics in the early 1900s...which had evolved into the study of racial differences and was defined as 'the study of agencies under social control that may improve or impair the racial qualities of future generation, either physically or mentally.'"[47] By the time race had come to be understood as the exclusive consideration for citizenship within the state, its corollary, the unlimited power of government, had become legitimized. The new regulatory power of government offered the possibility of using the science of eugenics not merely for making distinctions among immigrant groups, but also for establishing ranks among citizens as well.

Citizenship, the American Founders had argued, need not be established on the basis of a common faith or common blood. Rather, they believed that a common idea, the belief in the abstract truth that all men are created equal, must provide the only foundation of citizenship. But, once again, with the new authority of science and historicism, there would be a concerted attempt for the next half century to establish citizenship upon the foundation of race. Consequently, it was the principle of equality that would become the casualty of that transformation in the meaning of citizenship.

Daniel Tichenor has pointed to the change: "Drawing inspiration from the new scientific research, Progressive Era restrictionists aimed to build a national regulatory system that excluded immigrants of national and ethnic groups they deemed inferior. Certain that crucial *racial* distinctions existed between Europeans, they yearned for new immigration barriers to guard the nation from the contamination of southern and eastern Europeans."[48] In the next decades, many authors, including Clinton Stoddard Burr in *America's Race Heritage*, Madison Grant in *The Passing of the Great Race*, and Charles W. Gould in *America: A Family Matter*, insisted that the white race could be divided into a hierarchy of three races: the Mediterranean, Alpine, and Nordic. It was Mediterranean race, primarily southern and eastern Europeans, but particularly Russian Jews, who were lowest on the scale, with the Alpines on a somewhat higher level. But the Nordics were considered the superior race. Indeed, Burr goes so far as to suggest, that "Americanism is actually the racial thought of the Nordic race, evolved after a thousand years of experience."[49] If the European races could be distinguished in such a manner, it was not surprising that the other races were thought to be even further down the scale in terms of intelligence and capacity for self-government.

The first piece of legislation in American history, at the national level, to exclude immigrants on the basis of a scientific understanding of race did not occur until 1882. However, that act did not attempt to exclude Europeans because of race. Rather, the new immigration act resulted in the exclusion of the Chinese, who had become a political problem in California. The Chinese had not been assimilated easily into American society, so the case for exclusion was not difficult to make. But it was the growing awareness of the importance of race to membership in the new organic state that fueled the demand among many intellectuals and politicians for restricting those who could not be assimilated into society. Daniel Tichenor has observed that "Chinese exclusion called for the federal government to assume unprecedented regulatory authority over immigrant admissions and rights for the explicit purpose of guarding the racial purity of American society. Indeed, most advocates of Chinese exclusion shared a strong 'sense of the state'—one that linked national state-building to the preservation of existing orders of ethnic, racial, and religious hierarchy."[50]

The Chinese case is instructive, therefore, because that exclusion was defended on the ground of a new understanding of race and science as decisive for determining capacity for citizenship. It was thought that only those of common blood—whose superiority and thus qualification for membership in the state is determined by science—can be eligible for citizenship. If the state is the manifestation of a moral will, and will becomes intelligible as an embodiment of a people through race, citizenship in the state must be understood to be derived from the fundamental inequality of man as established by the differences among the races.

It is clearly the case that not everyone is entitled to citizenship in America, or any other sovereign nation. Immigrants can be excluded on the basis of race, religion, nationality, illiteracy, or many other reasons. That is because republican governments, unlike despotic regimes, must take into account the character of its potential citizens. Prior to the Civil War, the social compact was understood in terms of the principles of equality and liberty. Thus, as noted above, the problem of immigration was understood in terms of prudence or morality. Throughout the early part of the nineteenth century, there had been considerable political pressure to pass national legislation restricting immigration on the basis of religion, nationality, color, or language. Protestants wanted to restrict Irish Catholics because of their religion. But they could never persuade Congress to pass legislation banning immigration on the ground of religious differences. Nonetheless, there were numerous restrictions based on health, disease, mental disability, and character or morals—such as preventing prostitutes and criminals, or those of unsavory character, from becoming citizens.[51]

The Immigration Act of 1924 was the culmination of nearly a half century of effort on behalf of a view that celebrated the rational state as the embodiment of the moral will of a people. That will had come to be defined by blood, race, class, or culture. The scholarship in the defense of racial superiority had been generated in the empirical research of the new social and biological sciences. Many of those social science departments had established their legitimacy within the newly established research universities, and the research generated by social science would become important in bolstering the movement to restrict immigration on the basis of race.

The restrictionists had many influential supporters among the elites and the intellectual classes, as well as among labor unions. The labor unions opposed unrestricted immigration because they believed that it had caused a surplus of cheap labor, which kept down the wages of native American workers. The intellectuals, on the other hand, were in favor of restricting immigration because they thought it necessary that the economy and society should be brought under state control. In their view, it was the business interests that profited from unlimited immigration. Frank Julian Warne, the former secretary of the New York State Immigration Commission, insisted that mass immigration had made it easier for government to neglect the social and economic welfare of American citizens. Warne maintained that "factory laws, women and children in industry, workingmen's insurance, and widows' pensions...would in all probability have been established...several decades earlier if there had been no European immigration of the magnitude of the past three decades."[52]

In the view of many of the Progressive intellectuals, free immigration had made it possible to ignore the social ills brought about by unrestricted capitalism. As Tichenor has written, "the decentralized, self-regulating society that prevailed for much of American history was, in the view of the Progressive Era restrictionists, a luxury of the past."[53] Joseph Lee, a civic reformer, noted the difference in the meaning of liberty: "In political life, liberty meant until recently the minimum of control necessary to secure equal opportunity.... We have begun to realize the control of man over nature, and to see that the highest results come from the collective effort consciously directed to an end. These considerations have a direct bearing upon the question of immigration regulation."[54] In the new view, the responsibility for the social welfare of its members rests solely with the government of the state.

In 1916, the newly established Progressive publication, *The New Republic*, made this clear in an editorial: "Freedom of migration from one country to another appears to be one of the elements of nineteenth century liberalism that is fated to disappear. The responsibility of the state for the welfare of its individual members is progressively increasing. The democracy of today cannot permit...social ills to be aggravated by excessive immigration."[55] Of course, on practical grounds, every nation, including one based upon a social compact, must limit immigration to prevent social ills, or for many other reasons as well. But the Progressive rejection of the old liberalism was based upon a repudiation of the social compact in which private individuals and civil and economic associations, and not the state, determined the meaning of freedom and the welfare of the individuals.

In addition, many specialists in the social sciences, bolstered by the intelligence testing done in World War I, were quick to interpret the data as evidence for excluding certain races. This debate reached its peak after the Great War. In 1923, Henry Fairfield Osborn spoke enthusiastically about the results of intelligence testing carried out by the Army: "I believe those tests were worth what the war [World War I] cost, even in human life, if they served to show clearly to our people the lack of intelligence in our country, and the degrees of intelligence in different races who are coming to us, in a way which no one can say is the result of prejudice.... We have learned once and for all that the negro is not like us."[56] It is clear that social scientists such as Osborn could no longer understand the meaning of equality as a political principle. It was not possible for them to see what it is that men have in common by nature. Therefore, they had come to believe that the differences between blacks and whites were as fundamental politically as those between men and animals.

When Walter Lippmann questioned some of the interpretations of the psychologists, he was ridiculed by many social scientists, including Lewis Terman, who had published the Stanford-Binet scale of intelligence in 1916. Indeed, Dr. William McDougall, professor of psychology at Harvard, insisted that because of Lippmann's failure to accept the scientific explanation of the testing results, he was "denying also the theory of organic evolution, and he should come out openly on the side of Mr. [William Jennings] Bryan. For the theory of the heredity of mental qualities is a corollary of the theory of organic evolution."[57]

The denial of the principle of equality was stated most openly by Dr. Harry H. Laughlin, eugenics consultant to the House Judiciary Committee on Immigration and Naturalization. He noted, "We in this country have been so imbued with the idea of democracy, or the equality of all men, that we have left out of consideration the matter of blood or natural born hereditary mental and moral differences. No man who breeds pedigreed plants and animals can afford to neglect this thing."[58] In the same vein, Prescott Hall, writing in the *Journal of Heredity*, urged a worldwide application of Darwinian principles. Hall contended that "eugenics among individuals is encouraging propagation of the fit, and limiting or preventing the multiplication of the unfit. World eugenics is doing precisely the same thing as to races considered as wholes. Immigration restriction is a species of segregation on a large scale, by which inferior stocks can be prevented from both diluting and supplanting good stock."[59]

Immigration policy in America had gone from one based on an understanding of the natural rights of men to one based on historical and biological science. As Abba Schwartz has noted, "The National Origins provisions of the immigration law of 1924 marked the actual turning point from immigration control based on the asylum idea...[to one] definitely in favor of the biological basis."[60] The regime of civil and religious liberty had often provided asylum to those who had been persecuted because of religious belief. Religion, although a problem when allied with despotic governments, had also helped shape the kind of character necessary in a regime that required self-restraint and self-government. The authority of biology had come to determine the most important factor in establishing the capacity for citizenship. It is no small part of the tragedy of the period that by the time Hitler had come to power in the decade of the 1930s, the Immigration Act of 1924 made it nearly impossible for Jews to find an asylum in America.

The problem posed by unrestricted immigration would become a fundamental preoccupation of the nation after World War I. The Immigration Act of 1924, as a result of national or group quotas, seemed to have legitimized the view that the creation of a racial hierarchy to determine immigration policy was the primary motivation for the legislation. But that perception is not altogether accurate. There were numerous prudential reasons for restricting immigration; racial quotas would become only the most publicized reason for doing so. The war itself had temporarily resolved the problem; very little immigration had been possible during it. The war had fanned the flames of hostility against foreigners. Not surprisingly, however, because they were the enemy in that war, resentment against the foreign-born was directed first against a superior race, the Germans. As Tichenor has noted, "rallies held by the German-American Alliance in support of peace with Germany dismayed the American public in 1915–16, accentuating native fears about the loyalties of the country's large foreign-born population."[61]

That fear prompted suspicions about the character and reliability of nearly all foreign-born populations. By the end of the war, the Bolshevik Revolution in Russia had complicated the problem of immigration in a way that made it easier to defend restrictions based on race. Americans had begun to fear that a flood of refugees from Eastern Europe would include radicals and communist agitators. The racial theories seemed to support the view that southern and eastern Europeans lacked the proper intelligence and character for citizenship. Predictably, after the war, however, the hostility against the Germans would subside. But the racial theories would emerge once again to be used in support of the animus against the southern and eastern Europeans. Thus, in the early 1920s, there had been a flood of popular and academic books that decried the mixing of the races. In addition, the eugenics movement would gain an unprecedented respectability, not only in the social sciences but in the government, the courts, and the public at large.

In the aftermath of World War I, there was nearly universal agreement that some restrictions on immigration were necessary. Indeed, there was considerable public support for a ban on all immigration, in which case quotas would have been unnecessary. But there was little political support for closing the borders. In the absence of unrestricted immigration, it was necessary to determine who should be given preference in terms of immigration into the United States. The Quota Act of 1921, known as the Dillingham Act, was the first to establish immigration quotas based on the country of origin. Immigration would be limited to 3 percent of each European nationality living in the United States, with the total number of immigrants restricted to 355,000 per year.[62]

The practical problem of establishing quotas revolved around the necessity of determining an accurate way of distinguishing American citizens and establishing their country of origin. That was not an easy task. As Mae M. Ngai has noted,

> The census of 1790, the nation's first, did not include information about national origin or ancestry. The census did not differentiate the foreign-born until 1850 and did not identify the places of birth of parents of the native-born until 1890. Immigration was unrecorded before 1820 and not classified according to origin until 1899, when it was arranged, not by politically defined nation-states, but according to a taxonomy called "races and peoples."[63]

Thus, it was difficult to determine the country of origin for purposes of establishing quotas before the census of 1900. Moreover, many of the immigrants had come into the United States in the last decade of the nineteenth century. The new immigrants wanted the most recent census for the purpose of determining the numbers of each nationality living in the country. In the Dillingham Act, it was decided that the 1910 census would be used to establish that number for purposes of establishing quotas. This decision was not unnecessarily divisive and it appeared that most could live with those restrictions based on that census.

The problem arose when it came time to reauthorize the Dillingham Act. By 1924, the demand for racial quotas had gained momentum in Congress, and particularly in the House. When the Republicans took control of Congress in 1919, Albert Johnson (R-WA) took over the Immigration Committee. He had a long association with the Immigration Restriction League (IRL). Beginning in the 1890s, the IRL had attempted to lobby Congress using social science expertise to buttress the case for immigration restriction. Subsequently, Johnson hired Harry Laughlin to serve as the committee's expert on eugenics. Experts had long argued for "the proper eugenic selection of the incoming alien millions." They insisted that this could be done "not by killing off the less fit, but by preventing them from coming into the State, either by being born into it or by migration."[64] With Johnson in charge, the House committee went to great lengths to limit the quotas of those races thought to be inferior.

The provision of the Immigration Act of 1924 that caused the greatest outcry was the change that would require that the 1890 census—rather than the 1910 census—be used to determine national quotas. It was based on the assumption that those Americans who had arrived before 1890, largely of the Nordic and Alpine races, were to be preferred to the later immigrants. In terms of actual numbers, the act did not result in significantly reducing the number of immigrants from southern and eastern Europe. The restrictions on the total number of immigrants allowed in the Dillingham Act had already done that. The number of new immigrants from southern and eastern Europe were very small. The damage that was done resulted from the fact the new law appeared to establish a rank among citizens that would be based upon racial group characteristics. Moreover, there was no quota for immigrants from the Western hemisphere. Thus, immigrants from Mexico and Latin America were not affected.

Significant elements of both political parties and most elites had supported immigration policies based on racial superiority. But the Republican Party—perhaps because it dominated electoral politics during the 1920s—came to be viewed as the party most responsible for defending a new kind of inequality. Subsequently, the party of Lincoln would have great difficulty in reestablishing itself as the defender of the principle of equality. As a result, many of those constituencies that had supported the Republican Party, including blacks and Jews who had voted in support of the Republicans in the election of 1920, would abandon the party.

Moreover, the newer immigrants who had come to America after the 1880s settled largely in the big cities and urban areas. They were assimilated by the Democratic Party machines that had dominated politics and elections in those cities. Although most of the ethnic immigrants voted for Democrats in local elections, many of them voted for Republicans nationally, beginning in the 1890s and continuing into the early part of the twentieth century. Indeed, Woodrow Wilson had to repudiate much of his academic writing on race in order to lure some of the new immigrants away from the Republican Party. By the end of the 1920s, those immigrants and their children were no longer competitive for the Republican Party and would not be for nearly a half century. Ironically, it was FDR's Democratic Party, which was committed to the establishment of a new administrative state, that would make its appeal on the basis of equality and equal citizenship. Roosevelt insisted, however, that it was the government of the modern state, and not the principles of the social compact, that would determine the meaning of equality and equal citizenship. Although many in Congress had worked to mobilize constituencies on the ground of race, there were many others who had argued for immigration restriction in a way that was compatible with an understanding of equality and character, too, as necessary for good citizenship. Although President Warren G. Harding and Vice President Calvin Coolidge were in favor of immigration restrictions, their rhetoric was far different from that coming out of Congress. Indeed, when Coolidge became president he appeared to handle the problem in a prudential manner. First, Coolidge defended immigration restrictions on the practical ground that "we should have no more aliens to cope with . . . than our institutions are able to handle."[65] Furthermore, his defense of those restrictions was not intended to polarize the nation by categorizing American citizens in terms of race. Therefore, he insisted that "restrictive immigration is not an offensive but a purely defensive action. . . . We must remember that every object of our institutions of society and government will fail unless America is kept American."[66] America must be understood not in terms of race but in terms of an idea.

The perpetuation of the social compact is, of course, in the hands of all who are a part of it. Therefore, Coolidge was determined to prevent immigrants from any nation who would undermine that compact from becoming American citizens. He maintained that "there is no room in our midst for those whose direct purpose is political, social, or economic mischief, and whose presence jeopardizes the physical or moral health of the community." In the final analysis, Coolidge understood the problem of immigration in the same way as the American Founders, on moral grounds. Therefore, he insisted that "American institutions rest solely on good citizenship and were created by people who had a background of self-government. New arrivals should be limited to our capacity to absorb them into the ranks of good citizenship."[67] Coolidge's rhetoric did not appear to give support to those who would attempt to understand America in terms of class or racial groups.

The Immigration and Nationality Act of 1965 was defended on the ground that the old national or group criteria, which had established the foundation for the 1924 and 1952 immigration acts, would be replaced by individual criteria. Senator Edward Kennedy noted that "favoritism based on nationality will disappear. Favoritism based on individual worth and qualifications will take its place."[68] President Lyndon Johnson also criticized the national origins quota system because

> the ability of new immigrants to come to America depended upon the country of their birth. Only three countries were allowed to supply seventy percent of all the immigrants.... This system violated the basic principle of American democracy—the principle that values and rewards each man on the basis of his merit as a man. It has been un-American in the highest sense because it has been untrue to the faith that brought thousands to these shores even before we were a country.[69]

Johnson did not say what that faith was.

Both Kennedy and Johnson had denied that immigration policy should be based on nationality or race. Rather, Johnson insisted that the new immigrants should be admitted on the basis of their skills. "Those who can contribute most to this country—to its growth, to its strength, to its spirit—will be the first that are admitted to this land."[70] Kennedy and Johnson may have believed that the neutral category of skill, unrelated to character, is the way in which the immigration policy would consider the capacity of individuals as opposed to groups. But both Kennedy and Johnson were well aware that as citizens of the administrative state, the new immigrants would be important as members of ethnic and racial groups. Thus, they must have known that the new immigrants, shaped by the expectations created by government, and not those of a free society, could become important constituencies for the perpetuation of the Democratic Party. Moreover, in denying any moral basis for determining the character of prospective citizens, they were promoting a policy that would encourage immigrants who would seek benefits from, or become dependent upon, the administrative state.

The immigrants who came to America after the 1965 Immigration Act had fewer reasons to become citizens of the United States. The administrative state had begun to expand and consolidate its grip on American politics. Those immigrants who came were often more interested in what the government could provide. It was becoming less important, therefore, to participate as members of a political community. Although economic opportunity still provided a stimulus for those coming to America, the role of the federal government had changed in regard to the understanding of the status and rights of immigrants and aliens. As Daniel Tichenor has observed, "The post-1960s 'rights revolution' gave immigrants fewer reasons to become citizens. Naturalized voters and parties were no longer the lifeblood of expansive immigration policies."[71]

In the next decades, there is no question that Mexicans and other Latin American immigrants naturalized at very low rates compared to the earlier periods. Why did this happen? As Peter Schuck and Rogers Smith have observed,

> The law…increasingly speaks of individual "rights," the language of entitlement, rather than of their "interests," the language of policy and accommodation. Moreover, the law increasingly emphasizes the values of equality, group interest, and nondiscrimination.… And it is welfare state membership, not citizenship, that increasingly counts. Political membership uniquely confers little more than the right to vote and the right to remain here permanently; the former is used by only a bare majority of eligible voters, while the latter, although undeniably valuable, is problematic for only a minority of legal aliens.[72]

Moreover, the 1965 act, when interpreted by the bureaucracy and courts, had created a new category of those who could become beneficiaries of government and constituencies of the administrative state— aliens, legal and illegal. As a result of those policies of the bureaucratic apparatus of the state, which blurred the distinction between entitlements and responsibilities, it had become difficult to distinguish between the rights and duties of citizens and noncitizens. With the consolidation of the administrative state, it is difficult to understand the policies of government in any way other than the conferring of benefits to various groups or constituencies without regard for a public good.

The legislative and judicial remedies of the last half century designed to deal with the problems of immigration and citizenship have not succeeded in lessening the conflict over the protection of fundamental rights. That is because citizenship is still understood in terms of those historical categories of race and class established in the notion of the state. It is not surprising that this failure to understand citizenship as a social compact of the people, based on the principle of equality, has resulted in undermining the distinction between citizens and aliens, legal and illegal. The apparatus of the administrative state has extended rights and privileges to noncitizens that would be incomprehensible were it not for the fact that it is the state, and not the people, that has become sovereign. As a result, the government of the administrative state has produced an immigration policy that has generated very little public support among American citizens.

Furthermore, the remedies for protecting the civil rights of every American have not united but divided the country. In the public debate on immigration reform there was an explicit linkage between civil rights and immigration reform. As Vice President Hubert Humphrey noted, "We have removed all elements of second-class citizenship from our laws by the Civil Rights Act.... We must in 1965 remove all elements in our immigration law which suggests that there are second-class people.... We want to bring our immigration law into line with the spirit of the Civil Rights Act of 1964."[73] Not surprisingly, the Civil Rights Act of 1964 and the Immigration and Nationality Act of 1965 were primarily justified by their intention to reverse the racism in a society that had sanctioned segregation and the quotas of the Immigration Act of 1924. But the remedies for both problems were achieved not by denying that group status or race ought to establish the ground of civil rights or citizenship but by giving preference to the previously excluded groups and races. In short, it had not been possible to reestablish civil rights, or immigration policy, on the ground of the equality of all individuals.

Conclusion

The pervasiveness of an understanding of man and citizenship in terms of race and class has persisted unabated in the past half century, despite the collapse of Nazism and Communism. In abandoning nature as the standard for political life, the thinkers of the late nineteenth century had turned to race or class as the means of providing an explanation for the historical differences among men and their differing achievements. Furthermore, the newly created social sciences, with the authority of history and biology behind them, were uniform in their insistence that race should become the foundation for the determination of citizenship. However much racial theories came to be discredited in the twentieth century, the theoretical ground—the philosophy of History—upon which the defense of race and class had been established, was never discredited or abandoned.

As a result, it has not been possible to reestablish the protection of the equal rights of citizenship on the ground of an understanding of the principle of equality—as an abstract truth derived from nature. It was that understanding of natural right that had been abandoned as the foundation of citizenship by the Progressives. Thus, it has become clear in light of what occurred in the wake of the passage of the Civil Rights Act of 1964 and the Immigration and Nationality Act of 1965 that the rights and duties of citizenship, and their enforcement in the courts and bureaucracies, could only be understood on the basis of the Progressive understanding of history and the acceptance of the moral authority of the administrative state.

In practice, therefore, the policies promulgated in the bureaucracies and courts relating to the rights of citizenship have become meaningful only with reference to the state, or group identity. And groups can be understood in an intelligible way only through the categories derived from race, class, ethnicity, or gender. The result was not a return to the principle of equality—of individual rights—but a new kind of group equality, which would seek to reverse the old hierarchies (white—or male—dominance, economic class privilege, or racial preference).

Furthermore, when politicians attempt to make prudential arguments concerning immigration policy or civil rights policy on the basis of individual rights—which run counter to the contemporary historicist meaning of group rights—they are considered racist. It becomes impossible, in a practical way, to defend the equal rights of all individuals without reference to race or social status. Ironically, the political defense of the equal rights of individuals, a genuinely nonracist position, becomes vulnerable to the charge of racism precisely because it does not take race, class, or social status, into account. Thus, it is not surprising that politicians are unwilling or unable to make a compelling defense of the equal rights of individual citizens.

There is a deeper reason for the failure to reestablish the ground of citizenship on the principle of equality as the foundation of the social compact. Such a defense would require an understanding of natural right. But, the modern state itself and the problems of immigration and citizenship have been understood only in terms of a philosophy of History. In the final analysis, perhaps, Hannah Arendt was right when she insisted, speaking about race and class, that "free public opinion has adopted them to such an extent that not only intellectuals but great masses of people will no longer accept a presentation of past or present facts that is not in agreement with either of these views."[74] In the absence of an understanding of natural right, History may be intelligible only on the ground of race or class, or some similar variation of historical consciousness derived from the Progressive understanding of the meaning of freedom.

8

Politics, Rhetoric, and Legitimacy: The Role of Bureaucracy in the Watergate Affair

IT HAS BEEN MORE THAN A DECADE and a half since the Watergate scandal resulted in the forced resignation of a president of the United States.[1] There have been millions of words spoken and written about the events surrounding one of the most important political scandals in American history. The Watergate affair has been called many things: "a second-rate burglary," a "political crime in high places," a "constitutional crisis," and a consequence of "the imperial presidency." Watergate has had a continuing influence on the politics surrounding the institutional tension between Congress and the president. It brought to light the collision course upon which Congress and the president were embarking in the aftermath of the Vietnam War by testing the legitimacy of the use of presidential power and putting an end to the overblown rhetoric concerning "the imperial presidency."

Rarely has a political crisis arisen in the interim without someone in authority insisting that the "lessons" of Watergate should not be forgotten. The passage of time, however, has not resulted in greater clarity concerning what it is we should have learned from the event, perhaps because we still lack an authoritative account of it. But the meaning of Watergate has continued importance, if only because the prevailing opinion concerning what transpired then largely has determined what was politically possible subsequently. The passion generated by the politics surrounding Watergate has long inhibited a dispassionate analysis of the forces responsible for it. It is only in recent times that historical distance has provided the conditions, and the calm, that can shed new light on what is now an old political controversy.

In the broadest sense, the issues of Watergate involved the question of legitimacy concerning the use of power in national politics. In the American constitutional system, power resides in separate political institutions that depend on different constituencies to guarantee the autonomy of the respective branches of government. The separation of powers ensures that the political institutions have the incentive and opportunity to exercise power in dealing with the various normal problems of government, not to mention the extraordinary contingencies that sometimes arise.

Power, however, does not confer legitimacy. In claiming the right to use power, the president or Congress can cite the authority of the Constitution, or the people, to legitimize the claim. Where constitutional authority is unclear, politicians have attempted to legitimize the use of power by virtue of authority of the people. In doing so, public opinion becomes decisive in determining whether the people support a claim to power in their name. The formal participation of the people and the ratification of the acts of its representatives take place in the voting booth, but elections do not clarify every important political question. The same electorate that elects a president has, in its various parts, also elected the legislature, the majority of which may be of a different party.

The claim to legitimacy by election necessitates clarity concerning what it is the electorate has consented to. Watergate, an institutional crisis as opposed to a legal one, pitted the president and Congress against each other in terms of controlling the permanent government, or the bureaucracy. The president claimed the legitimacy of a partisan presidential election as justification for the use of power that could have resulted in fundamental changes in direction and control of the federal bureaucracy. Congress denied that the 1972 election contained any such mandate. Moreover, it denied the president's claim to derive moral authority to lead the country, rather than merely administer the government, as a result of a principled, partisan appeal to a national majority in a national election. The Democrats, instead, insisted that a majority in both houses of Congress constituted a mandate to resist a change that would undermine many of the most important programs created during the New Deal and the Great Society. Since Watergate, executive leadership responsive to the will of a national majority has been weakened: bureaucratic or centralized administrative rule, compatible with organized interests and a diversified legislature, has become almost institutionalized.

In institutional terms, the bureaucracy played a far more important role in Watergate than is commonly admitted. It is not of great importance what individual bureaucrats did or did not do in particular cases. Rather, the bureaucracy as a whole held the key to the balance of power between the political branches. During the Nixon years, it became clear that Congress and the president both had a stake in controlling the bureaucracy. As Douglas Yates subsequently observed, "presidential reaction to the problem of bureaucratic control may well have reached its high-water mark in the Nixon administration."[2] The presence of the bureaucracy—largely the creation of a partisan majority—had become the key to the decline of partisanship in the United States. The superiority of the Democratic Party at the congressional and state level, coupled with the acceptance of the legitimacy of the goals of the New Deal and Great Society as the ultimate consensus by politicians (not to mention intellectuals), helped create a disjunction between presidential electoral politics and politics at other levels. As John Wettergreen noted,

Parties as national electoral organizations must decline out of disuse in proportion to the rise of a national, centralized bureaucracy as the chief instrument of government ("conflict resolution") and the chief governmental source of private or local benefits. Agencies are the new, stabilizing "political structures" for the resolution of social conflicts. Therefore, disjunction between particular private or local interests, which are administered to individually and not legislated for nationally, and the national or public interest, which is articulated by presidents or aspiring presidents, is likely to continue.[3]

Consequently, the rise of the bureaucracy furthered the demise of the principle of majority rule by denying the element of consent. The national majority has access to the national government primarily through the institution of the presidency. The weakening of the presidency could not but have an adverse impact on the power of the national majority.

The consequence of bureaucratization has been an increased tension between the executive and the legislative, regardless of party, and, increasing apathy among voters. This is so because most important political decisions are made in Washington by a centralized administration not accountable to the elected chief executive. Moreover, the interest of the legislature is closely allied with—and committed to the perpetuation of—an executive bureaucracy. Thus, the bureaucracy, ostensibly nonpartisan, will retain effective power when backed by Congress. Walter Dean Burnham has commented on the effect of this phenomenon:

> as party erodes both in the electorate and in the House, divergence in the electoral coalitions of President and Congress increasingly reinforce the separation of powers; incumbents tend increasingly to be protected or insulated....The responsiveness of the representational system to electoral change declines; and abstention from the polls become the largest mass movement of our time.[4]

It seems unlikely, however, that the separation of powers is reinforced or even sustained. More likely, it is undermined to the extent that the president is unable to control the administration and change the direction of government to conform with the demands of new majorities. Rather, the president, like the party, is rendered nearly impotent, the symbol of an impotent majority. In the absence of crisis, and without the necessity of a majority consensus, administrative rule replaces political rule.

The institutional or political quarrel between the branches was settled decisively in the wake of Watergate. Congress prevented presidential use of power in a direction it opposed. But the battle to shape public opinion could not end, nor could a new consensus be forged concerning the use of power without the animating force of a national majority. Watergate attempted to restore a new political and institutional balance between the branches. More accurately, it sought to achieve a new equilibrium—wherein both branches could have access to the bureaucracy—but none could rule it in a unified manner. In such circumstances, the bureaucratic-legislative interests could resist the political force of the majority and its representative, the president.

The imbalance in the second Nixon term, which precipitated the Watergate crisis, resulted from Nixon's unwillingness to recognize the neutrality of the bureaucracy. His attack on the governmental bureaucracy constituted an implicit repudiation of the Progressive view legitimized by the New Deal, and made operative in the Great Society, that government could be an "engine of compassion." It appeared to be Nixon's view that the presence of a nonpartisan bureaucracy had resulted in a distortion of the principle of representation. It had prevented the majority from ruling. The purpose of his policy of decentralization and executive reorganization—the heart of the New American Revolution—was to restore a representative government.

Those opposed to Nixon sought to retain a centralized administration and attempted to continue the tradition of consensus politics that every president, regardless of party, had adhered to since the New Deal. The Democratic Party, though firmly in control of the legislature, appeared unable to make a principled appeal of sufficient moral authority to animate a national majority. It was unable to win the presidency. However, it was increasingly able—largely as a result of nonpartisan appeals, that is, as ombudsmen—to ensure that incumbent congressmen would not be defeated. With continued control of the central political branch of government, the Democratic leadership had the institutional means to dominate the bureaucracy in its interest. With regard to public opinion, however, it remained merely a powerful faction. Unable to mobilize a national majority, it lacked the moral authority to govern. More simply, the people had not, and apparently would not, consent to its rule. Subsequently, it became clear to the congressional leadership that it could not allow a president to govern, regardless of his electoral mandate, who sought to destroy the structure that maintained its power. Republicans, too, in Congress were alarmed by what they perceived to be the growing institutional imbalance between the branches. Consequently, Republicans in the legislature did not support the president on partisan grounds. The perceived institutional imbalance threatened not only the prerogatives of Congress as a body but those benefits that make incumbency so advantageous to individual members. Hence, Watergate was not a partisan affair in the ordinary sense, nor was it simply a legal controversy. Rather, it was an institutional struggle between the political branches of government. Such an event could not but be political.

The 1972 Election

A number of observers have suggested that the practical effect of Watergate was the reversal of the election of 1972. Henry Kissinger has noted,

> Nixon in the final analysis had provoked a revolution. He had been reelected by a landslide in 1972 in a contest as close to being fought on ideological issues as is possible in America.... The American people for once had chosen on philosophical grounds, not on personality.... For reasons unrelated to the issues and unforeseeable by the people who voted for what Nixon represented, this choice was now being annulled—with as-yet unpredictable consequences.[5]

Was it indeed possible that the issues of Watergate were unrelated to the political and "philosophical" issues of the 1972 election? Or was Watergate political in a different way than the public debate would lead one to believe? Nearly a decade after Watergate, a presidential scholar suggested that

> Nixon triumphed in the 1972 election, but the fragility of his power was perfectly shown by the capacity of the Watergate break-in, an intrinsically trivial episode, to become the symbol of great awfulness and to fuel his destruction. Washingtonians destroyed him, but they, rather than he, by that time held the confidence of the people.[6]

What had happened to public opinion in the interim? The election was an explicitly partisan event; Watergate was not. Both events, however, sought to mobilize public opinion in support of partisan as well as institutional goals. If Watergate obscured the issues of the election, it was a crucial event in undermining the moral authority that the president derived from the majority in the election and transformed public opinion concerning the use of presidential power. Just after the election, the president appeared to be invulnerable; within a year, his opponents had the upper hand.

On the surface, Watergate was viewed narrowly as a case of political corruption in high places. The tone of the public debate is seen in its most characteristic fashion in the famous query of Senator Howard Baker, put to the many defendants who appeared before the Senate Watergate Committee: "What did the President know, and when did he know it?" The central focus was the cover-up, and the primary question was a legal one. Was Nixon guilty of a crime? Furthermore, the president's public defense against impeachment only reinforced the legal character of the public debate. His lawyers argued that an impeachable offense should be narrowly construed to be an indictable offense. The defense was reduced to the assertion that Nixon had committed no crime.

Beneath the surface of the public debate, staged largely through the media and presented as a legal question, was an intensely partisan, political battle, as well as an institutional or constitutional struggle. Ironically, the political battleground was the least understood dimension of Watergate; the public debate was as little partisan as such an event can be, because the ground of the debate was narrowed to encompass the legal question of criminal guilt or innocence.

A great deal of confusion concerning Watergate was the result of focusing too much on the details of the event and too little on the political circumstances surrounding it. Nelson Polsby noted the following in a symposium on presidential power: "I think a good bit of the thrashing around that constitutional scholars have recently engaged in is directly traceable to their unwillingness to deal directly with, yet their incapacity quite to ignore, the fact that impeachments are by design and, in any event, inescapably, political acts as well as constitutional events."[7] In order for a president to court impeachment, Polsby suggested, he "must be guilty of substantial misdeeds, abuses of power rising to constitutional dimension, and *in addition* [his italics] must have alienated the other centers of power in and out of government to which a President, in our complex and interrelated system, must render account."[8] There is no doubt that Nixon alienated nearly every center of power in American life.[9] We must consider the extent to which the political circumstances and events that existed during and after the election of 1972 contributed to Watergate.

The Mandate

In a crucial way, the election of 1972 shaped the contours of the subsequent events known as Watergate. In the decisive respect, particularly in regard to domestic affairs, the election was a referendum on the issues of centralization in American government. Theodore White, in *The Making of the President 1972*, brought to focus one of the central issues of that election: "Richard Nixon campaigned in 1972...against central power, against the idea of the omnipotent President doing his will from Washington. He was for returning home power to the people in their communities."[10]

On November 2, 1972, in one of his last radio addresses to the nation before the election, Nixon deplored the increasing growth in the size and power of the centralized administration. "If this kind of growth were projected indefinitely into the future," he observed, "the result would be catastrophic. We would have an America top heavy with bureaucratic meddling, weighted down by big government, suffocated by taxes, robbed of its soul."[11]

By the end of his first term, Nixon had come to believe that the problems of domestic government could not be solved by the leadership of the national government. Moreover, that leadership—and its creation, the centralized bureaucracy—had undermined the ability of the people to govern themselves by weakening the character of the individual citizen. The problem of government had become the machinery of government, which, though enshrouded in the humane purposes of the New Deal and the Great Society, had obstructed an essential element of democracy—the responsiveness of government to the people. The primary obligation of the president in domestic affairs was control of the executive bureaucracy so that government could become responsible to political leadership and responsive to the demands of the contemporary majority. Nixon attempted, in his second term, "to revive and restore the principles of individual enterprise, personal responsibility, and limited government that were the legacy of the Founders to us."[12]

The ensuing struggle between the president and Congress was not a typical party struggle, as James Sundquist has suggested, "dominated by the same fundamental dispute over the role of government that defined a new party alignment in the 1930s."[13] Rather, it was a battle over control of the bureaucracy, in which the interests of the legislature—and anyone committed to the maintenance of a centralized administration—and those of the executive diverged, regardless of party. Nixon's solution to the problem was the increased centralization of power into the White House and away from the permanent government. Such a strategy required a massive reorganization of the bureaucracy, on the one hand, and the reversal of the flow of power to Washington and back to the localities, on the other. Nixon was surely vulnerable to the charge that he was attempting to usurp power. As White noted, "in practice he took to himself more personal power, delegated to more individuals of his staff the use or abuse of that power, than any other President of modern times."[14]

It was inevitable that a rigorous attempt to manage the executive branch would result in a collision with organized interests and their allies in Congress, not to mention the elites, including the national media. White clearly recognized the battle lines at the time:

> Faced by a hostile Congress, a hostile vanguard of the press-television system, a recalcitrant party of his own, and a Democratic party committed by definition to opposition, he abandoned all the old conventions of party politics. His campaign was, therefore, a personal campaign, and above all, a campaign of issues.[15]

White further alluded to the danger that would subsequently threaten the Nixon presidency: "It was a campaign that never invited Americans to judge his use or manipulation of power but only its apparent end results and its stated direction. He personally stood above detail, above the nitty-gritty of political mechanics."[16]

However, what Nixon intended to do in his second term was centrally concerned with the "nitty-gritty of political mechanics." Unlike Franklin Roosevelt, who in 1936 sought to portray the president's enemies as enemies of the people, Nixon attempted to get a mandate concerning the issues or ends of power. He expected the people to trust him as regards the means, or the manner, in which he used power. As White noted, "Americans overwhelmingly responded to Nixon's presentation of the issues—they chose his directions...as against the directions offered by George McGovern."[17] McGovern had, indeed, raised the issue of Nixon's abuse of power in his campaign. He insisted throughout that Watergate was the issue. But, although McGovern tried "to turn national debate to a consideration of the style of power itself," says White, "he could not score the question through on the minds of the people." It was only after the election, when it became clear what Nixon intended to do with his mandate in the second term, that his opponents were able "to pose the question of inherent power within the Nixon Administration, and of how the president had let that power be used, and abused, to defile the laws of the country and the political process itself."[18] Although a majority of Americans agreed with Nixon concerning the issues or the ends to which he was committed, he neglected to make clear—in the campaign—what means would be necessary to achieve those ends, apparently expecting the people to trust him in the use of power. They trusted him only so long as he was considered trustworthy. It is not surprising then that the central issue subsequently became the character of Richard Nixon.

The Administrative Presidency

Nixon noted just before the 1972 election that the next "four years of my administration would become known as having advocated the most significant reforms of any administration since that of Franklin Roosevelt in 1932." But, unlike FDR's reforms, which "led to bigger and bigger power in Washington," his reforms would "diffuse the power throughout the country." He reportedly told his staff the day after the election, "there are no sacred cows[;] we will tear up the pea patch."[19] On January 5, 1973, Nixon submitted his plan for the reorganization of the executive branch. The rationale for reorganization was laid out in his message to Congress:

> Throughout the middle third of the 20th century, power flowed to the center at every level of American government.... The vigor and independence of State and local government ebbed as Washington's power grew.... [T]he President's ability to manage effectively was increasingly hamstrung,...the Cabinet Secretaries, were steadily weakened by balkanization of the departments and agencies and the resultant ill-planned growth of the Executive Office of the President. *Now the age of centralism in American Government is ending.*[20] (emphasis mine)

Nixon believed that revenue sharing had begun to turn the tide within the federal system, and reorganization "would do the same within the executive branch." It will, he suggested, "enhance my ability, to deliver...what the people voted for in 1972."[21] Reorganization would, he insisted, contribute to that "'energy in the executive' which Hamilton called 'a leading character in the definition of good government.'" [22]

Nixon's plans to reorganize the executive branch had been detailed in his State of the Union message in 1971. In it, he stated, "I shall ask not simply for more new programs in the old framework, but to change the framework itself—to reform the entire structure of American government so we can make it fully responsive to the needs and wishes of the American people."[23] He proposed to abolish the constituency- and clientele-oriented Departments of Agriculture, Labor, Commerce, HUD, Interior, HEW, and Transportation, and consolidate their functions among four "goal-oriented" super-departments. The new departments were to be Human Resources, Natural Resources, Community Development, and Economic Affairs. He spelled out in greater detail the rationale of his reform plans in his "Reorganization Message" to Congress two months later. He made it clear, in the latter message, that it was better political control, rather than a more efficient administration, that was his prime concern.

But it was precisely this better political control that frightened Congress. In the report of Chet Holifield's Committee on Government Operations, this is made clear:

> All members of Congress, in *principle*, would favor better regional organization and making Government more responsive. In *practice*, members of Congress would be greatly interested in the shifts of authority, patronage, money-disbursing privileges to regional offices for their political as well as administrative implications. For those members who now have established points of contact and channels of communication with the various departments and agencies of the executive branch, reorganization undoubtedly would entail extended periods of readjustment.[24]

In such a reorganization, Congress would lose control over single departments and agencies and would oversee broader functional areas. "Unlike the President," the report noted, "who can take the initiative for the whole executive branch in proposing reorganization, the committees of Congress, with their independent...chairmen, do not fit into an administrative hierarchy subject to a single course of command."[25] As one observer noted,

It was obvious from the outset that Congress would never enact this measure because its committee structure is closely tied to the departmental structure of the executive branch, and the legislation just languished in committee.... The effort to sell the reorganization bill... proved to be a monumental failure [because the White House could not] overcome the opposition of vested interests on the Hill which were determined enough to resist all... attempts at persuasion, influence and bargaining.[26]

Nixon noted subsequently in his *Memoirs* that his "attempts at reorganizing or reforming the federal government... had been resisted by the combined and determined inertia of Congress and the bureaucracy." Such resistance was not only a result of partisan differences, but also, he suggested, "because the plans and programs... threatened the entrenched powers and prerogatives that they had built up over many decades." He admitted that he could not but accept the fact that no major reform would come from Congress in his first term. But, he wrote, "now, however, armed with my landslide mandate and knowing that I had only four years in which to make my mark, I planned to force Congress and the federal bureaucracy to defend their obstruction and their irresponsible spending in the open arena of public opinion."[27]

Congress, Nixon observed, "had smothered my attempt in 1971 to streamline the government," so he requested John Ehrlichman and Roy Ash to "determine how much reorganizing I could legally do on my own."[28] They advised "that I could in fact create by executive authority a system closely resembling the one I had requested in the 1971 reform proposal."[29] This strategy became the basis of an "administrative presidency." Richard Nathan suggests that Nixon, "unlike his modern predecessors, did not seek to make his mark through the legislative route for the achievement of domestic policy objectives."[30] Rather, he sought to decrease the power of the national government and the national legislature by managing the bureaucracy and making policy by reorganization, budget impoundment and reduction, personnel shifts, and regulation writing. In his first term, Nixon observed, "we had done a very poor job in the most basic business of every new administration of either party; we had failed to fill all the key posts in the departments and agencies with people who are loyal to the President and his programs. Without this kind of leadership in the appointive positions, there is no way for a President to make any major impact on the bureaucracy." In his second term, he noted, "I was determined that we would not fail in this area again, and on the morning after my re-election, I called for the resignation of every non-career employee in the executive branch[;] my action was meant to be symbolic of a completely new beginning."[31]

Nixon hoped, in his words, to "break the Eastern stranglehold on the executive branch and the federal government." In his view, even "at the beginning of my second term, Congress, the bureaucracy, and media were still working in concert to maintain the ideas and ideology of the traditional Eastern liberal establishment that had come to dominate through the New Deal, the New Frontier, and the Great Society." His purpose was "to give expression to the more conservative values and beliefs of the New Majority...and use my power to put some teeth into my New American Revolution."[32] In his diary, recorded just after the election, Nixon contemplated the critical character of the direction he would take after the election. He wrote:

> This is going to be quite a shock to the establishment, but it is the only way, and probably the last time, that we can get government under control before it gets so big that it submerges the individual completely and destroys the dynamism which makes the American system what it is.[33]

Nixon's reorganization strategy to manage and control the bureaucracy was supplemented by his attempt to reorder national priorities. The key to such an attempt required control of the federal budget.[34] As Richard Nathan has observed, "the meaning of mandate for domestic affairs...was expressed not in the State of the Union message as is customary, but in Nixon's tightfisted budget for fiscal year 1974."[35] In his budget message, Nixon stated, "This budget concerns itself not only with the needs of all the people, but with an idea that is central to the preservation of democracy: the 'consent of the governed.'" The 1974 budget

> is the clear evidence of the kind of change in direction demanded by the great majority of the American people. No longer will power flow inexorably to Washington. Instead, the power to make many major decisions...will be returned to where it belongs—State and local

officials…accountable to an alert citizenry and responsive to local conditions and opinions.[36]

This budget, Nixon observed, "proposes a leaner Federal bureaucracy, increased reliance on State and local government…and greater freedom for the American people to make for themselves fundamental choices about what is best for them."[37]

Nixon intended in his second term to avoid the "lethargy" that characterized the Eisenhower administration. He wanted to be explicitly partisan:

> I had a sense of urgency about the need to revitalize the Republican Party lest the New Majority slip away from us. It was one thing for the Democrats to hold all four aces in Washington—the Congress, the bureaucracy, the majority of the media, and the formidable group of lawyers and power brokers who operate behind the scenes in the city. It was another thing to give them the fifth ace of a timid opposition party.[38]

Nixon's decision to begin seriously the process of decentralization led to a politics of confrontation. This alarmed both liberals and conservatives. Liberals were committed to a necessary diversity in American politics, and conservatives insisted on consensus. Nixon polarized American politics in an unusual way: it was not Republicans and Democrats, or even liberals or conservatives, but friends and enemies.

Nixon noted in his *Memoirs* that his budget, "with its proposed spending ceiling was sending shock waves through Congress," and his "plan for government reorganization was sending seismic tremors through the federal bureaucracy."[39] It was clear that Congress was determined to do battle: "No sooner had the Vietnam peace agreement been announced than the complaints began over the reorganization plans, the proposed budget cuts…and what was soon labeled as the attitude and style of the 'Imperial Presidency.'"

In Nixon's view, Congress could not lead but had developed an interest in preventing presidential leadership in the national interest, responsive to national majority. By 1973, he writes, "I had concluded that Congress had become cumbersome, undisciplined, isolationist, fiscally irresponsible, overly vulnerable to pressures from organized minorities, and too dominated by the media."[40] Nixon believed that Congress as a body had changed significantly in the years since he had served there. "In 1947," he noted, "it was still possible for a congressman to run his office, do his homework, keep in touch with constituents, and have his eye on his political fortunes. But the federal government had become so big and the business of government so extensive that even the most conscientious congressman had to delegate a large part of his responsibilities to the personal and committee staffs."[41] Moreover, he suggests, the media "had demonstrated their power to make a politician a national figure overnight, putting a premium on color and controversiality, rather than steady industriousness." The change in Congress not only transformed the relationship between the president and Congress, but affected "the traditional relationship within Congress itself." Increasingly, he suggested, "members refused to accept party discipline and . . . went into business for themselves."[42]

Perhaps the most decisive change in Congress, which strengthened the power of individual members, was the relationship the congressmen had developed with the executive branch bureaucracy. It was not long after Nixon's attempts at reorganization that Congress began a counterattack. In Nixon's words, "the Democratic leadership decided that the best way both to assert their party's majority power and to recover Congress's former prestige, would be to take a piece out of the executive branch's hide."[43] Nixon notes:

> The first battle lines were drawn in the ostensibly peripheral areas of procedural prerogatives. In early January the Senate Democratic caucus voted 35 to 1 to narrow the President's traditional authority to invoke executive privilege. The same day a bipartisan bloc of 58 senators introduced legislation that would for the first time in our history limit the President's war powers. On February 5, the Senate voted to require confirmation of the Budget Director, a position that had been filled by presidential appointment without confirmation for the 52 years since it had been created.[44]

As Chet Holifield noted in the congressional hearing for passage of the confirmation requirement for a director of the Office of Management and Budget, "the larger issue at stake is the prerogative of the Congress, its power and prestige as an institution."[45]

As Nixon has written in his *Memoirs*, "in the midst of this developing confrontation between Congress and the presidency, the Senate Democratic Caucus called for a full-scale investigation of 1972 campaign practices."[46] It was on January 11, 1973, that the Senate Democratic caucus voted in favor of a Watergate investigation. Senator Mike Mansfield, the majority leader, "announced that Senator Sam J. Ervin Jr., the chairman of the Senate Committee on Government Operations as well as the Senate Judiciary Subcommittee on Constitutional Right and Separation of Powers...would head the investigation." Mansfield had requested that Ervin "press for an investigation by a Judiciary subcommittee, saying: 'the question is not political, it is constitutional.... At stake is the continued vitality of the electoral process.'"[47] Needless to say, Nixon viewed it in a distinctly partisan light. He writes in his *Memoirs*: "Mansfield is going to be deeply and bitterly partisan without question. The Democrats actually are starting four years early for their run for the White House."[48]

The details and outcome of Watergate are well-known. The political fortunes of Nixon and Congress were dramatically reversed. As the editors of the *Congressional Quarterly* noted in their review of the Ninety-Third United States Congress:

> When the 93rd first convened in January 1973, President Nixon's sweeping assertions of executive authority posed a threat to the viability of the legislative branch. Even as Congress braced for confrontations with Nixon over spending, war powers and other issues, its defiance was tempered by doubts as to whether it was indeed any match for the newly re-elected President. But by the time Congress adjourned December 20, 1974, the balance of power had shifted dramatically. Both Nixon and...Agnew had been driven from office in disgrace—replaced by men whom Congress had a hand in selecting. Meanwhile, moving into a vacuum created by the disintegration of executive leadership, Congress had staked out a commanding role for itself.[49]

Theodore White has noted,

> the Watergate affair is inexplicable in terms of older forms of corruption in American history where men broke laws for private gain or

privilege.... The men involved were involved at a moment, in 1972, when history was moving their way. They were trying to speed it by any means, fair or foul. By so doing, perhaps, they wrecked their own victory. And that, as history may record, compounds their personal felonies with national tragedy.[50]

If Nixon had history on his side in 1972, he also had adversaries who opposed his reading of those events. Watergate, to be sure, tended to obscure (to the public, at least) the collision course Nixon had embarked upon in early 1973; but, given the revolutionary nature of that course, the equivalent of a Watergate was an absolute necessity for the defenders of the New Deal order. As a result of Watergate, and after the resignation of several top White House aides, the press was advised, without fanfare, "that the President was reinstituting a 'direct line of communication with the Cabinet' and discontinuing the experiment with Counselors."[51] The attempt to reorganize and manage the bureaucracy was over. Gerald Ford, in his first address to Congress, pledged an administration that would seek "unity in diversity" and restore an open presidency. American pluralism and the constitutional order were apparently saved from the imperial presidency of Richard Nixon.

Afterword: January 15, 2018

This article was originally written for a panel on Watergate presented at the annual meeting of the American Political Science Association in Washington, DC, in 1984. At that time, there was little disagreement concerning the meaning of Watergate. It was and remains the political scandal by which all scandal is measured. Moreover, the political and intellectual elites of both parties, liberals and conservatives, agreed that Richard Nixon was the problem. His removal was meant to bring about the solution to a crisis of democratic government posed by executive abuse of power. That view of Nixon, and the popular understanding of Watergate as the greatest constitutional crisis of all time, remains unshaken after more than forty years.

I was not convinced then, or now, that the crisis could be understood in purely personal or legal terms. Nearly every political scandal in American politics has been transformed into a legal one in order to expose and reveal guilt as violation of law. It is fought out in the public, or political arena, on legal grounds to establish culpability, again with reference to the law. If successful, it is justified as upholding the rule of law. Although it provides clarity in terms of simplifying the issues in a manner suitable for presentation to a mass public, it often obscures the deeper, or more fundamental, problems that give rise to the necessity of political scandal. Nearly every administration has potential scandal that lies just below the surface of public or political life. They rarely erupt into a full-blown crisis of the political order.

I thought then that it was not personality alone that made it impossible to establish a consensus on fundamental issues. Rather, it was precisely the inability to prevent such political disagreements between the parties and the branches of government that made Watergate possible, and perhaps necessary, for the defenders of the new order. Why did the political branches, and the parties, diverge in such a manner as made it impossible for them to pursue a common good in tandem? What was at stake was not merely the prerogatives of the branches, or the protection of partisan differences. Rather, what made consensus impossible was a disagreement over what constituted a fundamentally good or just regime. Was the modern administrative state—that progressive innovation that took shape in the New Deal and was greatly expanded in the Great Society—more fundamentally just than the political structures that had been established centuries before in the Constitution itself?

Although this was a theoretical disagreement, it revealed itself as a political problem during Nixon's second term. As Henry Kissinger subsequently noted: "Nixon in the final analysis had provoked a revolution. He had been reelected by a landslide in 1972 in a contest as close to being fought on ideological issues as is possible in America.... The American people for once had chosen on philosophical grounds, not on personality.... For reasons unrelated to the issues and unforeseeable by the people who voted for what Nixon represented, this choice was now being annulled—with as-yet unpredictable consequences."[52] It was apparent then, and more clearly revealed subsequently, that the fundamental problem was that posed by the crisis of constitutionalism itself, brought about by the rise of the administrative state. The political essence of the Constitution is not contained in its written language but in its political structure, which requires a separation of the branches of government. It was the constitutional principle of separation of powers that had come to be undermined by the growth of the administrative state. The Great Society had changed the institutional dynamic of Washington politics. After the election of 1964, both branches participated in establishing greater political power in Washington, by expanding and centralizing administrative authority in the executive branch bureaucracy. That centralization of administrative authority created a political reaction in the electorate that began the process of undermining the policies that were established in the wake of the 1964 election. The Republican Party, led by Richard Nixon, established itself as the partisan opponent of centralized administration. Although Nixon's first term required political concessions that often required the expansion of federal power, it was done primarily in order to garner support for the Vietnam War in a Congress controlled by the opposition party. His second term was not a continuation of the first. Even the *New York Times* noted that the transformation demanded by Nixon of his administration after his reelection was as extreme as if an opposition party had won the election.

By the time of Nixon's reelection in 1972, he posed the greatest danger to the authority of the bureaucracy and the administrative state. Although he won one of the greatest popular and electoral victories in American history, he lost his office and power within the following two years. However, Nixon's removal from office did not end the political turmoil that had roiled Washington. Ronald Reagan's election in 1980 witnessed a renewal of the political animosity that had consumed the Nixon presidency. Although Reagan did not attempt a direct confrontation with the defenders of the administrative state, he did attempt to mobilize a public opinion based on the assumption that government is not the solution to our problems. His view that "government is the problem" resonated with a considerable portion of the electorate. Moreover, by the end of the second Reagan administration, politics in Washington had again become exceedingly contentious. The divisions between the parties and the branches seemed almost insurmountable. By the end of the twentieth century, it appeared to be the case that American politics could no longer be structured by the ordinary, or practical, operation of separation of powers. Rather, the actual conduct of the political branches of government was shaped by the ongoing necessity of accommodating, and ratifying, the actions of the rational, or administrative, state. In other words, it was an element of government itself, the bureaucracy, which had established the purpose and unity of the political branches, and with the blessings of the courts. In short, after nearly a half century of its growth, the bureaucracy has become the conservative defender of the liberal or rational state. Once established, the bureaucracy, and the political forces beholden to it, have sought to progressively replace politics by substituting administrative rulemaking for general lawmaking and rule by rational knowledge in place of political choices made by elected officials. In short, political rule of law gives way to executive or administrative discretion.

In our time, both political branches of government, and in some ways both parties, have accommodated themselves to the administrative state. Much greater authority resides in the administrative realm under executive control, often with the blessings of Congress. The growth of the administrative state has made it possible to politicize the culture by undermining the institutions of civil society, including the family, church, and nearly all private associations. That transformation was not brought about politically but administratively, through the bureaucracy and the courts. The various nationally organized interests, whether political, economic, social, media, entertainment, educational, scientific, cultural, or religious, have accommodated themselves to centralized rule. Moreover, they are well served by Washington, in terms of access to the political branches and the bureaucracy. But it is not clear that the American people are convinced that government now operates on behalf of a public good. For that reason alone, the administrative state has not been able to establish its legitimacy. But the difficulty of revitalizing political rule in a manner compatible with constitutional government remains a problem yet to be solved.

What did Watergate reveal? At the time, I thought it important to look at the institutional structures and the incentives of those who had become a part of the modern administrative state. I attempted to show the importance of the bureaucracy as an institution that could utilize its influence on behalf of one political branch or the other. The necessity to preserve those administrative structures had become essential to modern government. It led many within those organizations to consider institutional loyalty as fundamental to the defense of democratic government itself. For that reason, the nonpartisan character of bureaucracy, its avowed neutrality, could be cast aside. It became a defender of the administrative state, a faction on behalf of government that could no longer be regulated by government.

It was many years after Watergate that we learned the identity of the source of the leaks that led to the removal of a president. It was not surprising that Deep Throat, the source for Bob Woodward and Carl Bernstein, turned out to be a high-level official of the Federal Bureau of Investigation (FBI). Mark Felt had access to all of the classified information generated by the agencies of the government. He leaked that information to the *Washington Post* over the course of a year or more. It served to delegitimize the president and alienate him from the electorate and his party. Although Woodward and Bernstein were lauded as investigative reporters, they served merely as a conduit by which the bureaucracy could undermine the authority of an elected officeholder. In modern organizations, those who work in the administrative structures often understand their interest in terms of institutional loyalty and their professional association, rather than the larger political good understood in terms of the nation or the Constitution. In short, the bureaucracies have developed the instinct for self-preservation at all costs. They do not, however, defend themselves on the basis of self-interest. Rather, they see themselves as defenders of institutional rationality, as a part of the social intelligence that establishes the legitimacy of rule within the administrative state.

PART THREE

THEORY AND HISTORY OF THE ADMINISTRATIVE STATE: THE "NEW DESPOTISM" REPLACES SELF-GOVERNMENT

Bureaucratic government has existed since ancient Egypt and Imperial China, but the modern version is different not only in its origins but also in its distance from the republican self-government. The administrative state is the modern face of tyranny—an issue on which thinkers as diverse as Leo Strauss and Carl Schmitt apparently agree. In his study of centralized administration in *Democracy in America*, Alexis de Tocqueville contrasts the types of humans found under that "new despotism" and in a free society. But unlike the American Founders, Tocqueville did not base his defense of liberty on natural right. Contrary to political theorist and Tocqueville interpreter Harvey Mansfield Jr., Marini does not rely on Tocqueville to "understand politics," in particular American politics, even though Tocqueville anticipated many features of the administrative state.

Widespread American rejection of Lockean natural rights and legitimacy conferred by the consent of the governed paved the way for Progressive utopianism and for Darwinian racial teachings as well. In some forms, this rejection of moderation and embracement of radicalism took the notion of the universal and homogeneous world state (as in Alexandre Kojève), and in others became an embracement of fascism (as in Carl Schmitt's work). Whatever the direction, when History replaced natural right, it meant the rejection of reason and the rule of law. The absolute authority to act against the Depression that President Franklin Roosevelt demanded in his first inaugural provided the political foundation for the administrative state.

Grounded in the study of political philosophy, Marini's essays underscore how the administrative state is a different form of regime or government than that established by the Declaration of Independence and the Constitution.

9

Tocqueville's Centralized Administration and the "New Despotism"

ALEXIS DE TOCQUEVILLE is well known for his elaboration of the principle of equality as the animating force of modern democratic politics. Less well known, and often less well understood, is his analysis of the concept of centralization. Centralization was a primary concern of Tocqueville throughout much of his life. From the time he attended François Guizot's lectures on the *History of Civilization in Europe*, at age twenty-four in Paris, to his own classic account of centralization in *The Old Regime and the Revolution*, he became increasingly and ever more profoundly concerned with this issue. Tocqueville was so impressed with Guizot's historical analysis of the development of modern society that he wrote Beaumont: "We must re-read this together this winter my dear friend; it is prodigious in analysis of ideas."[1]

In that work, Guizot "developed the theme that European civilization was shaped by the theory and practice of monarchy, aristocracy, and democracy, and that the victory of the democratic force was the essential thread of Europe's history."[2] However, Guizot observed, the development of free political institutions was constantly challenged by the irresistible centralizing tendencies of modern government. Guizot was among the first to consider the modern state as a form of administration. In his lectures, he noted,

> Under the most general point of view, administration consists in an aggregate of means destined to propel, as promptly and certainly as possible, the will of the central power through all parts of society and to make the face of society, whether consisting of men or money, return again, under the same conditions, to the central power.[3]

Modern society really begins in the sixteenth century, Guizot maintained, by virtue of the "silent and hidden process of centralization, both in social relations and in the opinions of men—a process accomplished without premeditation or design."[4] Centralization, then, is the inevitable concomitant of democracy. Tocqueville, although impressed with Guizot's method and his analysis, never appeared to believe that the process of centralization was a providential fact. But, for reasons of his own, he devoted much of his scholarly life to the elucidation and elaboration of this idea of providence. In Tocqueville's hands, centralization received its most profound treatment.

In Tocqueville's view, it is the principle of equality that is the irresistible force of modern times. All democratic regimes are characterized by a commitment to equality, and all modern regimes will be democratic. In postdemocratic times, it is no longer principled issues that are of decisive importance in practical life, but the growth and development of the administrative state that shapes the essential character of social life. Centralization, though not fated, is the silent, continuous, almost natural tendency, that threatens to undermine that legitimate passion for equality that is compatible with liberty. Alongside the "manly and legitimate passion for equality," Tocqueville asserts, there is "a depraved taste for equality in the human heart that brings the weak to want to draw the strong to their level and that reduces men to preferring equality in servitude to inequality in freedom."[5] The modern bureaucratic state becomes the vehicle that reduces the individual to servitude. It does so by supplying all the needs of the body; in the process it enslaves the soul. The centralized administrative state becomes the "tutelary power...which alone takes charge of assuring [men's] enjoyments and watching over [their] fate." This power, Tocqueville noted, was

> absolute, detailed, regular, far-seeing, and mild. It would resemble paternal power if, like that, it had for its object to prepare men for manhood; but on the contrary, it seeks only to keep them fixed irrevocably

in childhood.... It willingly works for their happiness; but it wants to be the unique agent and sole arbiter of that; it provides for their security, foresees and secures their needs, facilitates their pleasures, conducts their principal affairs, directs their industry, regulates their estates, divides their inheritances; can it not take away from them entirely the trouble of thinking and the pain of living?[6]

The "slow process of bureaucratic government," Seymour Drescher has observed, "is the Frankenstein of the egalitarian process... it silently subverts the integrity of individuals and associations."[7] Tocqueville hoped to call attention to this process, almost before it began, by elaborating the theoretical and practical aspects of centralization.

In *The Old Regime and the Revolution*, Tocqueville documented the growth and development of the centralized administrative state. He traced its origin to the theory and practice of modern democratic egalitarianism. The French intellectuals and philosophers, as well as the monarchy, contributed to the administrative centralization that would become the hallmark of the modern nation-state. Moreover, the French Revolution succeeded in accelerating those centralizing tendencies, while destroying the elements in French society that could resist them. However, it was "towards the middle of the eighteenth century," he observed, "that a group of writers known as the 'Physiocrats' or 'Economists' who made the problem of public administration their special study, came on the scene."[8] The form of tyranny "sometimes described as 'democratic despotism'... was championed by the Economists well before the Revolution." In fact, he suggested, "the germinal ideas of practically all the permanent changes effected by the Revolution can be found in their works."[9] Their chief targets of attack "were those institutions which the Revolution was destined to sweep away forever." More importantly, he noted, "their writings had the democratic-revolutionary tenor characteristic of so much modern thought. For they attacked not only specific forms of privilege but any kind of diversity whatsoever; to their thinking all men should be equal even if equality spelled servitude."[10] Tocqueville analyzed their political program:

They were for abolishing all hierarchies, all class distinctions, all differences of rank, and the nation was to be composed of individuals almost exactly alike and unconditionally equal. In this undiscriminated mass was to reside, theoretically, the sovereign power, yet it was to be carefully deprived of any means of controlling or even supervising the activities of its own government. For above it was a single authority, its mandatory, which was entitled to do anything and everything in its name without consulting it. This authority could not be controlled by public opinion since public opinion had no means of making itself heard; the State was a law unto itself and nothing short of a revolution could break its tyranny.[11]

In Tocqueville's opinion, the Economists or Physiocrats were forerunners of those socialist thinkers who called for "the unlimited rights of the State." He believed that "socialism and centralization thrive on the same soil; they stand to each other as the cultivated to the wild species of a fruit."[12] Tocqueville's theoretical analysis of the concept of centralization required bringing to light the development of the modern bureaucratic state. At the same time, he hoped to shed new light on the character of modern despotism. In the process, he hoped to preserve the civic spiritedness necessary to allow men to be free.

Tocqueville was impressed with the absence of a centralized administration in the America of the 1830s. He noted in the first volume of *Democracy in America*, "We have seen that in the United States administrative decentralization does not exist.... But in the United States, governmental centralization exists to the highest point."[13] What Tocqueville most admired was "not the administrative effects of centralization, but its political effects."[14] The most important political effect of decentralization—or provincial institutions—was the creation of a kind of civic spiritedness and love of liberty necessary to keep individuals from becoming completely preoccupied with their own private interests and pleasures.

He observed,

> What does it matter to me, after all, that there should be an authority always on its feet, keeping watch that my pleasures are tranquil, flying ahead of my steps to turn away every danger without my even needing to think about it, if this authority, at the same time that it removes the least thorns on my path, is absolute master of my freedom and my life, if it monopolizes movement and existence to such a point that everything

around it must languish when it languishes, that everything must sleep when it sleeps, that everything must perish if it dies?[15]

Tocqueville was convinced that the democratic tendency was toward centralizing administrative and governmental authority in the same hands: the central power. In the past several decades, American government has become centrally administered at the national level. Tocqueville's predictions of the political effects of such centralization have been largely borne out. However, his warning concerning the despotic character of centralization has been widely ignored, especially by that most sophisticated and informed segment of society: the intellectuals. Intellectual, or elite, opinion—which often shapes the most influential public opinion on these matters—sharply diverges from the common-sense understanding of what is now called bureaucratization. The intellectual elite's acceptance of a certain "taste" for equality, which necessitates those "general ideas" and the kind of uniformity from which administrative centralization inevitably springs, has undermined Tocqueville's treatment of the despotic character of such centralization. Tocqueville's "philosophic analysis" of centralization was aimed at a similar intellectual elite, whose views began to dominate public discourse on this issue in the nineteenth century. It was not the first time that decent political practice required such a defense.

Recently, Henry Steele Commager criticized Tocqueville for what he described as "Tocqueville's Mistake."[16] Commager insisted that "centralization and a strong national government have extended, not curtailed, our liberties." He implies that the contemporary conservative criticism of centralization is only part of an attack on the social programs of liberal governments.

He suggests, therefore, that "those who declaim against Big Government as the enemy of liberty are ignorant of American history."[17] He contends that the central government abolished slavery and extended the civil rights of various minority groups. Consequently, he is unable to comprehend the contemporary popular animus against centralization. He states, "perhaps the most astonishing feature of the current attack on centralization, an attack that President Reagan has turned into a crusade, is the argument that the United States today has not a strong national government but a Big Government."[18] Commager insists that the national government is not "Big Government" when compared with most governments of the world. Moreover, he implies that Tocqueville's analysis is no longer relevant. "What Tocqueville failed to see," he asserts, "was that in a federal system like the American, the problem of the role of local and central governments has taken on a new character."[19]

Unlike Commager, most Americans believe that the national government is a "big government," and for that reason not as strong as it ought to be. Popularly understood, *big government* is bureaucratic government, government concerned not with the general or public principles of the regime but, increasingly, the minute regulations of the private and particular details of social existence. This view is closely akin to the distinction Tocqueville makes between government and administration. Commager appears not to have considered the importance of this crucial distinction in Tocqueville's analysis of centralization. Tocqueville observed, "for my part, I cannot conceive that a nation can live or above all prosper without a high degree of governmental centralization." He noted, however, "I think that administrative centralization is fit only to enervate the peoples who submit to it, because it constantly tends to diminish the spirit of the city in them."[20] Free men must take an active part in the conduct of their affairs. Elite opinion appears to have championed a conception of equality that denigrates liberty and leads to ever-greater uniformity. The contemporary intellectual understanding of centralization is so alien to the spirit of Tocqueville's views that his analysis must be recovered by considering its origins.

Centralization – "A Philosophic Analysis"

"Centralization," John Stuart Mill observed in 1862, is "one among the political questions of the age which bears the strongest marks of being destined to remain a question for generations to come."[21] The importance of this question, Mill asserted, "is constantly tending to increase, by the perpetual growth of collective action among mankind and the progress made in the settlement of other questions which stand before it in the natural order of discussion." The more "exciting subject of Forms of Government," which had for so long dominated political debate, he suggests, "is likely to be much sooner, at least theoretically settled." This is so because "it is simpler in itself," and "it admits . . . of a more definite answer."[22] The question of the legitimacy of popular government, not to mention its form, appears to admit almost no further debate. "Centralization; or in other words, the limits which separate the province of government from that of individual and spontaneous agency, and of central from local government" is the issue, Mill asserts, "which is destined to dominate political discourse for the foreseeable future."[23]

There is little doubt that Mill's understanding of this question was decisively shaped by Tocqueville. Mill recorded his debt in his *Autobiography*. He noted there that a

> subject on which I derived great benefit from the study of Tocqueville was the fundamental question of Centralization. The powerful philosophic analysis which he applied to American and to French experience, led him to attach the utmost importance to the performance of as much of the collective business of society, as can safely be so performed by the people themselves.[24]

The value of Tocqueville's contribution, quite apart from his practical conclusions, derived from his "philosophic analysis," which elevated the issue of centralization to a new theoretical level.

Mill suggested that it was as a result of Tocqueville's powerful analysis of this issue that he himself was alerted to the danger of centralization. European attitudes toward central and local government and administration derived largely from experience and habit. Mill noted that in England, unlike the Continent, "centralization was...the subject not only of rational disapprobation, but of unreasoning prejudice; where jealousy of Government interference was a blind feeling preventing or resisting even the most beneficial exertion of legislative authority."[25] If popular opinion depended upon habit and circumstance, and perhaps chance, Tocqueville was responsible for informing "philosophic" opinion. As Mill observed, "The more certain the public were to go wrong on the side opposed to Centralization, the greater danger was there lest philosophic reformers should fall into the contrary error." Mill himself was "actively engaged in defending important measures" that would have led to increased administrative centralization, and "had it not been for the lessons of Tocqueville,"[26] he would have failed to see that the prejudice of his countrymen was more enlightened than the opinions of the philosophic reformers. "The reaction...against governmentalism and centralization, and in favor of individual and local agency is at present intense," Mill noted, and "the renewed and more serious movement in this beneficent direction is usually dated from the publication of the great work of M. de Tocqueville."[27]

Mill insisted that Tocqueville's thought was indispensable in the creation of the "serious movement" in the direction "against governmentalism and centralization and in favor of individual and local agency." There were few issues that Tocqueville considered with greater care or seriousness than the problem of centralization. Indeed, he commented in a letter concerning this subject, "I sense that I am treating there the most important idea of our time."[28] In his *Journeys to England and Ireland*, Tocqueville recorded in his notes the following observation: "Centralization...Preparation for despotism."[29] Tocqueville always believed that "despotism would be the inevitable but (almost) silent companion to the centralized state."[30] In focusing on centralization, Tocqueville hoped to expose the sinister aspect of the passion for equality. Toward the end of the second volume of *Democracy in America*, Tocqueville observed,

> Every central power that follows these natural instincts loves equality and favors it; for equality singularly facilitates the action of such a power, extends it, and secures it. It can also be said that every central government adores uniformity; uniformity spares it the examination of an infinity of details with which it would have to occupy itself if it were necessary to make a rule for men, instead of making all men pass indiscriminately under the same rule. Thus the government loves what citizens love, and it naturally hates what they hate. This community of sentiments which, in democratic nations, continuously unites each individual and the sovereign in the same thought, establishes a secret and permanent sympathy between them. The government is pardoned for its faults for the sake of its tastes.[31]

Consequently, Tocqueville suggests, "the first, and in a way the only, necessary condition for arriving at centralizing public power in a democratic society is to love equality or make it believed [that one does]. Thus the science of despotism, formerly so complicated, is simplified: it is reduced, so to speak, to a single principle."[32] For this reason, Tocqueville believed that "it is easier to establish an absolute and despotic government in a people whose conditions are equal than in any other."[33] Although "democratic peoples are instinctively drawn toward centralization of powers," he noted, "they tend to do it in an unequal manner. That depends on particular circumstances that can develop or restrict the natural effects of the social state."[34] In America, those circumstances were extremely propitious. Tocqueville's practical task was to clarify the meaning of centralization. His philosophic analysis required a clarification of the idea that lay at the heart of modern political practice.

The Practical Problem

If centralization were to be recognized as an issue of the first magnitude, it was imperative that Tocqueville clarify its meaning and establish the ground upon which the issue would be debated. "When we speak of centralization," he noted, "we are always fighting in the shadows because of a failure to make the distinction between governmental and administrative centralization."[35] In his famous definition, he seeks to make this distinction with precision:

> Certain interests, such as the enactment of general laws and the nation's relations with foreigners, are common to all parts of the nation.
>
> There are other interests of special concern to certain parts of the nation, such, for instance, as local enterprises.
>
> To concentrate all the former in the same place or under the same directing power is to establish what I call governmental centralization.
>
> To concentrate control of the latter in the same way is to establish what I call administrative centralization.[36]

However, it is almost impossible, theoretically, to maintain this celebrated distinction; it is full of ambiguity in practice. Tocqueville was aware of the difficulty. He noted, almost in the same breath, "There are some points where these two sorts of centralization become confused."[37]

The difficulty is a practical one: how does one distinguish national from local interests? There cannot be a principle to regulate this distinction that would not succumb to necessity—particularly war. Far from defending decentralization, Tocqueville makes it clear that in America, administrative decentralization has been carried too far in ordinary times. "We have seen that the Americans have almost entirely isolated the administration from the government," he observed. "In doing this they seem to have overstepped the limits of sane reason, for order, even in secondary matters, is still a national interest."[38] Is it possible that Tocqueville was unaware of this difficulty? It seems unlikely. Marvin Zetterbaum has noted in this regard,

> Tocqueville not only does not provide a simple formula to distinguish matters concerning the general interest, from matters that may safely be left to local authorities; he recognizes that if a nation is subject to significant external pressures, local autonomy in anything other than trivial matters is impossible. In such a case, the distinction between national and local becomes arbitrary and meaningless.[39]

But Tocqueville was not concerned to resolve the issue as a practical matter; it is practically insoluble. In bringing the distinction to light, he hoped to expose the practical consequences of modern philosophic or ideological politics. Hence Tocqueville served a theoretical rather than a practical need. In his elaboration of the distinction between administration and government, Tocqueville brought to light the inherent tension between the general and particular, the common and self-interest, and the public and private spheres.

Mill's comments on centralization are helpful in clarifying Tocqueville's purpose. Mill, in his definition of centralization, distinguishes the governmental from the private, as well as from the central and local. This juxtaposition is not without significance, for he recognized two separate kinds of authority: the private, individual, and self-interested he associates with local government, or what Tocqueville called "administration," and the general, uniform, and the public interest form the heart of central authority, or what Tocqueville characterizes as "government." This analysis is instructive for it offers a corrective to the interpretation commonly held in our time. The contemporary understanding falls prey to the very tendency Tocqueville sought to expose in his analysis. Tocqueville, like Mill, was of the opinion that the different kinds of authority, implicit in the distinction "of central contrasted with local authority, as of government contrasted with the individual," ought to be preserved with the view to tempering in practice the principle of popular sovereignty.

The contemporary understanding admits to a single legitimate center of authority: the public, the general, or the governmental. If the locus of that authority had shifted from the states to the national legislature since Tocqueville's time, the principle is clear: there is nothing that government—primarily the legislature—cannot do. The democratic instinct that tends toward the nation-state also moves in the direction of uniform government and legislative supremacy. In Tocqueville's time, it was the state legislatures that he looked to as the "locus of the tendency towards democratic centralism."[40] He noted:

> The duties and the rights of the federal government were simple and easy enough to define, because the Union had been formed with the goal of responding to a few great general needs. The duties and rights of the state governments were, on the contrary, multiple and complicated, because these governments entered into all the details of social life.[41]

It is now the national government that has become involved in all the "details of social life," but the principle remains the same. Tocqueville observed that the legislative power is the "power that emanates most directly from the people, it is also the one that participates the most in its omnipotence."[42] A recent observer, John Koritansky, has stated, "the legislature tends to be supreme because, strictly speaking, legislative supremacy is a necessary implication of democracy...not only is the legislature most directly responsible to the people...it is the legislative function that corresponds to the kind of political activity the people themselves would perform if they actually assembled."[43] Legislative supremacy appears to be the closest thing to direct popular rule, but it tends also "in the direction of a simple rule of law unimpeded by any perception of the need for administrative discretion or provincial autonomy."[44] The tendency is toward greater centralization as a consequence of the necessity to treat everything in a uniform manner. As Koritansky notes,

> Any argument that limits the ability of the law to govern every last detail of human life always involves some allegation of complex circumstances

that need special, particular accommodation. But democracy is always impatient with such claims. The image that corresponds most closely to the democracy's vision of society is a social atomism; the atoms them-selves being simple and perfectly interchangeable are suitably gov-erned by a few majestic generalities. Democratic citizens always suspect the allegation of special circumstances to be a cover for inequality, and they reject inequality in turn because it is the source of these complexities that impede the simple rule of law.[45]

This leads necessarily to the creation of an "administrative class" formed to handle in a uniform and general way the details of everyday life.

This tendency in the direction of legislative supremacy and admin-istrative unity, not to say uniformity, is so compelling—the notion of popular sovereignty so pervasive—that Tocqueville's analysis of centralization has been undermined. Administrative centralization becomes necessary in democratic times to ensure greater efficiency and rationality, not to mention equity. Furthermore, the distinction between government and administration in Tocqueville's sense has been replaced by the distinction between policymaking and execution. As Martin Diamond observed,

> The most common understanding of Tocqueville's distinction is the fol-lowing: Government centralization means that policy should be made centrally, the power of legislation belongs to the central government, administrative decentralization requires that central policies be locally administered; the power of execution belongs to the localities.[46]

However, in Tocqueville's view, both government and administra-tion form an autonomous whole. Both are concerned with lawmaking and execution. The difference lies in the kind of authority characterized by each—administrative authority concerns the details of social life; it is private and self-interested, not to say particular. Governmental authority is principled and uniform, not to say general.

According to Tocqueville, the proper reconciliation of these two kinds of authority can occur only on the level of the community or town-ship. It is there that both public and private interests can be properly considered. Such a resolution involves the necessity of abstracting from one's private interest in the conduct of the ordinary details of life. Such an abstraction leads to the realization that every citizen must consider the whole or the common good first, or at least at the same time that he considers his own good. As a result, every citizen's private interest is inseparable from his public duty. Private interest moderates public policy by attempting to preserve individual autonomy or freedom, and public spiritedness is engendered in the act of self-legislation. "There will be no stable order," Tocqueville noted in *Le Commerce*, "as long as the law does not give to each citizen a political existence which bestows on each person both rights and duties; and thereby, a civic conscience, a respect for authority...a reasoned respect for the law."[47]

The Theoretical Problem

Tocqueville's analysis is, in the fundamental respect, primarily theoretical. It involves nothing less than the attempted reconciliation—on the level of political history—of the inherent tension that exists between the public and private, the general and particular. In the process, he hoped to forestall the worst aspect of democratic life—the tendency to administrative despotism. "To what degree," he asked, "can these two principles of private and public welfare be blended? To what point can a conscience born of reflection and calculation overcome political passions not yet visible, but which cannot help arising?"[48]

Tocqueville's distinction provided the conceptual means of isolating the tendency of modern government toward unity or centralization. He hoped to buttress those elements—provincial institutions—which could serve to mitigate its growth. He was aware that provincial institutions and local liberty are not the "natural government" of the modern world. They grew "almost secretly in the bosom of a half-barbaric society." Left to themselves, "the institutions of township can scarcely struggle against an enterprising and strong government."[49] Their existence depends upon the civic virtue of a people. Thus, Tocqueville insisted that "decentralization, like liberty, is a thing which leaders promise their people, but which they never give them. To get and keep it, the people must count on their own sole efforts; if they do not care to do so the evil is beyond remedy."[50]

In teaching democratic man the necessity of civic virtue, he would show them how to remain free.

Nonetheless, it is hard "to make the people take a share in government." And "it is more difficult still to furnish them with the experience and to give them the sentiments that they lack to govern well."[51] Such a task requires the service of a legislator. The difficulty of Tocqueville's project was nowhere better stated than in Rousseau's *The Social Contract*:

> Sages who wish to use their own language in addressing the vulgar instead of vulgar language cannot possibly make themselves understood. For ... there are a multitude of ideas which it is impossible to express in the language of the people. Views that are too general ... objects ... too remote, are equally beyond their comprehension; and every individual, relishing no scheme of government but that which promotes his own private interest, cannot easily be made sensible of the benefits to be derived from continual privations imposed upon him by wholesome laws. For a newborn people to relish wise maxims of policy and to pursue the fundamental rules of statecraft, it would be necessary that the effect should become the cause; that the social mind, which should be the product of such an institution, would prevail even at the institution of society; and that men should be, before the formation of laws, what those laws alone can make them. The legislator being, from these reasons, unable to employ either force or argument, he must have recourse to an authority of another order, which can bear men away without violence, and persuade without convincing them.[52]

To what authority did Tocqueville have recourse to assist in the legislator's task? He seems to have turned to "historical philosophy" to accomplish his purpose.

In his review of *Democracy in America* in 1840, John Stuart Mill stated, "It is perhaps the greatest defect of M. de Tocqueville's book, that ... his propositions even when derived from observation have the air of mere abstract speculation."[53] This criticism is rarely noted. Subsequently, Tocqueville's own work was praised for the soundness of his practical observations. It was not "abstract speculation" that characterized his work but incisive analysis of sociological and political phenomena. His work is often thought to be a series of brilliant observations without theoretical coherence. One commentator, Marvin Zetterbaum, has remarked, "like other nineteenth-century theorists, Tocqueville was in revolt against those of his predecessors who had looked on political things in an abstract way."[54] Paradoxically, both Mill and Zetterbaum are right. Tocqueville was concerned with placing politics within a proper historical framework, but he was aware that every society is animated by certain ideas. Tocqueville believed that the science of politics gave

> birth or at least form to those general concepts whence emerge the facts with which politicians have to deal, and the laws of which they believe themselves the inventors. They form a kind of atmosphere surrounding each society in which both rulers and governed have to draw intellectual breath, and whence—often without realizing it—both groups derive the principles of action. Only among barbarians does the practical side of politics exist alone.[55]

It is for this reason that Tocqueville desired a new political science for a new age.

America appeared to offer Tocqueville the historical material from which he could undertake an analysis of democracy. In his first letter written from American soil, Tocqueville seemed to have grasped the meaning of the opportunity presented to him. He wrote:

> Picture to yourself...a society which comprises all nations of the world...people differing from one another in language, in beliefs, in opinions; in a word, a society possessing no roots, no memories, no prejudices, no routine, no common ideas, no national character....The whole world over here seems to consist of malleable matter which forms and fashions to his liking.[56]

America offered Tocqueville the opportunity to "form those general concepts" of democratic society, in the process of describing "the general facts with which politicians have to deal."

He noted his purpose in another way in another context: "I must find somewhere a solid, lasting basis of fact for my ideas. I can find this only as I write history."[57] If his study of the French Revolution provided an opportunity in this regard, he pointed to the greatest difficulty he encountered in pursuing his method. "The one that troubles me most," he wrote, "arises from the mingling of history proper with historical philosophy.

I do not yet see how I can mix the two things (and it is most important that this should be done, for one can put it that the former is the canvas, the latter the color—and both these are necessary to make a picture)."[58]

In blending history and historical philosophy, Tocqueville's task is at once practical and theoretical. It was only by proceeding in this way that he could hope to moderate a politics that was in the process of becoming ideological. He noted,

> It was political science, and often that science at its most abstract, which put into our father's heads the germs of those new ideas which have since suddenly blossomed into political institutions and civil laws unknown to their forebears.... Among all civilized peoples the political sciences create, or at least give shape to, general ideas, and from these general ideas are found the problems in the midst of which politicians must struggle, and also the laws which they imagine they create. The political sciences form a sort of intellectual atmosphere breathed by both governors and governed in society, and both unwittingly derive from it the principles of their action.[59]

As a consequence of the unification of politics and a certain kind of modern philosophy, which occurred as a result of the French Revolution, the "natural link" between "opinions" and "tastes," "acts" and "beliefs," "feelings" and "ideas" had been severed. It "was the French," Tocqueville observed in the chapter in which he described the "philosophical approach of the Americans," who "turned the world upside down." The reason "is not because the French changed their ancient beliefs and modified their ancient mores that they turned the world upside down; it is because they were the first to generalize and to bring to light a philosophic method with whose aid one could readily attack all ancient things and open the way to all new ones."[60] Tocqueville had observed the result in his Introduction to *Democracy in America*:

> I search my memories in vain, and I find nothing that should evoke more sadness and more pity than what is passing before our eyes; it seems that in our day the natural bond that unites opinions to tastes and actions to beliefs has been broken; the sympathy that has been noticeable in all times between the sentiments and ideas of men appears

destroyed; one would say that all the laws of moral analogy have been abolished.[61]

Tocqueville's purpose is to inspirit democratic man by forging artificial links to replace the broken natural link. In the process he will have established new laws of moral analogy. "Whereas only observations and facts are necessary to demonstrate mathematical truths," Tocqueville noted, "to understand and believe moral truths, mores are needed."[62]

Centralization and Despotism

At its most fundamental level, centralization is derivative of the desire for perfectibility and the taste for general ideas, or the quest for rationality and uniformity. It is the practical culmination of the transformation of modern political life and institutions, brought about by modern political philosophy and science. "One cannot believe," Tocqueville observed, "how many facts naturally flow from the philosophic theory according to which man is indefinitely perfectible, and what a prodigious influence it exerts even on those who, always being occupied only with acting and not thinking, seem to conform their actions to it without knowing it."[63] What is the idea to which theory and practice are made to conform? Tocqueville wrote,

> Equality suggests several ideas to the human mind that would not otherwise have come to it, and it modifies almost all those already there. I take as an example the idea of human perfectibility because it is one of the principle ones which intelligence can conceive and because it alone constitutes in itself a great philosophic theory whose consequences are displayed at each instant in the practice of affairs.[64]

Like Rousseau, Tocqueville regards perfectibility as the distinguishing characteristic of man. "Although man resembles the animal in several points," Tocqueville noted, "one feature is peculiar to him alone: he perfects himself and they do not perfect themselves."[65]

"[P]erfectibility," Tocqueville asserted, is "as old as the world," but equality "gives it a new character." When citizens were classified by rank, profession, birth, men believed they could see the "furthest boundaries of human power near himself, and none seeks any longer to struggle against an inevitable destiny." In his view, aristocratic societies thought in terms of "improvement, not change." They imagined "the conditions of coming societies as better, but not different."[66]

When "castes disappear, as classes get closer to each other," when "mixed tumultuously, and their usages, customs, and laws vary," Tocqueville remarked, "the image of an ideal and always fugitive perfection is presented to the human mind." Under these circumstances, "continual changes then pass at each instant before the eyes of each man"; they observe that "man improves his lot," and they conclude "that man in general is endowed with indefinite faculty for improvement."[67] When change occurs and conditions become more equal, Tocqueville observed that "each man in particular becomes more like all the others, weaker and smaller[;] one gets used to no longer viewing citizens so as to consider only the people." Individuals are forgotten "so as to think only of the species." At such times, he noted, "the human mind loves to embrace a host of diverse objects at once; it constantly aspires to be able to link a multitude of consequences to a single cause." The "idea of unity" then "obsesses the mind."[68] Throughout much of the second volume of *Democracy in America*, Tocqueville attempted to show the manner in which the "predominating taste of democratic people for very general ideas" manifested itself in politics, philosophy, and religion.

Centralization appeared to be the almost inevitable concomitant of the desire for uniformity and the taste for general ideas. In a conversation with John Stuart Mill in England in 1833, Mill made it clear to Tocqueville that it was the English abhorrence of general ideas that was largely responsible for the administrative decentralization in that country. In his notes, published as *Journeys to England and Ireland*, Tocqueville recorded his conversations with Mill on this subject. In questioning Mill on the danger of centralization, he asked if he feared "the present tendency of his country toward centralization." Mill replied that he did not, because "up to now centralization has been the thing most foreign to the English temperament." He noted further,

> Our habits or the nature of our temperament do not in the least draw us towards general ideas; but centralization is based on general ideas; that is the desire for power to attend in a uniform and general way,

to the present and future needs of society. We have never considered government from such a lofty point of view. So we have divided administrative functions up infinitely and have made them independent of one another. We have not done this deliberately, but from our sheer inability to comprehend general ideas on the subject of government or anything else. The tendency of English politics up to now has been to remain as free as possible to do what was convenient. The taste for making others submit to a way of life which one thinks more useful for them than they do themselves, is not a common taste in England.[69]

But "could it not be," Tocqueville asked, "that what you call the English temperament is the aristocratic temperament?" Mill admitted he had not considered the possibility. Is it not the "aristocratic temperament," Tocqueville inquired, which is likely "to isolate oneself... to be more afraid of being disturbed in one's own domain, than wishful to extend it over others?" Is not "the instinct of democracy exactly opposite," Tocqueville asked, "and may it not be that the present tendency which you consider as an accident is an almost necessary consequence of the basic cause?"[70] The demise of the aristocracy, Tocqueville implied, leads almost inevitably to centralization. Why is this so?

Tocqueville's analysis of the problem was developed in his study, *The Old Regime and the Revolution*. This work only strengthened his belief that the destruction of the aristocracy accelerated the tendency toward centralization. But, in one of the novel findings of his research, Tocqueville discovered that centralizing tendencies were already apparent in the old regime. However, there was no principle involved in centralization prior to the French Revolution. It was the greed of the aristocracy and the desire for money and power on the part of the monarchy that resulted in increased centralization prior to the Revolution. In the decades preceding the Revolution, "feudal institutions had broken down to such an extent that the nobility had retained many of the privileges, but virtually none of its political authority."[71]

In *The Old Regime*, Tocqueville demonstrated the means by which "the monarchy centralized all administrative power under its own authority." The central power "controlled either directly, or indirectly, virtually every aspect of provincial and local life including public order."[72] Local autonomy nearly disappeared, and the nobility ceased to play an administrative role in the community—it was virtually powerless. Moreover, it ceased to concern itself with public affairs and was wholly preoccupied with its private pleasures. The aristocracy in France relinquished its power in exchange for its privilege—primarily the exemption from taxes. Tocqueville asserted that the old regime succumbed on the day that the French people "permitted the king to impose a tax without their consent and the nobles showed so little public spirit as to connive at this, provided their own immunity was guaranteed—it was on that fateful day that the seeds were sown of almost all the vices and abuses which led to the violent downfall of the old regime."[73]

The lack of public spiritedness on the part of the French aristocracy stood in sharp contrast to the British nobility. "The English aristocracy," Tocqueville noted, "took upon itself the heaviest public charges in order that it would be allowed to govern; in France the nobility retained to the very end its exemption from taxes to console itself for having lost control of the government."[74] If the French nobility lost its political virtue and ceased to be an aristocracy, becoming instead what Tocqueville called a caste—composed of individuals concerned with private economic advantage—with its destruction, every barrier to centralization was removed.

However, when "that ancient institution, the French monarchy, after being swept away by the tidal wave of the Revolution, was restored in 1800," Tocqueville asked, "how was it possible for this part of the old regime to be . . . integrated into the constitution of modern France?" The centralization of power "did not perish in the Revolution," he noted, because "whenever a nation destroys its aristocracy, it almost automatically tends toward a centralization of power."[75] The revolutionaries, despite their hatred of central power, could not prevent even greater centralization of authority. Nonetheless, prior to the Revolution, "it (was) due to habits and not to ideas that . . . centralization remained strongly established." In spite of the fact that "the future revolutionaries themselves"—in their pamphlets—were "opposed to centralization and in favor of local rule."[76] Tocqueville demonstrated that "the democratic revolution, though it did away with so many institutions of the past, was led inevitably to consolidate this one; centralization fitted in so well with the program of the new social order that the common error of believing it to have been a creation of the Revolution is easily accounted for."[77]

In his *Correspondence with Gobineau*, Tocqueville took Gobineau to task for asserting that *The Old Regime* was a book about "administrative institutions." As Tocqueville recorded in his "Notes" on what was to have been the second volume of *The Old Regime*, "The influence of administrative practices on the destiny of a people should not be exaggerated. The principal source of these (political) vices and virtues are always to be found in the original ideas."[78] He outlined the principle "ideas at the base of the new social and governmental system" in his *Notes*:

> Natural equality must be represented in all institutions.... The sovereign power resides in the nation. It is one and omnipotent. It is not from traditions, not from examples, not from precedents, not from the particular rights of certain bodies or classes, not from the rights achieved, not from established religions that these principles derive, but from *general* reason, from the natural and primordial laws regulating the human species.[79]

The triumph of general ideas goes hand in hand with the destruction of all intermediate powers. Thus Tocqueville noted, "centralization does not develop in a democratic people only according to the progress of equality, but also according to the manner in which that equality is founded."[80] It is true, he observed, that "in democratic peoples[,] government is naturally presented to the human mind only in the form of a lone central power and that the notion of intermediate powers is not familiar to it." This is particularly true in regard to "democratic nations that have seen the principle of equality triumph with the aid of a violent revolution." In such a circumstance, because "the classes that directed local affairs disappear all at once in this storm and the confused mass that remains still has neither the organization nor the habits that permit it to take the administration of its own affairs in hand, one no longer perceives anything but the state itself that can take charge of all the details of government." Centralization "becomes a fact, and in a sense, a necessity."[81]

For this reason, Tocqueville insisted that "one must neither praise nor blame Napoleon for having concentrated almost all administrative powers in his hands alone; for after the abrupt disappearance of the nobility and the haute bourgeoisie, these powers came to him of themselves; it would have been almost as difficult for him to repel them as to take them up." However, this was not the case in the United States, because the Americans derived from the aristocracy of England "the idea of individual rights and the taste for local freedoms; and they have been able to preserve both because they have not had to combat aristocracy."[82]

In Tocqueville's view, aristocratic institutions form a bulwark against those tendencies in democratic society toward centralization. He commented in detail on the differences in the old societies. Unity and uniformity "were nowhere to be found." Nor had there developed a taste for general ideas in aristocratic societies. Tocqueville more than once points to the fact that the English had an aversion to generalization. But, he noted, "a more or less highly developed culture is not by itself enough to account for a taste for or aversion from generalization." Rather, it is in aristocratic societies that he discerns a distaste for generalization:

> When conditions are very unequal and the inequalities are permanent, individuals little by little become so unalike that one would say there are as many distinct humanities as there are classes; one always discovers only one of them at a time, and losing sight of the general bond that brings all together in the vast bosom of the human race, one ever views only some men, not man. Those who live in these aristocratic societies, therefore, never conceive very general ideas relative to themselves, and that is enough to give them a habitual distrust of these ideas and an instinctive distaste for them.[83]

Tocqueville traced the origin of the taste for generalization to Christianity. Societies in antiquity were aristocratic. To illustrate his point, Tocqueville argued that "the most profound and vast geniuses of Rome and Greece were never able to arrive at the idea, so general but at the same time so simple, of the similarity of men and of the equal right of freedom that each bears from birth." They were at pains to show that slavery was natural and would always exist: "all the great writers of antiquity," Tocqueville insisted, "were a part of the aristocracy of masters, or at least they saw that aristocracy established without dispute before their eyes; their minds, after expanding in many directions, were therefore found limited in that one, and it was necessary that Jesus Christ come to earth to make it understood that all members of the human species are naturally alike and equal."[84] Christianity made egalitarian societies possible, and unity and uniformity in politics and society likely.

Unlike man in aristocratic society, democratic man "finds near him only beings who are almost the same; he therefore cannot consider any part whatsoever of the human species without having his thought enlarge and dilate to embrace the sum." Truths which apply to himself seem equally to apply to all men. "Having contracted the habit of general ideas in the one study with which he most occupies himself and which most interests him, he carries the same habit over to all the others." Thus, says Tocqueville, "the need to discover common rules for all things, to enclose many objects within the same form, and to explain a collection of facts by a single cause becomes an ardent and often blind passion of the human mind." The equality of conditions and standards brings "each to seek the truth by himself." It is "easy to see that such a method will imperceptibly make the human mind tend toward general ideas." When traditions of class, of profession, and of family are repudiated and men "escape the empire of example to seek by the effort of [their] reason alone the path to follow," Tocqueville observed, "I am inclined to draw the grounds of [my] opinions from the very nature of man, which necessarily leads [me], almost without [my] knowing it, toward a great number of very general notions."[85]

However, Tocqueville insisted that "general ideas do not attest to the strength of human intelligence, but rather to its insufficiency, because there are no beings in nature exactly alike: no identical facts, no rules indiscriminately applicable in the same manner to several objects at once."[86] Nature is hostile to uniformity. Nonetheless, a central power attempts to oversee all the details of the life of a nation. But, such a power, Tocqueville asserted, "however learned one imagines it, cannot gather to itself alone all the details of the life of a great people." It cannot do so "because such a work exceeds human strength."[87] Tocqueville noted the sterile character of such an attempt in the following observation:

> Men put the greatness of the idea of unity in the means, God in the end; hence it is that the idea of greatness leads to a thousand [instances] of pettiness. To force all men to march in the same march, toward the same object—that is the human idea. To introduce variety into actions, but to combine them in a manner so that all these actions lead

by a thousand diverse ways toward the accomplishment of one great design—that is a divine idea.[88]

Democratic peoples "naturally favor the concentration of powers." The idea of secondary powers, "between sovereign and subjects, naturally presented itself to the imagination of aristocratic peoples because these powers contained within them individuals or families whom birth, enlightenment, and wealth held up as without peer and who seemed destined to command."[89] However, Tocqueville suggested, "for contrary reasons, the same idea is naturally absent from the minds of men in centuries of equality; it can only be introduced artificially then, and it is retained only with difficulty; whereas they conceive, so to speak without thinking about it."[90]

Consequently, Tocqueville noted, "in politics, moreover, as in philosophy and religion, the intellect of democratic peoples receives simple and general ideas with delight. Complicated systems repel it, and it is pleased to imagine a great nation in which all of the citizens resemble a single model and are directed by a single power." Once the idea of a single central power is grasped,

> the one that presents itself most spontaneously to the minds of men in centuries of equality is the idea of uniform human legislation. As each of them sees himself little different from his neighbors, he hardly understands why the rule that is applicable to one man should not be equally so to all others. . . . The slightest dissimilarities in the political institutions of the same people wound him, and legislative uniformity appears to him to be the first condition of a good government.[91]

Democratic man as a result of the breakup of intermediate powers, the uniformity of ideas and feelings, comes at this moment to place all powers into the hands of the only authority that stands above all equally: the central power.

It is at the time when all things have conspired to deprive the individual of any support in the society, when he is most isolated and alone, that the central power assumes the greatest authority over the individual. Moreover, it is in these circumstances that the individual is least concerned with the conduct of public affairs. Tocqueville noted, "it is above all at the moment when a democratic society succeeds in forming itself on the debris of an aristocracy that this isolation of men from one another and the selfishness resulting from it strike one's regard most readily."[92] Because every person finds his beliefs within himself, "he turns all his sentiments toward himself alone." Thus Tocqueville alerts us to the new and dangerous element of democratic society, what he calls "individualism." "Individualism is a reflective and peaceable sentiment that disposes each citizen to isolate himself from the mass of those like him and to withdraw to one side with his family and friends, so that after having thus created a little society for his own use, he willingly abandons society at large to itself."[93] The individual becomes isolated and alienated and is concerned primarily with his pleasure and physical comfort. At such time, Tocqueville remarked, "men are swept away and almost beside themselves at the sight of the new goods that they are ready to grasp.... [A]nd to watch better over what they call their affairs, they neglect the principal one, which is to remain masters of themselves."[94] Men are following two separate roads to servitude. He observed that "the taste for well-being turns them away from being involved in government, and the love of well-being puts them in an ever stricter dependence on those who govern."[95]

Despotism, Tocqueville wrote, "sees the most certain guarantee of its own duration in the isolation of men, and it ordinarily puts all its care into isolating them." The problem is that "[e]quality places men beside one another without a common bond to hold them. Despotism raises barriers between them and separates them. Equality disposes them to think of those like themselves, and for them despotism makes a sort of public virtue of indifference."[96] How is it possible, Tocqueville asked, "that a society should escape destruction if the moral tie be not strengthened in proportion as the political tie is relaxed?"[97]

Recently, Roger Boesche has suggested that "previous theorists assumed that despotism required an extremely hierarchical society. Tocqueville agrees that despotism hinges on isolation, but he recognizes a new and modern historical development encouraging a despotism that need not rely on force (but instead can make servitude delightful)."[98] This new despotism is particularly to be feared because it may be unrecognizable. Tocqueville attempted to teach democratic man the "feeling" and "attitudes" of oppression, for modern despotism will be accompanied by ever-greater physical comforts. It endangers not the body but the soul.

As Tocqueville noted:

> Fetters and headsman were the coarse instruments that tyranny for-
> merly employed; but the civilization of our age has perfected despotism
> itself, though it seemed to have nothing to learn.... Under the absolute
> sway of one man the body was attacked in order to subdue the soul;
> but the soul escaped the blows which were directed against it and rose
> proudly superior. Such is not the course adopted in democratic repub-
> lics; there the body is left free, and the soul is enslaved.[99]

In Tocqueville's view, only freedom could forestall the worst aspects of
the new despotism. In his Foreword to *The Old Regime*, he articulated
his mature reflection on the issue:

> Freedom and freedom alone can extirpate these vices, which indeed
> are innate in communities of this order; it alone can call a halt to their
> pernicious influence. For only freedom can deliver the member of a
> community from that isolation which is the lot of the individual left
> to his own devices and, compelling them to get in touch with each
> other, promote an active sense of fellowship. In a community of free
> citizens every man is daily reminded of the need of meeting his fel-
> low men ... of exchanging ideas, and coming to an agreement as to
> the conduct of their common interests. Freedom alone is capable of
> lifting men's minds above mere mammon worship.... It alone replaces
> at certain critical moments their natural love of material welfare by a
> loftier, more virile ideal.[100]

Tocqueville insisted that "in the democratic centuries that are going to
open up, individual independence and local liberties will always be the
product of art. Centralization will be the natural government."[101] In his
"most enlightened speculation" on the issue of administrative centralization, Tocqueville offered the legislator's art in the service of genuine
liberty.

In an important respect, Tocqueville has been remarkably influential in shaping the "attitudes" and "feelings" of the individual in modern
society, particularly with regard to the problem of what is now called

"bureaucracy." His success can be seen in the remark of a contemporary observer:

> The contempt in which bureaucracy is held in modern thinking and prejudice, the insensitivity to honour that is also present in this function of government—this contempt was for all time given respectability by Tocqueville's history.[102]

10

On Harvey Mansfield's Jefferson Lecture: How to Understand Politics

H ARVEY MANSFIELD WAS GIVEN the high honor of delivering the Jefferson Lecture in the Humanities in Washington in 2007.[1] That privilege, not often given to a political scientist, is the highest honor the federal government confers for distinguished intellectual achievement in the humanities. This panel, in a much smaller way (and with the blessing of the American Political Science Association), is also an attempt to honor his achievement. We here, I think, understand and appreciate the importance of Harvey Mansfield's contribution to our understanding of politics. This discipline, which is perhaps reluctant to praise its most severe and honest critics, too, owes him a debt of gratitude not only for his scholarship, but for his extraordinary influence as a teacher as well. I need only look at the other presenters on this panel—I believe nearly all of them were his students at various times. Consequently, we have not only his work, but his influence on the many contributions of his students as well. In his lecture, Mansfield raised the question of how to understand politics by asking "How to Understand Politics: What the Humanities Can Say to Science." In doing so, he expressed his reservations concerning the dominant way of trying to understand politics—the scientific study of politics. The fundamental problem of a political science that seeks to be scientific in the manner of natural science is that it must ignore the question of importance, which he says "is the central question in politics." "Politics is about who deserves to be more important: which leader from which party with which ideas. Politics assumes that the contest for importance is important: in a grander sense it assumes that human beings are important."

In the attempt to establish scientific truth as the ground of objective knowledge, political science has become dependent upon a method that seeks to comprehend only behavior, and only in the aggregate, and only on behalf of universal abstractions. In doing so, scientific political science alienates itself from what is of paramount importance in political life: the individual human being. "Human beings and their associations always have names," Mansfield says. "They maintain their individuality by the use of proper names." They might even have souls and may sometimes insist upon their own importance. Mansfield offers some suggestions for improving our understanding of politics. First, he thinks that political science should "recapture the notion of *thumos*" (spiritedness, a philosophic concept derived from Plato and Aristotle), which refers, he says, "to a part of the soul that makes us want to insist on our own importance." The "second improvement," he tells us, "is the use of names—proper to literature and foreign to science." "Literature," he says, "tells stories of characters with names, in places with names, in times with dates." We come to understand in the course of his lecture that the humanities, understood broadly as philosophy, and history as well as literature, knows something that science does not: "the human resistance to hearing the truth.... While science aims at agreement among scientists, in literature as in philosophy the greatest names disagree with one another."

Mansfield, it becomes clear, is not only interested in the importance of importance, but the importance of the most important. Thus, we are confronted with human greatness. "Human greatness," he notes, "is the height of human importance, where the best that humans can do is tested, and it is the work of great individuals. The great Tocqueville—and I refuse to give a lecture on politics without mentioning his name—alluded to himself and his favorite readers as 'the true friends of liberty and human greatness.' Somehow liberty and human greatness go together." I have no doubt about Tocqueville's greatness, or his attachment to liberty. But when a certain understanding of liberty becomes the foundation of a political theory, perhaps it is necessary to look at the disagreement that exists among theorists and democratic statesmen.

Tocqueville understood liberty as the highest good of democratic society. It stands in uneasy tension with equality, a providentially or historically fated fact that is a product of the taste for general ideas that arise in post-Christian democratic societies. Thus, although the desire for equality and the passion for uniformity of social conditions accompany democracy, equality is compatible with freedom or despotism. The greatest danger to liberty arises as a result of the unification of governmental and social or administrative centralization. Therefore, the fate that awaits democratic man is either the preservation of local and individual liberty or the establishment of administrative despotism.[2] The desire for equality of conditions accelerates the process of individual isolation and the subsequent rationalization of human life.[3] Therefore, it is not equality but the passion for *liberty* that must be nurtured and preserved. Thus, Tocqueville believed freedom is the closest thing to a principle of nature or, more specifically, of humanity. Consequently, it is the defense of freedom that becomes the fundamental problem of democratic times.[4] Tocqueville did not understand the idea of equality, as the American Founders had, in philosophic terms, as a political principle derived from nature and theoretical reason. In fact, Tocqueville seems to have minimized the importance of theory; his explanation rests upon a fundamental change in social conditions that leads to theories that seem to be by-products of social change. Similarly, Tocqueville's understanding of freedom is not the same as the earlier tradition, either philosophic or religious. The older philosophic and religious traditions and the American Founders understood liberty as subordinate to the moral law (made manifest through reason or revelation). It presupposed the necessity of subordinating passion, or will, to rational limits.[5] In the older view, it is nature and reason, or God's revelation, that established and discerned the limits upon human freedom.

Tocqueville's view of equality must be understood in terms of providence, or history, as a general idea that shapes and takes its shape in democratic times. If the democratization of society leads to equality of conditions or centralization, there can be no natural beneficial order that is intelligible through the use of human reason or the comprehension of natural human equality. The idea of equality therefore cannot be rooted in the laws of nature or nature's God. For that reason, the principle of equality cannot serve as the ground of political justice. Rather, for Tocqueville, man's humanity is established in the exercise of freedom or free will over the course of time or history. Nonetheless, the outcome of the use of man's freedom is dependent upon the earlier use of his freedom and is therefore always in doubt.[6] Historical circumstances, it seems, will determine whether equality is compatible with freedom or despotism. In order for freedom to become the ground of justice, self-interest, individual will, or desire, must be rationalized by being generalized.[7] Nonetheless, the will of each individual remains as the irreducible ground of freedom. Consequently, as Strauss has indicated, for Rousseau, freedom becomes "a higher good than life."

In fact, Strauss goes on about Rousseau, he tends to identify freedom with virtue or with goodness. He says that freedom is obedience to the law which one has given to one's self. This means, in the first place, that not merely obedience to the law but legislation itself must originate in the individual. It means, secondly, that freedom is not so much either the condition or the consequence of virtue as virtue itself. What is true of virtue can also be said of goodness, which Rousseau distinguished from virtue: freedom is identical with goodness; to be free, or to be one's self, is to be good—this is one meaning of his thesis that man is by nature good. Above all, he suggests that the traditional definition of man be replaced by a new definition according to which not rationality but freedom is the specific distinction of man.[8] Tocqueville's understanding of freedom is not substantially different from that of Rousseau. The reconciliation of the individual and the general will is the fundamental problem of politics. That reconciliation is only possible when freedom is exercised at the level of local or parochial institutions.[9] Only there is it possible for the individual to abstract from his particular interests in a manner compatible with the interest of the community. Freedom understood in this way cannot be subordinate to the moral law; it becomes the foundation of the moral law. Indeed, as Strauss suggested, with reference to Rousseau, "the ultimate outcome of this attempt was the substitution of freedom for virtue or the view that it is not virtue which makes man free but freedom which makes man virtuous."[10]

It is not surprising that for Tocqueville every political order must be judged from the point of view of its capacity to defend individual, or local, liberty, which is the foundation of virtue and justice. As Leo Strauss subsequently noted, it was Rousseau who thought it "necessary to abandon altogether the attempt to find the basis of right in nature, in human nature. And Rousseau seemed to have shown an alternative. For he had shown that what is characteristically human is not the gift of nature, but is the outcome of what man did, or was forced to do, in order to overcome or to change nature: man's humanity is the product of the historical process."[11] Consequently, it is providence or history, not nature, that enabled man to see himself as what he is or may become. For Rousseau and Tocqueville, freedom, or individual freedom, or will, becomes and remains the indissoluble ground of virtue. The political problem for both is one of reconciling the individual and the general will.[12] It is free will, not reason, that distinguished man from the animals.[13] If history or perfectibility, not nature, had determined what man is capable of, then free will, not reason, is the distinctive characteristic of man, as that which separated him from the animals.[14] If the law of reason was severed from the law of nature, a new foundation for rationality and morality had to be established. It was to be found in the passionate and self-interested awareness of the fact that the rights of each depend upon the recognition of the rights of all. Or the will of the individual, in order to become legitimized, must be generalized. Again, it was Rousseau who provided the analytical framework for the understanding of will as the foundation of a new law of reason and morality.[15] "Rousseau may be said to have indicated the character of such a law of reason," Strauss suggested, "by his teaching concerning the general will, by a teaching which can be regarded as the outcome of the attempt to find a 'realistic' substitute for the traditional natural law."[16] It is the recognition in all others of the same right that one claims for one's self; all others necessarily take an effective interest in the recognition of their rights, whereas no one, or but a few, take an effective interest in human perfection of other men. This being the case, my desire transforms itself into a rational desire by being "generalized" (i.e., by being conceived as the content of a law that binds all members of society equally); a desire that survives the test of "generalization" is, by this very fact, proved to be rational and hence just.[17] Nonetheless, Tocqueville's historical analysis, unlike that of those thinkers who were influenced by Kant and Hegel, still seemed to place a premium on the importance of practical reason, or prudence, in human affairs. His concern with the practical and political led one observer, Marvin Zetterbaum, to suggest that "Tocqueville was in revolt against those of his predecessors who had looked on political things in an abstract way."[18]

Yet, his new political science may have conceded too much to fate or History. In denying the authority and primacy of theoretical or metaphysical reason, the autonomy of practical reason is wholly undermined. Prudence, as well as common sense, is without a theoretical defense. In such circumstances, no political science could establish a viable defense against the forces of History. Any moderate or constitutional regime based upon an understanding of nature and reason would be wholly disarmed. Once the historical conditions, which sustained a view of equality compatible with liberty, were transformed, equality itself would become a principle of despotism. After the transformation, prudence could provide no further guidance for a political defense of individual freedom.[19] Indeed, in the subsequent history of political thought, no such defense was attempted. In fact, just the opposite occurred. In Hegel and his successors, rational or bureaucratic rule—or the rule of organized intelligence—would replace individual freedom and self-rule in civil society. Civil associations would become professional associations, like the American Political Science Association (APSA). Furthermore, the later historicists, such as Hegel and Marx, demanded a reconciliation of the individual and general will, which required the unification of the social and political, the public and private, making citizenship in the rational state the ground of freedom and virtue. Tocqueville denied that such a reconciliation is possible because he believed that the will, like freedom, is essentially private or individual. Therefore, the defense of human freedom would require a defense of individual and local liberty. Only a small democratic community could prevent the centralization of administration and the rationalization of society.

If Leo Strauss is right, it was Jean-Jacques Rousseau who originated the new philosophy of freedom. It is no doubt the case that the new philosophy of freedom paved the way for Hegel's philosophy of History. Tocqueville was in nearly full agreement with Rousseau's philosophy of freedom. Nonetheless, he would not acquiesce in the Hegelian attempt to rationalize will in a manner that would transcend the particular and individual. He did not believe that a new ground of positive freedom could be established on the basis of citizenship in the rational state. However, like

Hegel, he agreed that history was moving almost inevitably toward universalizing rights of man (equality and liberty). Furthermore, he agreed that Christianity had provided the moral foundation for the democratic, or rational, state. However, whereas Hegel regarded the rational state as a kind of secular deity, and bureaucracy as the embodiment of rationality, Tocqueville saw it as the end of freedom and the beginning of a new kind of despotism. Tocqueville's defense of freedom was a defense of the private and particular elements of individual will. He did not think it possible for man to universalize, or rationalize, the will. He thought it was impossible to do so in a manner that was compatible with freedom. In other words, he was not persuaded, as Hegel was, that the historical process is rational.

The challenge posed by Rousseau's theory was to determine whether or not it was possible "to seek the standard of human action in the historical process." As Strauss observed, "this solution presupposed that the historical process or its results are unambiguously preferable to the state of nature or that that process is 'meaningful.'" Strauss contended that

> Rousseau could not accept that presupposition. He realized that to the extent to which the historical process is accidental, it cannot supply man with a standard, and that, if that process has a hidden purpose, its purposefulness cannot be recognized except if there are trans-historical standards. The historical process cannot be recognized as progressive without previous knowledge of the end or purpose of the process. To be meaningful, the historical process must culminate in perfect knowledge of the public right; man cannot be, or have become, the seeing master of his fate if he does not have such knowledge. It is, then, not knowledge of the historical process but knowledge of the true public right which supplies man with the true standard.[20]

Tocqueville remained within the horizon of Rousseau, in his rejection of the view that the historical process is rational and therefore meaningful. Thus, he could not accept the Hegelian claim that it is possible to unite "true knowledge of public right" with perfect knowledge of the end or purpose of the historical process.[21] As a result, he refused to believe that the rational or bureaucratic state could be anything other than a new kind of despotism.

Nonetheless, his analysis of the subsequent progress of equality of conditions and its effect upon democracy was so prescient and accurate because it derived from a theoretical understanding of man in which the primacy of History had replaced nature. In that respect, he acquiesced in the view that will had replaced reason as the distinctive characteristic of man.[22] Therefore, the process of centralization, or rationalization and bureaucratization, was almost an historical inevitability for Tocqueville. As a result, he could find no rational defense of the principle of equality in nature itself, as did the American Founders. Consequently, Tocqueville could not provide a theoretical or intellectual defense of constitutionalism, or limited government. Such a defense would have required a recovery of the philosophic ground of natural right, which was not forthcoming until the twentieth century.[23] It was Leo Strauss who made the defense of constitutional government possible once again by distinguishing, in a meaningful way, the theoretical and practical differences in the understanding of natural right and history.

In 1953, in *Natural Right and History*, Strauss noted that "the problem of natural right is today a matter of recollection rather than of actual knowledge. We are therefore in need of historical studies in order to familiarize ourselves with the whole complexity of the issue. We have for some time become students of what is called 'the history of ideas.'"[24] Harvey Mansfield and his many students have contributed to a renewed understanding of the problem of natural right by their historical studies, which have illuminated the history of ideas. Nonetheless, Tocqueville's warning concerning the dangers of centralized administration have taken on a new meaning with the possibility of the coming into being of a universal homogeneous state. In the absence of a meaningful defense of natural right and a decent constitutionalism, there seems no reason to doubt that Tocqueville's diagnosis of the problem of democracy, understood historically, is an accurate depiction of the advent of a universal tyranny. Tocqueville's analysis of the despotic character of centralized administration is therefore more relevant than ever before. But the important question remains: Is it possible to defend the principles of equality and liberty, understood in a manner compatible with constitutional government, without meaningful knowledge of natural right?

11

Roosevelt's or Reagan's America?
A Time for Choosing

O N JANUARY 11, 1944, President Franklin D. Roosevelt sent the text of his Annual Message to Congress.[1] Under normal conditions, he would have delivered the message in person that evening at the Capitol. But he was recovering from the flu, and his doctor advised him not to leave the White House. So he delivered it as a fireside chat to the American people. It has been called the greatest speech of the century by Cass Sunstein, a prominent liberal law professor at the University of Chicago.[2] It is an important speech because it is probably the most far-reaching attempt by an American president to legitimize the administrative or welfare state, based on the idea that government must guarantee social and economic security for all.

Thirty-seven years later, in his first inaugural on January 20, 1981, President Ronald Reagan would deny that government could provide such a broad guarantee of security in a manner consistent with the protection of American liberty.[3] Indeed, he would insist that bureaucratic government had become a danger to the survival of our freedom. In looking at the differences between the views of Roosevelt and Reagan, we can discern the distinction between a constitutional regime—in which the power of government is limited so as to enable the people to rule—and an administrative state, which presupposes the rule of a bureaucratic or intellectual elite.

FDR's New Bill of Rights

When Roosevelt spoke to the nation that January night, he was looking beyond the end of World War II. In recent years, he said,

> Americans have joined with like-minded people in order to defend ourselves in a world that has been gravely threatened with gangster rule. But I do not think that any of us Americans can be content with mere survival. Sacrifices that we and our Allies are making impose upon us all a sacred obligation to see to it that out of this war we and our children will gain something better than mere survival.

And what was this "sacred obligation?" Roosevelt continued:

> The one supreme objective for the future, which we discussed for each nation individually, and for all the United Nations, can be summed up in one word: Security. And that means not only physical security which provides safety from attacks by aggressors. It means also economic security, social security, moral security—in a family of Nations.

Government has a sacred duty, in other words, to provide security as a fundamental human right. Roosevelt was well aware that this was a departure from the traditional understanding of the role of American government:

> This Republic had its beginning, and grew to its present strength, under the protection of certain inalienable political rights—among them the right of free speech, free press, free worship, trial by jury, freedom from unreasonable searches and seizures. They were our rights to life and liberty. As our Nation has grown in size and stature, however—as our industrial economy expanded—these political rights proved inadequate to assure us equality in the pursuit of happiness. We have come to a clear realization of the fact that true individual freedom cannot exist without economic security and independence. "Necessitous men are not free men." People who are hungry and out of a job are the stuff of which dictatorships are made. In our day these economic truths have become accepted as self-evident. We have accepted, so to speak, a

second Bill of Rights under which a new basis of security and prosperity can be established for all.

Among these new rights, Roosevelt said, are

> The right to a useful and remunerative job in the industries, or shops or farms or mines of the Nation; The right to earn enough to provide adequate food and clothing and recreation; The right of every farmer to raise and sell his products at a return which will give him and his family a decent living; The right of every businessman, large and small, to trade in an atmosphere of freedom from unfair competition and domination by monopolies at home or abroad; The right of every family to a decent home; The right to adequate medical care and the opportunity to achieve and enjoy good health; The right to adequate protection from the economic fears of old age, sickness, accident, and unemployment; The right to a good education.

The Constitution had established a limited government that presupposed an autonomous civil society and a free economy. But such freedom had led inevitably to social inequality, which in Roosevelt's view had made Americans insecure in a way that was unacceptable. He had lost faith in the older constitutional principle of limited government. Rather, he thought that the protection of political rights—or of social and economic liberty, exercised by individuals unregulated by government—had made it impossible to establish a foundation for social justice (i.e., what he called "equality in the pursuit of happiness"), He assumed that a fundamental tension exists between equality and liberty that can only be resolved by a powerful, even unlimited, administrative or welfare state.

Rejecting the Founders

The American Founders, by contrast, thought that equality and liberty were perfectly compatible—indeed, that they were opposite sides of the same coin. The principle of natural equality had been set forth in the Declaration of Independence, which clearly spelled out the way in which all human beings are the same: They are equally endowed with natural and inalienable rights. But along with this similarity, the Founders knew that differences are sown into human nature: some people are smarter, some are stronger, some are more beautiful, some are musically inclined while others have a predilection for business. Political equality, which requires the protection of individual rights, produces social inequality (or unequal achievement) precisely because of these unequal natural faculties. The preservation of freedom, in the Founders' view, requires a defense of private property, understood in terms of the protection of the individual citizen's rights of conscience, opinion, self-interest, and labor. They thought that a constitutional order, by separating church and state, government and civil society, and the public and private sphere, makes it possible to reconcile equality and liberty in a reasonable way that is compatible with the nature of man. Thus the Constitution limits the power of government to the protection of natural rights.

Roosevelt and his fellow Progressives rejected the idea of natural differences between men, insisting that those differences arise only out of social and economic inequality. As a result, they redefined the idea of freedom, divorcing it from the idea of individual rights and identifying it instead with the idea of security. It was in the cause of this new understanding of freedom that America's constitutional form of limited government was gradually replaced—beginning with the New Deal and culminating in the late 1960s and 1970s—by an administrative or welfare state. Roosevelt had made it clear, even before he was elected president, that government had a new and different role to play in American life than that assigned to it by the Constitution. In an October 1932 radio address, he stated: "I have further described the spirit of my program as a 'new deal,' which is plain English for a changed concept of the duty and responsibility of Government toward economic life."[4] In his view, selfish behavior on the part of individuals and corporations must give way to rational social action informed by a benevolent government and the organized intelligence of the bureaucracy. Consequently, the role of government was no longer the protection of the natural or political rights of individuals. The old constitutional distinction between government and society—or between the public and private spheres—as the ground of liberalism and a bulwark against political tyranny had created, in Roosevelt's view, economic tyranny. To solve this, government itself would become a tool of benevolence working on behalf of the people.

This redefinition of the role of government carried with it a new understanding of the role of the American people. In Roosevelt's Commonwealth Club address of 1932, he said:

> The Declaration of Independence discusses the problem of government in terms of a contract. . . . Under such a contract, rulers were accorded power, and the people consented to that power on consideration that they be accorded certain rights. The task of statesmanship has always been the re-definition of these rights in terms of a changing and growing social order. New conditions impose new requirements upon Government and those who conduct Government.[5]

But this idea of a compact between government and the people is contrary to both the Declaration of Independence and the Constitution. Indeed, what links the Declaration and the Constitution is the idea of the people as autonomous and sovereign, and government as the people's creation and servant. Jefferson, in the Declaration, clearly presented the relationship in this way: "to secure these [inalienable] rights, governments are instituted among men, deriving their just powers from the consent of the governed." Similarly, the Constitution begins by institutionalizing the authority of the people: "*We the People* of the United States, in Order to form a more perfect Union, establish Justice, insure domestic Tranquility, provide for the common defence, promote the general Welfare, and secure the Blessings of Liberty to ourselves and our Posterity, do ordain and establish this Constitution for the United States of America."

In Roosevelt's reinterpretation, on the other hand, government determines the conditions of social compact, thereby diminishing not only the authority of the Constitution but undermining the effective sovereignty of the people.

Reagan's Attempt to Turn the Tide

Ronald Reagan addressed this problem of sovereignty at some length in his first inaugural, in which he observed famously: "In this present crisis, government is not the solution to our problem, government is the problem." He was speaking specifically of the deep economic ills that plagued the nation at the time of his election. But he was also speaking about the growing power of a bureaucratic and intellectual elite. This elite, he argued, was undermining the capacity of the people to control what had become, in effect, an unelected government. Thus it was undermining self-government itself.

The perceived failure of the US economy during the Great Depression had provided the occasion for expanding the role of the federal government in administering the private sector. Reagan insisted in 1981 that government had proved itself incapable of solving the problems of the economy or of society. As for the relationship between the people and the government, Reagan did not view it, as Roosevelt had, in terms of the people consenting to the government on the condition that government grant them certain rights. Rather, he insisted:

> We are a nation that has a government—not the other way around. And this makes us special among the nations of the Earth. Our government has no power except that granted it by the people. It is time to check and reverse the growth of government, which shows signs of having grown beyond the consent of the governed.

In Reagan's view it was the individual, not government, who was to be credited with producing the things of greatest value in America:

> If we look to the answer as to why for so many years we achieved so much, prospered as no other people on Earth, it was because here in this land we unleashed the energy and individual genius of man to a greater extent than has ever been done before. Freedom and the dignity of the individual have been more available and assured here than in any other place on Earth.

And it was the lack of trust in the people which posed the greatest danger to freedom:

> [W]e've been tempted to believe that society has become too complex to be managed by self-rule, that government by an elite group is superior to government for, by, and of the people. Well, if no one among us is capable of governing himself, then who among us has the capacity to govern someone else?

Reagan had been long convinced that the continued growth of the bureaucratic state could lead to the loss of freedom. In his famous 1964 speech, "A Time for Choosing," delivered on behalf of Barry Goldwater, he had said:

> [I]t doesn't require expropriation or confiscation of private property or business to impose socialism on a people. What does it mean whether you hold the deed or the title to your business or property if the government holds the power of life and death over that business or property? Such machinery already exists. The government can find some charge to bring against any concern it chooses to prosecute. Every businessman has his own tale of harassment. Somewhere a perversion has taken place. Our natural, inalienable rights are now considered to be a dispensation of government, and freedom has never been so fragile, so close to slipping from our grasp as it is at this moment.[6]

Reagan made it clear that centralized control of the economy and society by the federal government could not be accomplished without undermining individual rights and establishing coercive and despotic control.

> "[T]he full power of centralized government" was the very thing the Founding Fathers sought to minimize. They knew that governments don't control things. A government can't control the economy without controlling people. And they knew when a government sets out to do that, it must use force and coercion to achieve its purpose. They also knew, those Founding Fathers, that outside of its legitimate functions, government does nothing as well or as economically as the private sector of the economy.

Over the next fifteen years, Reagan succeeded in mobilizing a powerful sentiment against the excesses of big government. In doing so, he revived the debate over the importance of limited government for the preservation of a free society. And his theme would remain constant throughout his presidency. In his final State of the Union message, Reagan proclaimed, "the most exciting revolution ever known to humankind began with three simple words: 'We the People,' the revolutionary notion that the people grant government its rights, and not the other way around." And in his Farewell Address to the nation, he said: "Ours was the first revolution in the history of mankind that truly reversed the course of government, and with three little words: 'We the People.'" He never wavered in his insistence that modern government had become a problem, primarily because it sought to replace the people as central to the American constitutional order.

Like the Founders, Reagan understood human nature to be unchanging—and thus tyranny, like selfishness, to be a problem coeval with human life. Experience had taught the Founders to regard those who govern with the same degree of suspicion as those who are governed— equally subject to selfish or tyrannical opinions, passions, and interests. Consequently, they did not attempt to mandate the good society or social justice by legislation, because they doubted that it was humanly possible to do so. Rather they attempted to create a free society, in which the people themselves could determine the conditions necessary for the good life. By establishing a constitutional government of limited power, they placed their trust in the people.

Up or Down, Not Right or Left

The political debate in America today is often portrayed as being between Progressives (or the political left) and Reactionaries (or the political right), the former working for change on behalf of a glorious future and the latter resisting that change. Reagan denied these labels because they are based on the idea that human nature can be transformed such that government can bring about a perfect society. In his 1964 speech, he noted:

> You and I are told increasingly that we have to choose between a left or right. Well I would like to suggest that there is no such thing as a left or right. There is only an up or down—up to man's age-old dream, the ultimate in individual freedom consistent with law and order, or down to the ant heap of totalitarianism. And regardless of their sincerity, their humanitarian motives, those who would trade our freedom for security have embarked on this downward course.

In light of the differences between the ideas and policies of Roosevelt and Reagan, it is not surprising that political debates today are so bitter.

Indeed, they resemble the religious quarrels that once convulsed Western society. The Progressive defenders of the bureaucratic state see government as the source of benevolence, the moral embodiment of the collective desire to bring about social justice as a practical reality. They believe that only mean-spirited Reactionaries can object to a government whose purpose is to bring about this good end. Defenders of the older constitutionalism, meanwhile, see the bureaucratic state as increasingly tyrannical and destructive of inalienable rights.

Ironically, the American regime was the first to solve the problem of religion in politics. Religion, too, had sought to establish the just or good society—the city of God—upon earth. But as the Founders knew, this attempt had simply led to various forms of clerical tyranny. Under the American Constitution, individuals would have religious liberty, but churches would not have the power to enforce their claims on behalf of the good life. Today, with the replacement of limited-government constitutionalism by an administrative state, we see the emergence of a new form of elite, seeking to establish a new form of perfect justice. But as the Founders and Reagan understood, in the absence of angels governing men, or men becoming angels, limited government remains the most reasonable and just form of human government.

12

Theories of the Legislature: The Changing Character of the American Congress

Congress in the Theories of Self-Government

The first day of April 1989 marked the two-hundredth anniversary of the first meeting of the United States Congress. In the long history of that body, Congress has been the object of countless jokes, and a good deal of scorn, which was aptly summed up in Mark Twain's comment that Congress is America's only "distinctly criminal class." If recent public opinion polls are any indication of the current status of this central institution of American government, Congress has been held in "contempt" by the American public.[1] Nonetheless, individual members of Congress continue to be held in high regard and have become increasingly immune from defeat at the polls.

The ambivalence concerning generally hostile perceptions of Congress as a body, and a favorable public attitude in regard to individual members, has led one observer to conclude, "there is not one Congress but two." Roger Davidson pointed out that "One of these two entities is Congress as an institution.... It is Congress, the lawmaking and policy-determining body.... It is Congress acting as a collegial body, performing its constitutional duties and deliberating legislative issues." The second Congress, he regards as "the Congress of 535 ... individual senators and representatives. They possess diverse backgrounds and follow varied paths to win office. Their electoral fortunes depend not upon what Congress produces as an institution but upon the support and goodwill of voters hundreds or thousands of miles away."[2]

Why does the American public, on the one hand, scorn the institution that serves collectively as the representative body of the people, and on the other hand, often admire and vote for the individual member? Why do we observe, with increasing regularity, individual candidates for Congress—including incumbents—who run for national office by running against Congress as an institution?[3] Perhaps the reason for this is to be seen in the fact that, as Morris Fiorina has observed, "the individual members can achieve their primary goals independently of (and even in opposition to) the ends for which the institution was created." If this is the case, Fiorina was perhaps correct when he insisted that a primary objective in contemporary government is to "harmonize the desires of the individual member for re-election and the integrity of the institution as a democratic, policymaking assembly." He suggested that a solution "involves making the fate of individual members more dependent on institutional performance and less dependent on their personal efforts."[4]

There is little doubt that the growth of a centralized bureaucracy has contributed to the difficulty of reconciling the conflicting demands and interests of members of Congress with those of the institution of Congress itself. What is good for the member is not necessarily good for the body as a whole, let alone the nation. However, any attempt to explain this apparent paradox must consider the inherent tension, which exists within a large or diverse liberal republic, between the public and private spheres, or the state and society. This tension provides a basis for the distinction between local and national interests, or the private as opposed to the public good. In the past, the private and parochial interests of citizens were most often administered at the local and state level, or in society, in the economic marketplace. At that level, it was possible to resolve, in a satisfactory manner, the differences implicit in the distinction between the public and private, the general and particular, or the governing as opposed to the administrative elements of a regime. The nation was characteristically governed on the basis of general principles; it was both governed and administered at the state and local level.

The secret to successful reconciliation of the differences involved in the public and private spheres lay in the decentralized character of the American regime. Prior to bureaucratization, Congress as an institution was held to the standard of governing in the national or general interest. After centralization, individual congressmen were judged by their ability to satisfy the private interests of their constituents. Political centralization thus undermined a crucial ingredient of liberal democracy, what Tocqueville called "local institutions" or "provincial liberties." It also blurred the distinction, crucial to liberal societies, between the public and private, or the state and society. The devitalization of local institutions, which made the distinction between the general and particular politically unintelligible, also made it practically impossible to achieve a reasonable reconciliation of those respective interests. As Tocqueville noted, "when the central administration claims completely to replace the free concurrence of those primarily concerned, it is deceiving itself, or trying to deceive you." This is so, he suggests, because, "a central power, however enlightened and wise one imagines it to be, can never alone see to all the details of the life of a great nation. It cannot do so because such a task exceeds human strength. When it attempts unaided to create and operate so much complicated machinery, it must be satisfied with very imperfect results or exhaust itself in futile efforts."[5]

The distinction between the public and private, or the general and particular, is best observed, in a practical way, by focusing on the difference between governing and administering. This difference, articulated and made practically intelligible by Tocqueville, requires recognition of two kinds of political activity, or rule. John Wettergreen has elaborated this point. "The one is proper to personal or parochial interests," he observes, "and the other to general or national interests." Unlike contemporary students of politics or public administration, who see administration as synonymous with "execution." Tocqueville insisted that "both kinds of political activity are characterized by deliberation or lawmaking, by adjudication, and by execution." Consequently, as Wettergreen indicates, "Tocqueville refuses to reduce the one kind of politics to the other, not because private interests and the national interest are often involved with one another, but because he supposes that the principle of administrative authority is radically distinct from the principle of governmental authority. Administrative authority is personal or partial, not to say partisan; it is rooted in the personal attachments of kinship, friendship, and neighborliness. Governmental authority is impersonal or general, not to say nonpartisan: it proceeds from general ideas or universal truths (e.g., "that all men are created equal").[6] As a result, Wettergreen maintains, "administrative excellence is something more than 'prompt and salutary execution of the laws,' because administration involves more than enforcement of laws. It involves, above all, the sound judgment of particulars."[7]

Alexander Hamilton recognized the inherent difficulty in distinguishing the governing and administrative function, and the necessity of careful delineation of the administrative sphere. In *Federalist 72*, he observed that "the administration of government, in its largest sense, comprehends all the operation of the body politic, whether legislative, executive, or judiciary; but in its most usual and perhaps precise signification, it is limited to executive details, and falls peculiarly within the province of the executive department." What are those particular things which "constitute what seems to be most properly understood by the administration of government," and therefore should fall under the province of the "chief magistrate," according to Hamilton? They are "the actual conduct of foreign negotiations, the preparatory plans of finance, the application and disbursement of the public money in conformity to the general appropriations of the legislature, the arrangement of the army and navy, the direction of the operations of war." In Hamilton's view, these are all details of administration, and executive in nature. Moreover, as Wettergreen makes clear, these "distinctly administrative actions of our national government cannot be ordered by law (if for no other reason than that they require secrecy). More importantly, administration of the law itself cannot be ordered by law: the executive must be left free to decide which law to enforce first, and even, sometimes, whether to enforce the law at all; no law can change this circumstance."[8]

It was precisely because of the requirement that administration must be concerned with particular details that Tocqueville believed it impossible for a great nation to wholly centralize administration in a way that is compatible with the preservation of local liberties, and the distinction of the public and private sphere, or government and society. Wettergreen has examined and clarified this important point in Tocqueville's work. He noted, "if humans could think like the Deity, seeing both universals and particulars at once, then both government and administration could and ought to be centralized. In that case, humans could govern themselves and the world providentially, providing for the general or public interest and the private or particular interests—at one stroke and in a perfectly harmonious manner." However, he suggests, "given the limits of the human moral and intellectual capacities, Tocqueville concluded that it would be desirable to establish one political order—government—with authority over humans insofar as they are alike or similar, and many other distinct political orders—decentralized administrations—to rule men insofar as they are different."[9]

Until recently, the American regime was centrally governed but administratively decentralized. In the period between 1965 and 1975, Congress created a bureaucracy capable of centrally administering the details of American life. Many congressmen objected to the fact that the political function of Congress as a body was changed by its increased preoccupation with the administrative process. Representative Gillis Long (D-LA) complained: "we (Congress) were turning ours from an institution that was supposed to be a broad policymaking institution with respect to the problems of the country and its relationship to the world, into merely a city council that overlooks the running of the store every day."[10] Such objections were ineffectual and short-lived. Subsequently, after several years of experience, Congress came to prefer administration and regulation to legislation. The growth in size and the centralization of the administrative and regulatory bureaucracy only serve to confirm this fundamental change. In the period 1970–1974, Wettergreen wrote, "not only did the number of commercial regulatory agencies increase from fifty to seventy-two, but also thirty-five of those fifty established agencies were substantially reformed. For the first time, agencies with 'economy-wide' (in fact, 'society-wide') purview and vast administrative discretion were established."[11]

Indeed since 1975, the characteristic activity of the central government has become the regulation or the administration of the details of the social, political, and economic life of the nation. Such a development could not but strengthen the organized interests and their ties with the legislature, as well as the judiciary, at the price of executive control of the details of administration. As Seidman and Gilmour have suggested, the courts, too, have developed an important role in administrative decision-making and execution. They have observed:

> Perhaps the most important consequence of the growth of the regulatory state is the increasing involvement of the courts in administrative decision making and execution. Up to now public administration literature and theories have almost totally ignored the role of the judicial branch. This is no longer possible when substantially less than 10 percent of the federal budget is spent on domestic programs performed directly by federal employees and the lion's share of federal programs are administered by independent third parties through grants, contracts, and transfer payments. Such arrangements not only invite litigation, but since disputes among parties in these relationships cannot be resolved authoritatively within the executive branch, they virtually command a litigation strategy by third parties and their supporting interest associations as vital means of dealing effectively with federal monitors, rule makers, and enforcers. In addition, Congress has added commands of its own in the form of direct requirements for public participation in the judicial review of administrative decision making and appropriations for attorneys' fee awards. Once judges accepted the appropriateness of their courts as sites for the resolution of such disputes, they became significant, sometimes the most significant actors in the administrative process.[12]

Moreover, the expansion of federal governmental power in this period was not merely accomplished through creation of public agencies but the proliferation of government-sponsored enterprises that are privately controlled, the so-called twilight zone bodies. The links between the public and private sector were forged and maintained through the growth of state budgets and increased control over economic and social relations. Nonetheless, public growth could not be calculated simply by looking at the size of state *budgets*. Public authority consisted of more than public expenditures or tax subsidies, not to mention regulatory power. Government could and did provide loan guarantees and other means by which certain public or even private enterprises were provided the opportunity to obligate the Treasury. In response to the passage of the Congressional Budget and Impoundment Control Act of 1974, these so-called "off-budget" expenditures could be excluded from the official budget process and the necessity of annual appropriations.

As Seidman and Gilmour have indicated: "off-budget agencies are not covered by the new Congressional process and they are not included in the aggregate or functional amounts set forth in the Congressional budget resolutions." Those programs or off-budget agencies, such as the Federal Financing Bank, Pension Benefit Guaranty Corporation, Synthetic Fuels Corporation, to name only a few, have grown tremendously in a short time. "The excluded outlays of government-sponsored enterprises have jumped from relatively small amounts in the 1960s to an estimated $44.3 billion for 1985."[13] Such expenditures are not harmful merely because they have increased the scope and power of the central government, or because they may constitute less efficient use of economic resources. They obscure responsibility and distort important distinctions in liberal governments. Seidman and Gilmour have suggested that

> labeling as "private" what is in reality "public" for cosmetic reasons or to obtain fictitious budget reductions can contribute to loss of faith in our democratic institutions.... Distinctions between what is public and what is private are becoming increasingly blurred, but we cannot abandon these distinctions altogether without fundamental alterations in our constitutional system. The maintenance of this distinction has been considered essential both to protect private rights from intrusion by the government and to prevent usurpation of government power.[14]

Bureaucratic regulation is a kind of administration most impervious to the maintenance of a constitutional separation of powers and most destructive of control of the "details of administration" by the political executive. Moreover, unlike the political branches of government, regulatory agencies are explicitly prevented from attempting to deliberate in a comprehensive manner concerning the public good. As Wettergreen has stated: "what defines each branch is the comprehensiveness of its public functions. All three branches have comprehensive functions, in the sense that they, unlike any agency, act for the whole nation.... No administrative agency, whether independent or dependent, performs any function comprehensively."[15] Furthermore, the status of the regulatory agencies, in their relation to the chief executive, was changed after 1973. Seidman and Gilmour observed,

> Until 1973, the regulatory commissions in some areas enjoyed less independence than some executive agencies. The president, through OMB review of budgets, legislation, and data questionnaires, and Department of Justice control of litigation, was able significantly to influence commission policies, administration, and operations. The Congress in 1973 overrode White House objections and amended the Alaska pipeline bill (1) to authorize the Federal Trade Commission to represent itself in civil court proceedings and (2) to transfer authority for review of independent regulatory commission data requests under the Federal Reporting Services Act from OMB to the General Accounting Office.[16]

The independent regulatory commissions may have become less dependent upon executive supervision in recent years, but they appear to be more responsive to congressional intervention.

The importance of these changes in the standard of political life, which occurred as a result of the regulatory revolution, can be seen in Wettergreen's concise formulation of the problem. He suggests that "the constitutional distinction of regulation from government ought to be observed: simply stated, in the Constitution, 'government' is the adjustment of private interests to the public good and 'regulation' is the adjustment of private interests to each other. A shift of the government's activities from governance to regulation implies a shift of the political standard from the public interest to private interests."[17]

Administrative centralization did not strengthen the governing capacity of the national institutions; on the contrary, it weakened them. As government's role was expanded and its functions increased, it became more intrusive and bigger, but not stronger and more decisive. Rather, as Walter Lippmann pointed out long ago, "to be big is not necessarily to be strong." Indeed, Lippmann insisted that the growth of modern or bureaucratic government threatened "the devitalization of the executive power." The ensuing "disorder," he suggested, "results from a functional derangement in the relationship between the executive power on the one hand, the representative assemblies and the mass electorates on the other hand."

Lippmann contended that "democratic states are susceptible to this derangement because congenitally the executive... is weaker than the elected representatives.... And the normal tendency of elections is to reduce elected officers to the role of agents or organized pluralities."

Such governments, he maintained, are, "to be sure, big governments, in their personnel, in the range and variety of their projects, the ubiquitousness of their interventions." But they are not strong governments. "They are, in fact," he noted, "swollen rather than strong, being too weak to resist the pressure of special interests and of the departmental bureaucracies."[18] Hence, modern democratic governments, when bureaucratized, are faced with the apparent paradox of being less able to govern the more they try to administer the details of life in society. *Centralized administration almost requires decentralization of government.*

Administrative centralization, moreover, has exacerbated the tension between the executive and the legislature in a way that subsequently worked to undermine the separation of powers. As Wettergreen has observed, "the difference of interest between the President and Congress, which bureaucratization has produced, ought to be distinguished from the traditional rivalry of the branches, which is the consequence of separation of powers. The Presidency, as the only truly national elective office, is ultimately subversive of central administration, while Congress, especially the House, has a natural sympathy with administration because of its closer ties to narrower interests." When administration is centralized, Wettergreen suggests, "it does not naturally fall under the authority of any one branch.... Instead, it becomes a bone of contention among them." Moreover, Congress gets "the better of the division because of its superior attention to localized interests (and its superior part in deliberations)." Before centralization, Wettergreen contends, "congressmen surveilled the president, to protect non-national interests from the untoward effects of national executions. The ultimate protection was to refuse to make laws touching these interests on the ground that they were not national interests."[19]

In the same manner, "the President surveilled Congress with an eye to the national (or, at least, trans-sectional) interest, if only because his political interest required a broader coalition." Hence, Wettergreen noted, "before the choice to centralize was made, separation of powers was an important prop for decentralized administration, in which congressmen have an interest (even during the New Deal), and for centralized governance, in which the President has a special interest. In sum, the whole central government had a common interest in deliberating the national interest, and in distinguishing it from narrower interests." Administrative centralization makes it far less necessary for Congress to subordinate private and parochial interests to a national interest. Rather, Congress in the period during and after the Great Society, "brought all the partial interests to the center, where they do almost nothing but try to compromise national execution and legislation." Consequently, Wettergreen concluded: "decrees, i.e. bureaucratically promulgated regulation, have replaced public laws as the typical expression of public authority."[20]

In the aftermath of administrative centralization, Wettergreen suggests, "the President still has a political interest in central governance, but the Congress has lost its interest in decentralized administration." The constitutional separation of powers, Wettergreen maintains, "did not deadlock national governance on national issues, but encouraged it by making the cooperation of the two branches necessary. However, administration does not require that cooperation. So today, the branches stand divided against themselves, one wishing to govern and the other to administer." Hence, he concluded, "the conflict between the two branches is no longer the result of differing opinions of the national interest."[21]

Even before the election of 1972, it had become clear that a president's ability to govern in the national interest was undermined by administrative centralization, and every recent president has sought to control the bureaucracy in order to decentralize administratively, with a view to governance in accord with general principles or a public interest. On the other hand, Congress has benefited from and has become the defender of a centralized administration. In practice, this has often required obstructing the president's ability to govern by preventing unified presidential control of the bureaucracy. Furthermore, Congress inhibited its own capacity to govern in accord with a general or national interest by deemphasizing its legislative or lawmaking and its deliberative function, while at the same time strengthening its administrative oversight capability. Hence Congress reorganized itself in such a way as to disperse power broadly among its members in committee or subcommittee, with a view to allowing individual members the ability to intervene routinely in the execution phase of the governing process. As a result, some of the most important political battles between the president and Congress revolve around the question of which branch will control the bureaucracy, and in whose interest. In these circumstances, it has become almost as difficult to distinguish the executive and legislative function of the respective political branches as it is to discern the difference between the public and private sphere in the post-bureaucratic society.

In the public mind, Congress as an institution is expected primarily to deliberate and legislate or make general laws in the national interest. Secondly, it is to represent and serve the particular or private interests and constituencies of the localities that make up the nation. When it is judged as a body or an institution, Congress is judged on its ability to make good public law in the national interest. On the other hand, individual members of Congress are more often judged on the basis of their ability to provide the kinds of goods and services that can satisfy the private interests of organized groups, or electorally decisive minorities, within a district. The problem posed by this dilemma is that it is not possible to make good general laws in the public interest and, at the same time, provide the particular necessities sought by the private interests. At the national level, it seems to be impossible to govern and administer at the same time. However, this problem was solved in a satisfactory way for individual members, but not for the institution of Congress, by the creation of a bureaucracy whose public mandate was so large, its purposes so broad, that the impact of its rules and regulations touched upon nearly every interest and detail of life in society. By delegating authority to the bureaucracy, Congress could avoid responsibility for the obtrusive regulations foisted upon society. The bureaucracy could be blamed for its meddlesome rules rather than congressional failure to provide proper guidelines in its delegation of authority, assuming national legislation was necessary in the first place.

In this period of administrative centralization, Congress apparently had concluded that nearly every social and economic, not to mention political, problem required a national solution. But Congress was unable to pass general laws that were sufficiently detailed to accomplish its purposes. This was particularly true when those purposes were so vague— such as a general desire to clean up the environment—that any specific measure could not get majority, let alone presidential, support. What Congress did, as Wettergreen has shown, was "deliberately leave the law 'unfinished,' wait and see what bureaucratic discretion would do with the law, and then, if necessary, correct the bureaucracy."[22]

The precedent for this kind of delegation of authority on a broad scale, with vague standards of enforcement, was the Federal Trade Commission (FTC) Act of 1913. Wettergreen has called this act "one of the poorest pieces of legislation ever written." As he noted, "according to that act, the FTC's authority was to be exercised to prevent 'unfair methods of competition in commerce.' Moreover, the FTC Act explicitly declares that the 'reason' of the commission should determine which methods are unfair; Congress explicitly refused to reason about this and meant to deny the president's reasoning." Such broad and vague delegation of authority had the effect of substituting administrative discretion for congressional deliberation in a vast area of public policy. As a result of the difficulties posed by this act, Wettergreen noted that "Congress never deliberately created agencies with broad, vaguely defined purpose and purview. Never, that is, until the regulatory revolution of the early 1970s, when it created society-wide regulatory agencies with intentionally vague purposes after even less deliberation than the FTC."[23]

Once administration is centralized, no legislative body can legislate, in a general manner, all of the details of the life of a great nation. Congress had to delegate authority to administrative bodies. Of course, it could continue to play a significant in role in the administrative process, or void an exercise of delegated authority, through the use of a legislative veto. But Congress has a number of ways of ensuring that the bureaucracy is responsive to its members. Perhaps the most important formal power is the statutory authority of Congress to create departments and agencies, as well as determine their size, not to mention the ability to control their budgets. Ripley and Franklin have pointed to several means by which Congress keeps the bureaucracy responsive to its will. As they have observed: "in the technical sense, only statutes have the force of law. However, Congress has also made its will felt in programmatic terms through language contained in committee reports. And the executive branch often treats this language as binding." Also, "Congress may require that parts of the bureaucracy make certain information available to it through reporting requirements in statutes." Perhaps, most important for ongoing control, is control of authorizations and appropriations, which require numerous formal and informal contacts between administrators and congressmen. Consequently, as Ripley and Franklin have suggested, "Congress inevitably is the focus of attention from bureaucrats requesting and defending their agencies' budgets, and budget decisions are an important congressional technique for influencing programmatic performance in the executive branch."[24] It is not surprising that career civil servants are often more attentive to the wishes of relevant members of Congress than to their elected or appointed superiors in the executive branch.

The implicit premise of legislative delegation, and the necessity of administrative oversight, is the belief that administrative bodies, scientifically neutral and technically rational, can best carry out the will of the people. The political reason of the people, or the deliberation of the partisan representative legislative bodies, is ineffective in fulfilling the people's intention. Furthermore, administrative bodies benefit from the technical rationality of the social sciences. The scientific method is superior to the political process as the means of serving the will of the people. As Harvey Mansfield has commented, "The trick, then, is to leave the people their will and take away their reason; then social science can bring its reason to serve their will, showing them how to get more of what they want. The value neutrality of social science is the best or only means by which government can bring value to the people."[25] It is no wonder that legislative bodies have become increasingly apprehensive concerning the necessity of public deliberation and the efficacy of political reason as the means by which modern problems can be solved. Thus, within the legislatures, public deliberation and lawmaking has given way to delegation of authority to those administrative bodies capable of utilizing the expertise of those trained in the scientific method, or the technical rationality of the now authoritative social sciences, in solving the problems of modern society.

The rationale for the legality of the delegation of power, and the use of a congressional negative, was stated in Justice Jackson's opinion in *Federal Trade Commission v. Ruberoid* (1952). As Wettergreen commented, "according to that opinion, the laws establishing administrative agencies were '... unfinished law which the administrative body must complete before it is ready for application.'" But, as he points out, such a view "appears to be unreasonable: an unfinished law is not yet a law; it is not really a law at all."

Nor can the bureaucracy complete the law. Indeed, Wettergreen opines, "the same reasons which prevented Congress from 'finishing' the law in the first place—the threat of a presidential veto, the lack of majority support for any possible finished law—kept the law from ever being 'finished' by the bureaucracy. How could anyone suppose that, if Congress could not 'finish' a law, a bureaucratic agency which is by nature politically weaker than Congress could 'finish' that same law!" In fact, Wettergreen insists, "no law defining 'consumer product safety' could get through Congress and past the President today for the same reasons that none could in 1972."[26]

In terms of practical effect, Wettergreen concluded, the use of the legal device of "unfinished law" was just a means of centralizing administration. "The laws could not be 'finished,' [he contends] because they invariably dealt with administrative, not governmental problems." If Congress could not govern concerning the details of administration, it learned to benefit from overseeing the administrators. Furthermore, in terms of constitutional government, Wettergreen has observed that "the passage of intentionally 'incomplete laws,' which would be 'completed' by the fiats of the bureaucracy, and the development of the congressional veto, which is essentially a declaration of the will of Congress, moved the nation away from the rule of law."[27] Those "details of administration," which Hamilton thought executive in nature, had become the province of the legislature. Also, the capacity of deliberation, which is a peculiar virtue of the legislature, and the exercise of will, or energy, which is a function of the executive, is curiously reversed.

Administrative centralization allowed members of Congress to take credit for providing those subsidies or services, including regulatory relief, which benefited particular constituents. As Fiorina has observed, "Congress maintains a federal bureaucracy deliberately organized to make it permeable to congressional intervention—not only to the chamber as a whole, but to subgroups and even individuals. So long as an agency cooperates when members make specific requests, it is unlikely to suffer long-term losses no matter how poor its performance." Moreover, Congress disguises its responsibility in the delegation of authority. "Why take political chances by setting detailed regulation sure to antagonize some political actor or another?" Fiorina asks, "Why not require an agency to do the dirty work and then step in to redress the grievances that result from its activities? . . . Let the agency take the blame and the member of Congress the credit. In the end everybody benefits. Members successfully wage their campaigns for re-election. And while popularly vilified, bureaucrats get their rewards in the committee rooms of Congress."[28] While individual members of Congress have benefited from this arrangement with the bureaucracy, the institution of Congress has had greater difficulty in performing its primary function as a body, which is general lawmaking in the public interest. Seidman and Gilmour have suggested that "the particularistic elements in our society will always triumph over the general interest as long as they are nourished and supported by committees and subcommittees that share their limited concerns."[29]

The Crisis of Constitutional Government

In the American Constitution, Congress was to be the central political branch in a government of separated powers. Its chief purposes were lawmaking, deliberation, and representation. As a legislative body, Congress was thought to be primarily concerned with making law. However, in recent years, it has done so with difficulty and reluctance. Moreover, Congress found it easy and useful to delegate authority to executive branch agencies or independent regulatory commissions. It became necessary to do so when the functions of the national government became so varied and thoroughgoing, that no single body could legislate reasonably, or in a general manner, when faced with such detail. In a time when the power and presence of the federal government has become nearly all-pervasive, it is significant to note that "the total output of Congress in a typical session is usually no more than 400 pieces of legislation." Moreover, not all such laws are general public laws; many are private or individual pieces of legislation. "By contrast, the total number of regulations each year is now in the neighborhood of 7000."[30] Rulemaking by executive branch agencies has surpassed legislative lawmaking in importance. In this new environment, members of Congress have found it convenient to emphasize the oversight function at the expense of lawmaking or general legislation.

Congress Ceases Deliberation: Notes from John Locke, *The Federalist*, and Carl Schmitt

An equally important function of the legislature was thought to be rational deliberation, or public discussion of policy issues, that would culminate in legislation or general public law. Harvey Mansfield Jr. has pointed to the fact that the "purpose of the Constitution is to transform the people's will both by settling it into a determined intent (a 'cool and deliberate sense,' *Federalist* 63) and by elevating it from whim into deliberate choice. This is the work of reason, and it is 'the reason, alone, of the public that ought to control and regulate the government. The passions ought to be controlled and regulated by the government.'"[31]

Of course, a reasonable or constitutional government does not depend exclusively upon the reasonable character of the legislative body, for otherwise there would be no need of a separation of powers, let alone a Constitution. Nonetheless, it was assumed that Congress would be a deliberative body, which could "refine and enlarge the public views." As Mansfield explains, "through elections of the people's representatives, the legislature not only puts a distance between itself and the people's momentary inclinations but also draws the virtue out of the people (for virtue does exist there) and sets it to work (*Federalist* 55, 57)."[32] Congress no longer functions primarily as a deliberative body. Moreover, as a representative body, it is less effective in reconciling, in a reasonable way, particular interests in light of the general interest. The deliberative function of Congress was eroded by the attack on reason itself, which was a product, in philosophical thought, of the triumph of historicism. Public reason was no more defensible than the faculty of reason itself, against the corroding influence of Darwin and Marx, and the success of the experimental method in science, which dominated nineteenth-century thought. Edward S. Corwin long ago pointed to the effectiveness of that attack. He observed that the principal affinity between Darwinism and Marxism

> becomes clear when we turn to the philosophy of instrumentalism or experimentalism and its conception of thought as planning. Such a conception simply passes by as obsolete the idea of thought as the fine fruit of a cognitive, reasoning faculty which, just because of its detachment from the daily concerns of men, is able to arrive at abstract

and permanent truths. . . . The autonomous reason of the eighteenth-century Enlightenment, the power to see things sub specie aeternitatis, is demoted by instrumentalism to a planning device for meeting the shifting demands of an ever changing environment, and is then further reduced to the ignoble role of a tool of propagandists. The eternal verities become, first, relative truths, then half-truths, or less than half truths, even deliberate falsehoods.[33]

Such an attack could not but succeed in undermining the idea of a common good, which is discerned by rational deliberation.

In America, the Progressive Era critique of the Constitution was part of a systematic attempt to compromise the older concept of reasonable government by undermining the authority of constitutionalism itself. Paul Eidelberg accurately and concisely formulated the character of that attack. The Constitution, he noted:

embodies or reflects fundamental notions of what is right and reasonable. Subject that law to frequent change and the very notion of what is right and reasonable will change as frequently. So undermine respect for that law and respect for all forms of authority will crumble beside it, above all, "the authority of reason, justice and truth."

Moreover, says Eidelberg:

as the laws will be in a constant state of flux, so too will public opinion. But this means there will be no public philosophy, no unifying sense of tradition, no venture in a common destiny, but rather a restless pursuit of private interests, a general state of anomie or alienation. Hence, with the mutability of public opinion, the very notion of a "public" will become questionable. . . . All opinions will come to enjoy an equal status, except the opinion which renders everything equal. This being so, public standards or the rule of law will have been replaced by subjective feelings or the rule of numbers. The passions of ever-changing majorities, or of a dominant majority, will gain ascendancy. Temporary interests, expediency, unqualified pragmatism will dominate political life. As a consequence, the powers of government (no longer restrained by the principles of a permanent law) will vastly increase, although its purposes will be as obscure as "public opinion" or as variable as the passions of popular majorities.[34]

In such circumstances, legislation and deliberation will cease to be the primary function of the legislature. Public government, Eidelberg implies, will soon give way to private government, or a government without public purpose or principle. Ironically, this kind of society, without public purpose or principle, now called a pluralist society—or interest-group liberalism—has become the political ideal for twentieth-century democratic social scientists. This is not the first time that the foundations of constitutional government have been threatened. Carl Schmitt witnessed the collapse of constitutionalism in the overthrow of the Weimar Republic in Germany. His thoughtful analysis of the causes of the erosion of the function of deliberation, as an essential element of constitutional government, was made in that turbulent decade of the 1920s. In his critique of the "crisis of parliamentary democracy," Schmitt scrutinized the connection between openness and discussion, not to mention reason, as crucial elements of the function of the legislature. Schmitt likens the distinction of the legislative and executive to the difference between law and decree, or reason and will. "Only a universally applicable law," he observed, "not a concrete order, can unite truth and justice through the balance of negotiations and public discussion." As a result, he noted, "Bluntschli...set out as an essential characteristic of modern parliament that it should not conclude its business in committees as the old corporate assembly had done."[35]

Schmitt repeatedly emphasized the fact that "openness and discussion are the two principles on which constitutional thought and parliamentarism depend.... What was to be secured through the balance guaranteed by openness and discussion was nothing less than truth and justice itself." He asserted that the "whole complex fabric of constitutional and parliamentary thought" can be summed up in the following: "All progress, including social progress, is realized 'through representative institutions, that is regulated liberty—through public discussion, that is, reason."[36] If public discussion no longer culminated in general—not to say reasonable—legislation, the primary function of the legislative body is not legislation or deliberation, but the representation of interests.

Indeed, the modern state itself came subsequently to be viewed as one more interest, albeit a public interest because of its comprehensive character. By the second decade of the twentieth century, Max Weber could write "that the state was sociologically just another large business and that an economic administrative system, a factory, and the state are today no longer essentially different."[37] However, as Schmitt retorted, "a political form of organization ceases to be political if it is, like the modern economy, based on private law."[38] A government which is merely a faction is without moral authority. A representative of such a government is nothing more than a public entrepreneur as opposed to a private one.

If Congress no longer legislates or deliberates as the characteristic activity of that body, what role does it play? In the wake of the flurry of legislative activity that occurred in the mid-1960s, Congress erected a centralized administrative apparatus whose task was to solve, in a technically rational way—using the methods of science and social science—the social and political problems of industrial or postindustrial society. However, if Harry McPherson, a top Johnson aide, is to be believed, the animating force behind the Great Society was not the desire to legislate reasonable public policy. Rather it had its origins in the malaise of the intellectuals and the leadership class. It was essentially driven by the private passions of troubled elites. Their guilt could be alleviated by a creative public effort on behalf of the poor and middle classes. Public policy was apparently no longer a product of reason but derived from passion. McPherson observed that:

> a new philosophy of government had emerged since New Deal days. In essence it held that our problems were more of the spirit than of the flesh. People were suffering from a sense of alienation from one another, of anomie, of powerlessness. This affected the well-to-do as much as it did the poor. Middle-class women, bored and friendless in the suburban afternoons; fathers, working at "meaningless" jobs, or slumped before the television set; sons and daughters desperate for "relevance"— all were in need of community, beauty, and purpose, all were guilty because so many others were deprived while they, rich beyond their ancestors' dreams, were depressed. What would change all this was a creative public effort; for the middle class, new parks, conservation, the removal of billboards and junk, adult education, consumer protection,

better television, aid to the arts; for the poor, jobs, training, Head Start, decent housing, medical care, civil rights; for both, and for bridging the gap between them, VISTA, the Teacher Corps, the community action agencies, mass transportation, model cities.[39]

Such an effort required the wholesale utilization of the expertise of the modern university. Rational deliberation of the public interest, which was not beyond the ken of an ordinary legislator, was replaced by a bureaucratic rationality designed to solve in a minute way all the problems of a technological society. As James Ceaser has written, "it is undeniable that social scientists helped supply the ideas that underlay many of the Great Society programs. It was, in fact, the heyday for social science, as the 'new professionals' within the government who had been trained in the social sciences stepped in to help devise the new programs, borrowing freely from current theories floating around academia. The era of the policymaking state had arrived."[40]

With the arrival of the policymaking state, the kind of detailed information necessary to run it was not at the disposal of the typical legislator. The knowledge of the expert became the most valuable commodity of such a government. Furthermore, as Theodore Lowi noted, such "government is almost impossible to limit. Liberalism tends to universalize the scope and responsibility of government, and science then makes the liberal argument almost unassailable." This explains, Lowi observed, "why legislation has grown broader and broader in scope, has become more and more abstract in definition, and is more and more universal in its applicability." Lowi concluded that "the liberal approach to government has made government a magnet and has rendered representatives powerless to say no or to establish priorities among theories and needs. If a theory points to consequences, there is an obligation to act upon it. In fact, during the last two or three decades, the legislative process has not even required that legislators be knowledgeable about what to do or how to do it. It simply accepts the theory ('whereas…') and indicates that there is an injury and a likely cause ('here's the problem…'); then it delegates to an administrative agency the responsibility for doing something about it ('go deal with it…')."[41]

In a bureaucratic state, it is not much of an exaggeration to say that the typical activity of a member of Congress is the superintendence of the details of administration. Power has been decentralized and dispersed among numerous subcommittee chairs. At the same time, personal and committee staff has grown tremendously. Party and leadership authority has only been centralized when it has been necessary to prevent presidential use of power that could undermine congressional domination of the bureaucracy.

In such areas as fiscal policy formation or budget control, not to mention impoundment of funds, presidents of either party could no longer be trusted. Nonetheless, majority control of the House continued to be of great importance to the Democratic Party. That party created the bureaucracy and learned to benefit from its existence. If deprived of majority status, the Democrats would lose the ability to organize and control the House and determine its ends. If the members' connection with the bureaucracy were severed, incumbency would be far less important, making electoral success much more precarious. Thus, Congress has organized itself in such a way as to allow individual members the ability to control, on a day-to-day basis, the various areas of public policy legally assigned to the federal bureaucracy. As individual entrepreneurs defending particular and organized interests, members of Congress have become very adept at advancing those interests, while at the same time obscuring responsibility for the growth of the administrative state. Their skill is reflected in the stunning rate of incumbent electoral success. In nearly every election since 1960, more than 90 percent of House incumbents have been reelected. In the most recent election, the election of 1990, 98 percent of incumbents in the House of Representatives were returned to office.[42]

A Constitutional Legislature

When the 101st Congress convenes in January 1991, it will not serve the same general functions and reflect the same constitutional purposes and principles as the body that met two centuries ago. In the minds of the Founders, the principle tasks of the legislature were lawmaking, deliberation, and representation. Practical experience under the Articles of Confederation and in the state constitutions revealed the difficulty of legislative domination of government. Few would have denied Madison's sagacity, even before he became a member of that first Congress, when he noted in the famous fifty-first *Federalist Paper*, that "in republican government, the legislative authority necessarily predominates." However, Madison had learned from John Locke that the legislative authority can predominate without the necessity of allowing the legislative body the ability to predominate in the governing process itself. Indeed, the practical success of constitutional government may depend upon preventing the domination of government by the legislative body.

John Locke had attempted to solve this problem by balancing executive prerogative against the legislature's claim that the law is sovereign. As Locke noted in the *Second Treatise*, "because the laws, that are at once, and in a short time made, have a constant and lasting force, and need a perpetual execution, or an attendance thereunto: therefore tis necessary there should be a power always in being, which should see to the execution of the laws that are made, and remain in force. And thus the *legislative* and *executive* powers come often to be separated."[43]

At first, as Harvey Mansfield has reminded us, "an executive power is needed...only in a subordinate capacity for the execution of the laws passed by the legislature." But "as Locke's exposition of rightly constituted government proceeds, he becomes more and more doubtful that government can be directed merely by laws," says Mansfield. He notes that "foreign affairs cannot be directed by 'antecedent, standing, positive Laws' and requires the use of prudence; and even domestic matters. . . must be left in good part to the 'discretion' of the executive, soon called the 'Supream Executor.'" Hence Mansfield concludes, "we have two supreme powers, one representing law, the other representing extralegal, even illegal, discretion."[44]

The success of Locke's scheme was dependent upon a single executive, armed with prerogative—or the ability to act for the public good even if it required breaking the law—and a numerous legislature. His theory presupposed an uneasy tension between the executive, whose prerogative and claim to rule derives from necessity, and the rational authority of the rule of law, which provided the moral claim of legislative dominance. Or as Carl Schmitt later formulated this dilemma: "whether the impersonal law or the king personally is sovereign." Schmitt insisted that "it will always be necessary to make exceptions to the general rule in concrete circumstances, and that the sovereign is whoever decides what constitutes an exception."[45] In Locke's view, the executive was in a better position to decide what constituted an exception, but there were no formal means of reconciling disputes between the executive and the legislature. The reason for this may be quite simple: in Locke's thought, there was not yet a place for a written Constitution. As Mansfield notes, "in Locke's conception, the constitution goes only so far as the law extends; there is no fundamental or constitutional law above the ordinary law, and the prerogative power of the executive goes as much against the constitution when necessary as against the law. It is limited only by the end for which it is entrusted by the people, which is the public good as interpreted by the people."[46]

The distinction between the legislature and the executive is analogous to the distinction between reason and will. As Schmitt explained, "the crucial distinction always remains whether the law is a general rational principle or a measure, a concrete decree, an order."[47] The legislature, a numerous body, is best able to make general laws, because such a body is most capable of reasoning or deliberating about public affairs. Consequently, Montesquieu insisted that "the great advantage of representatives is their capacity of discussing public affairs. For this the people collectively are extremely unfit, which is one of the chief inconveniences of a democracy."[48] It is the great diversity of the legislative body, which makes it most fit to deliberate and to represent diverse constituencies but also makes it unfit to act, or to exercise its will, in the manner of an executive. This difference can be seen in the observation of Carl Schmitt. The "idea of law," he noted, "has always been conceived as something intellectual, unlike the executive, which is essentially active. Legislation is deliberare, executive agere."[49]

Hamilton, moreover, had given perfect expression to this view in *Federalist* 70, when he noted: "Those politicians and statesmen who have been the most celebrated for the soundness of their principles and for the justice of their views, have declared in favor of a single Executive and a numerous legislature. They have, with great propriety, considered energy as the most necessary qualification of the former, and have regarded this as most applicable to power in a single hand; while they have, with equal propriety, considered the latter as best adapted to deliberation and wisdom, and best calculated to conciliate the confidence of the people and to secure their privileges and interests." Schmitt, too, pointed to the heart of the matter when he observed that "the universal criterion of the law is deduced from the fact that law (in contrast to will or the command of a concrete person) is only reason, not desire, and that it has no passions, whereas a concrete person 'is moved by a variety of particular passions.' In many different versions, but always with the essential characteristic of the 'universal,' this concept of legislation has become the foundation of constitutional theory."[50]

The American Constitution created an institutional tension between the executive and the legislature, which, in practice, subordinated both executive prerogative and ordinary lawmaking by legislative majorities to the authority, rationality, and balance of a written Constitution. Its success was dependent upon the ability of the executive to act energetically, exercising its will on behalf of the public good when necessary, and also its ability to prevent the legislature from governing in the details, or acting like an executive. The tendency of democratic government is toward legislative dominance of the governing function. It is for this reason that Madison speaks of legislative predominance as an "inconveniency," the "remedy" of which "is to divide the legislature into different branches; and to render them, by different modes of election and different principles of action, as little connected with each other as the nature of their common functions and their common dependence on the society will admit."[51]

But, even this, he knew, was not sufficient. "It may even be necessary to guard against dangerous encroachments by still further precaution," he insisted. "As the weight of the legislative authority requires that it should be divided," he noted, "the weakness of the executive may require...that it should be fortified."[52]

The consequence of the failure to do so had already been clearly stated by Montesquieu. He observed: "were the executive power not to have a right of restraining the encroachments of the legislative body, the latter would become despotic; for as it might arrogate to itself what authority it pleased, it would soon destroy all the other powers."[53] The separation of powers cannot be maintained if the distinction between the legislative and executive power is undermined by the legislature's attempt to substitute its will for the reason of the Constitution. In such a case, the legislative body, and not the law, will indeed predominate. Constitutional government requires the maintenance of a separation of powers that distinguishes legislative and executive, reason and will, or law and prerogative.

The practical distinction between the executive and the legislature collapses when the agents of the executive administration become the tools of the legislature. Montesquieu warned that "if…the executive power should be committed to a certain number of persons selected from the legislative body, there would be an end then of liberty; by reason the two powers would be united, as the same persons would sometimes possess, and would always be able to possess, a share in both."[54] The growth of the bureaucracy and its connection with the legislature has undermined the principle of the separation of powers. Although members of Congress do not serve in the executive branch, personnel of the executive bureaucracy have become the tools of the legislature.

Carl Schmitt clearly underscored the importance of the separation of powers in constitutional government. He asserted "that a constitution is identical with division of power." He pointed to article 16 of the Declaration of the Rights of Man and Citizens, which states, "Any society in which the separation of powers and rights is not guaranteed has no constitution." Schmitt goes so far as to suggest "that the division of powers and a constitution are identical and that this defines the concept of a constitution even appears in German political thought from Kant to Hegel as a given. In consequence such a theory understands dictatorship not just as an antithesis of democracy but also essentially as the suspension of the division of powers, that is, as a suspension of the constitution, a suspension of the distinction between legislative and executive."[55]

The undermining of this essential principle of constitutional government, which is a recent phenomenon of American politics, was already apparent to Schmitt in the 1920s when he witnessed the collapse of the Weimar constitution. He noted then that the

> great political and economic decisions on which the fate of mankind rests no longer result today…from balancing opinions in public debate and counter debate. Such decisions are no longer the outcome of parliamentary debate.…The participation of popular representatives in government—parliamentary government—has proven the most effective means of abolishing the division of powers, and with it the old concept of parliamentarism. As things stand today, it is of course practically impossible not to work with committees, and increasingly smaller committees; in this way the parliamentary plenum gradually

drifts away from its purpose (that is, from its public), and as a result it necessarily becomes a mere facade.

Schmitt argued that "parliamentarism thus abandons its intellectual foundation and that the whole system of freedom of speech, assembly, and the press, of public meeting, parliamentary immunities and privileges, is losing its rationale. Small and exclusive committees of parties or of party coalitions make their decisions behind closed doors, and what representatives of the . . . interest groups agree to in the smallest committees is more important for the fate of millions of people, perhaps, than any political decision." Schmitt concluded that "if in the actual circumstances of parliamentary business, openness and discussion have become an empty and trivial formality, then parliament, as it developed in the nineteenth century, has also lost its previous foundation and its meaning."[56]

The American Congress remains perhaps the most powerful legislative body in the world. But its power is no longer derivative of its constitutional purpose. Increasingly, its authority derives from the fact that the legislative body has succeeded in exercising its will rather than its capacity for reason, which has undermined the reasonableness of the constitutional order itself. Consequently, its influence has become dependent upon its ability to function like an executive. It has become, as we have argued in other chapters, an administrative congress.

Congress or Government as a Faction

The dangers that majority factionalism posed to stability and the protection of private rights in a small democracy is analogous to a similar danger in an extended republic. If the members of the legislature and the dominant interests in government (i.e., the bureaucracy) become no more than a faction on behalf of the interests of government or bureaucratic rule, deliberation and representation of a public interest, or a common good, would be unnecessary, not to say impossible. Government itself would no longer be the interest that transcends factionalism; it would be a faction. And, like "the will in the community independent of the majority—that is, of the society itself," which Madison spoke of in *Federalist* 51, it "may as well espouse the unjust views of the major, as the rightful interests of the minor party, and may possibly be turned against both parties." In short, such a will is unrestrained, and the government is no longer constitutional. Because of its overriding power and its unique connection to the people, the danger of legislative corruption has long been recognized as the gravest danger to free government. In *Federalist* 71, Hamilton expressed with perfect clarity the constitutional problems posed by legislative usurpation of power. He noted: "to what purpose separate the executive, or the judiciary, from the legislative, if both the executive and the judiciary are so constituted as to be at the absolute devotion of the legislative? Such a separation must be merely nominal and incapable of producing the ends for which it was established. It is one thing to be subordinate to the laws, and another to be dependent on the legislative body. The first comports with, the last violates, the fundamental principles of good government; and whatever may be the forms of the Constitution, unites all power in the same hands."

Some years before the American Constitution was written, the celebrated theorist of democracy, Montesquieu, pointed to the conditions under which liberty and democratic governments were likely to be destroyed. Like Hamilton, and the framers of the United States Constitution, he insisted that good government would require a viable separation of the powers of government. In addition, like the framers, he insisted that this principle of democratic constitutionalism would most likely be undermined through the corruption of the legislature. Montesquieu observed: "as all human things have an end, the state we are speaking of will lose its liberty, will perish. . . . It will perish when the legislative power shall be more corrupt than the executive."[57]

13

Progressivism, the Social Sciences, and the Rational State

SHORTLY BEFORE THE END of the twentieth century, Progressivism once again entered the popular vocabulary as the preferred term for what had long been described as liberalism.[1] When it came to be understood in political terms, Progressivism engendered heated opposition to the economic and social agenda of the modern administrative state. For much of the past century, triumphant liberalism had disguised the political character of Progressivism by portraying it as an inevitable historical movement. That movement or transformation of American life in the direction of the liberal or rational state was said to be spawned by urbanization, industrialization, and the corruption of state and local governments, as well as private economic corporations. The modern state, and the need for unlimited power in the national government, was thought to be the inevitable consequence of the progress of those economic and social forces unleashed by modernity.

It was not the conscious choice of politicians that had brought about the transformation of political life. Politicians could not oppose or derail those historical forces; they could only adapt to them. Such adaptation left political men with little choice but reform of the old order. As a result, partisanship came to be viewed in terms of progress: those who embraced History's advance toward a glorious future, the Progressives;

or Reactionaries, those who resisted change and attempted to cling to an outmoded past. Liberalism and conservatism is best understood from the same theoretical perspective, as a political reflection of the distinction between progressive and reactionary. Consequently, contemporary ideology and politics become intelligible only with reference to a philosophy of History, which originated in the political thought of Kant and Hegel.

At the beginning of the twentieth century, Progressivism was still understood explicitly as a political and social movement. Moreover, it was clear that Hegelian historicism, as a theoretical perspective, had already established itself as the authority to be reckoned with. Indeed, it clearly dominated the intellectual landscape of the newly emerging social science disciplines within the new and newly restructured university graduate schools. Subsequently, it would come to dominate the political landscape as completely as it had the intellectual. Some indication of that potential for political dominance was already apparent in the election of 1912, when three-fourths of the votes of the American people were cast for avowed Progressives; Woodrow Wilson, Theodore Roosevelt, and Eugene Debs. The other fourth went to the incumbent president, William Howard Taft, who, not to be outdone, called himself a progressive conservative.

Clearly, there were political differences among the Progressives concerning Progressivism's practical meaning and what should be done. Although it was and is a political movement, Progressivism, like liberalism, could not be understood simply in terms of politics or concern with agenda. Rather, Progressivism was the political manifestation of a theoretical revolution in political thought. Just as constitutionalism was dependent on a philosophic doctrine of nature and natural right, Progressivism derived its political and social agenda from a philosophy of History. In exposing the theoretical roots of Progressivism and the liberalism it spawned, it becomes possible to reveal the political agenda of both and to understand the common historicist roots it shared with economic and social conservatism. In short, it becomes possible to understand the political disagreements only after we have understood what it is that Progressives, liberals, and conservatives agreed on.

To put it simply, liberals and Progressives (as well as post–Civil War conservative economists and social scientists) were united in their opposition to the political theory of the American Founding. They were united in accepting the view of Kant, that the moral law could not be established on the foundation of natural law or natural right, which was derivative of philosophical or metaphysical reason.[2] In his revised view of practical and theoretical reason, Kant had argued that pure reason, or metaphysics, could reveal only natural or physical reality; hence natural laws would come to be understood in terms of natural science or physics. And the moral law, or political right, for Kant, could be understood only on the basis of practical reason. In short, later thinkers would come to view the moral law as a product of the exercise of human freedom or will.

Consequently, historicist thought, a century before Progressivism, had already undercut the ground of theoretical or metaphysical reason, and severed the connection with philosophic ethics, or natural right. Progressive intellectuals had come to understand natural laws only in terms of science, not ethics or morality. It was for this reason that many Progressive intellectuals, including Woodrow Wilson, would insist that the American Founders had wrongly derived moral and political authority from what they (the Founders) had thought to be natural laws of science. Wilson assumed, therefore, that the Founders' understanding of political principles had been derived from the authority of theoretical physics. It is clear, however, from any candid assessment of the American Founders, that they did not believe that their political principles had been derived from Newtonian physics. As a result, they would not have understood politics or its theory or practice from a modern historical or scientific perspective. Nor could they have agreed with those Progressive intellectuals in the next century who would insist that the Founders' political principles had or could become historically obsolete.

Woodrow Wilson, under the spell of Kant's views concerning theoretical and practical reason, had assumed that it was metaphysical reason in the form of a scientific law, Newton's physics, which had established the theoretical and scientific ground of American constitutionalism.[3] But it is clear that Wilson's understanding of science was already shaped by his understanding of History. Not surprisingly, the Progressives, like Wilson, assumed that the Founders lacked "historic sense" and were unable to see that their scientific views were a product of their time, which happened to be dominated by Newtonian physics. But Wilson, like most Progressive social scientists, was convinced that the new Darwinian science had rendered the static or mechanical understanding of *The Federalist's* political science (and its Constitution) obsolete.[4] Rather, they believed Darwin had vindicated, through the new science of *biology*, the Hegelian view of the historical process, and its vehicle, the rational state, as a living and evolving organism.

Consequently, it was the modern theoretical understanding of philosophy of History, and the concept of the rational state, that would establish the moral and intellectual foundations of modern progressive politics.[5] And it would establish the theoretical ground of both modern liberalism and conservatism.

Thus, Progressives (liberal and conservative) were united in their view, derived from Hegel, that the organic or rational state must replace the social compact, or constitutionalism. They were united in their view that rights and freedom were not natural or individual but social and dependent on historical development. They were united in the view that the replacement of philosophy by History made it possible to establish the conditions for the replacement of both static politics and religion by dynamic economics and society. Political life and religion must vanish to enable the perfecting of economic and social conditions through the establishment of new social sciences that could bring about an uncoerced rational society, thereby opening up the possibility of complete freedom, or self-fulfillment. The coming into being of the rational or administrative state is possible and necessary only at the end of History, when the rule of the philosopher or statesman can be replaced by the rule of organized intelligence, or bureaucracy.

The Rational State: Eclipsing Nature and the Social Compact

The idea of the state provided the unifying concept of the disciplines of the social sciences from the beginning. That idea, as it was developed by Hegel, rested on the discovery of the rational character of the historical process. With the concept of the state, Leo Strauss noted:

> Hegel had reconciled "the discovery of History"—the alleged insight into the individual's being in the most radical sense, the son or stepson of his time, or the alleged insight into the dependence of man's highest and purest thoughts on his time—with philosophy in the original meaning of the term by asserting that Hegel's time was the absolute moment, the end of meaningful time: the absolute religion, Christianity,

had become completely reconciled with the world; it had become completely secularized or the saeculum had become completely Christian in and through the post-revolutionary State; history as meaningful change had come to its end; all theoretical and practical problems had in principle been solved; hence, the historical process was demonstrably rational."[6]

Subsequently, the metaphysical concept of nature, as well as the political doctrine of natural right, as a theoretical perspective, would lose its authority in terms of establishing a meaningful ground of human understanding concerning politics, morality, and religion.

The end of History is the end of philosophy as the quest for knowledge, and the end of politics and religion as central to the understanding of the fundamental human dilemma. That dilemma was thought to have originated in nature and was revealed in human nature itself. In transcending rational limitations on human knowledge and nature, it becomes possible to transcend those limitations on human freedom that had been thought to be imposed by natural necessity. In denying the liberalism of Locke and the American Founders, the Progressives, influenced by Hegel, were convinced that the old conception of nature, and the political doctrine of natural right, had produced only a negative understanding of freedom. As a result, they had established the purpose of government to be the protection of the rights and property of the private individual. But, as Hegel noted: "The national spirit is the substance; what is rational must happen. The contractual form of constitutional development is not in fact the rational, but merely a form of property. But the rational must always find a way, for it possesses truth, and we must cease to fear that bad constitutions might be made."[7] In Hegel's view, new constitutions, now understood as states, are products of human freedom or will. As he noted, "Whether the State coheres on the basis of nature or of the freedom of the will is what forms the dividing line between constitutions. Every concept begins in immediacy, in nature, and strives toward rationality. Everything depends on the extent to which rationality has replaced nature."[8]

In moving beyond the contractual as a defense of property and individual rights, Hegel advanced a rational and positive view of freedom that made it possible to reconcile the antagonism between the particular and the universal, the private and the public, or the individual and society. Those antagonisms can be resolved within the unity created on a new intellectual and moral foundation established within the state. Hegel insisted that "the essential being is itself the union of two wills: the subjective will and the rational will. This is an ethical totality, the *state*. It is the reality wherein the individual has and enjoys his freedom—but only insofar as he knows, believes, and wills the universal" (Hegel's emphasis). As noted before, it was the protection of individual rights and property, based on an understanding of human nature that had made limited government necessary. Hegel insisted that such an understanding could provide only a "negative conception of freedom." But, he maintained: "As against this negative concept of freedom, it is rather law, ethical life, the state (and they alone) that comprise the positive reality and satisfaction of freedom. The freedom which is limited in the state is that of *caprice*, the freedom that relates to the particularity of individual needs" (emphasis mine).⁹ In the new society, man is not free as an individual, but as a self-legislating member of a community, or a *citizen* of the state.

The state, Hegel suggested, "is the realization of Freedom, i.e. of the absolute final aim, and...it exists for its own sake. It must further be understood that all the worth which the human being possesses—all spiritual reality, he possesses only through the State.... Thus only is he fully conscious; thus only is he a partaker of morality—of a just and moral social and political life. For Truth is the Unity of the universal and subjective Will; the Universal is to be found in the State, in its laws, its universal and rational arrangements. The State is the Divine Idea as it exists on Earth."¹⁰ Within the state, it becomes possible to transcend the antagonisms thought to be inherent in the nature of things. It was this understanding of nature that animated the earlier liberal political thought of John Locke and the American Founders. It was this philosophic view, derived from metaphysical reason, and religious belief dependent on faith (or the inability to ameliorate the tension between reason and revelation), that made the political-theological problem the fundamental human dilemma. If the historical process is rational, the moral order is created through the use of freedom or will as necessary for determining the ongoing conditions of progress. When rational freedom, or *will*, establishes the foundation of morality in each historical epoch, it becomes possible to transcend the political-theological problem. Moral will provides the unity that makes it possible to unite theory and practice on behalf of rational purpose, or History. Consequently, Progressivism, as a political movement, attempted to unify the sacred and secular (church and state), public and private (community and individual), or government and civil society, through the concept of the state. The state becomes the vehicle for the administration of progress.

Once the idea of the state established the ground of political legitimacy, the necessity of the unity of theory and practice within the state undermined the theoretical ground of nature, and natural right—understood in terms of metaphysical reason. Moreover, it undercut the necessity of political prudence, or practical reason, as the essential element of practical political science. In the old view, nature itself had established rational limits on human freedom. The political conditions of human life required recognition of the fact, as Madison noted, that factionalism is inherent in human nature. Although political philosophy could make the principles of natural right intelligible, prudence would always be necessary to determine the practical requirements of politics or political science. It was not possible to ignore the sphere of prudence by establishing a wholly theoretical and applied rational science. Constitutionalism, therefore, was thought to be the best practicable solution to the political problem of reconciling freedom, equality, and natural necessity. Consequently, although the human problem, like the political-theological problem, is capable of reasonable accommodation, the political and religious antagonism remains insoluble.

On the other hand, historicist political science rested on the assumption that the replacement of theoretical (and practical) reason by philosophy of History made it possible to actualize the conditions necessary for the replacement of politics and religion by administration and a rationalized science of economics and society (or culture). The final principles of politics—equality and liberty—would be embodied as the rights of man within the state itself. But political right, or morality, could no longer be derived from an understanding of nature or reason. Rather, positive freedom, or rational *will*, as it developed within the state, would establish the ground of morality, and hence, the legitimacy of *evolving human rights*.

With the end of politics and religion, the use of practical reason, or prudence, would become not merely superfluous as a political virtue but perceived as a reactionary defense of the irrationality of the past.

If will established the ground of legitimacy, or political right, it would be immoral *not* to carry it out. Administration, by replacing politics, would provide the technical or rational means of carrying out the will that establishes the moral legitimacy of law within the state. Thus, efficiency becomes the primary practical necessity of the modern state. As a result, in its origins, social science was intended to be the applied rational science of the state. When professionalized as specialized societies within the universities, it would generate the scientific knowledge required to solve every political, social, economic, or cultural problem. Consequently, for the Progressives, the human problem, as well as the political-theological problem, is theoretically and practically soluble in a technical or rational way. In their view, nature, and the human problems understood in terms of nature, including politics and religion, must be transcended on a higher plane, one that makes it possible to ameliorate human problems scientifically, within the framework of the *rational state*.

The discovery of the rationality of History would transform the theory and practice of politics in the nineteenth century. Progressive intellectuals, after Hegel, accepted the view that History, not nature, would establish the ground of meaningful knowledge concerning human affairs. They targeted the economy or society as the driving force of an evolving political organism, under the direction of organized intelligence, or bureaucracy. Freedom itself, would come to be redefined in terms of social rather than individual purpose. The state, consequently, would come to be understood as an ethical or moral organism, a vehicle for the rational administration of progress. It is within the state that a common ground of freedom and citizenship could be established by progressively discovering and securing rights.

One important American Progressive thinker, Mary Parker Follett, who published *The New State* in 1918, outlined the distinction between the old and new definitions of freedom and rights in a very clear way. She noted:

> Democracy has meant too many "natural" rights, "liberty" and "equality." The acceptance of the group principle defines for us in truer fashion those watchwords of the past. If my true self is the group-self, then my only rights are those which membership in a group gives me. The old idea of natural rights postulated the particularist individual; we know

now that no such person exists. The group and the individual come into existence simultaneously: with this group-man appear group-rights. Thus man can have no rights apart from society or independent of society or against society. Particularist rights are ruled out as everything particularist is ruled out.... The truth of the whole matter is that our only concern with "rights" is not to protect them but to create them. Our efforts are to be bent not upon guarding the rights which Heaven has showered upon us, but in creating all the rights we shall ever have.

Consequently, Follett insisted that as "the group process abolishes 'individual right,' so it gives us a true definition of liberty. We have seen that the free man is he who actualizes the *will* of the whole. I have no liberty except as an essential member of a group...to obey the group which we have helped to make and of which we are an integral part is to be free because we are then obeying our self. Ideally the *state* is such a group; it depends upon us to make it more and more so. The state must be no external authority which restrains and regulates me, but it must be myself acting as the state in every smallest detail of life. *Expression*, not restraint, is always the motive of the ideal state" (emphasis mine).[11]

The new understanding of rights required that government within the state should provide for the satisfaction of all human need. Men are free not as individuals, but as members of groups that form an ethical whole: the *state*. Rights are created in the process of self- or group expression. Creativity, or self-expression, becomes possible only when humans are free of necessity, natural or man-made. As FDR liked to say, "necessitous men cannot be free." Consequently, the power of government cannot be limited; its purpose is to relieve man of necessity by providing a rational solution to every human problem. Freedom of expression, or self-creation, then becomes a human reality.

Hegel's historical philosophy had provided the theoretical foundations for the revolution in thought that established itself as the intellectual and political authority for nineteenth-century Progressivism. But the thinker whose writings proved more immediately useful to the new academic disciplines established in the emerging American universities was August Comte. It was Comte's positive philosophy that would become the most successful attempt to establish a scientific methodology compatible with the new understanding of man as an historical being. The origins of the social sciences and the transformation of the American university were a product of that positivist view, which sought to combine the spirit of science with what Comte would call "the religion of humanity." Taken as a whole, the new theories of Hegel and Comte undercut the intellectual and moral foundations on which the theoretical structure of the old order was based. It brought into question the very possibility of preserving the kind of education and those moral virtues necessary for the perpetuation of a regime of civil and religious liberty. The social sciences, developed mainly in the universities, were meant to replace the theological and metaphysical foundations of human knowledge.

August Comte's positivism was dependent on a theory of the evolution of the mind, understood as an ongoing historical and rational development. It presupposed an acceptance of Hegel's philosophy of History, with the view that its rational character is revealed at the end of the process. Comte, in elaborating on historical evolution, insisted that the progress of the mind moves, as a kind of ascent, through three stages. In the first stage, it was theological knowledge that informed human understanding. Subsequently, in the second stage, theological knowledge was replaced by metaphysical, or abstract, but destructive knowledge. In the last stage, the highest and final stage of the development of the mind, human knowledge is informed by what Comte called scientific, constructive, or positive philosophy. At the positive stage, the scientific mind is complete; at that point man can begin to rationally order society. When the mind attains the positive, or scientific, stage, it recognizes the illusory character of every earlier stage in the evolution of knowledge.

Consequently, Comte's analysis made it possible to show that only empirical, or scientific, knowledge is genuine, meaningful, and useful knowledge for human, or social, life. He created a systematic theory of social science, which established a scientific methodology by which to transform society. In short, August Comte's positive philosophy was quite successful in undermining the theoretical foundations of metaphysical and theological knowledge. Philosophy and religion, relegated to the realm of normative *values*, subjective and meaningless in terms of genuine knowledge, would relinquish authority to science and empirical methodology.

The triumph of the philosophy of History had resulted in the secularization of society and the transformation of religion into what would become the absolute philosophy, *science*. The method of science would provide the foundation for overcoming the absolute or universal, but spurious, claims to knowledge once made by religion and philosophy. In Comte's formulation:

> All of our fundamental conceptions having thus been rendered homogeneous, philosophy will be constituted finally in the positive state. Its character will be henceforth unchangeable, and it will then have only to develop itself indefinitely, by incorporating the constantly increasing knowledge that inevitably results from new observations or more profound meditations. Having by this means acquired the character of universality which as yet it lacks, the positive philosophy, with all its natural superiority, will be able to displace entirely the theological and metaphysical philosophies. The only real property possessed by theology and metaphysics at the present day is their character of universality, and when deprived of this motive for preference they will have for our successors only a historical interest.[12]

August Comte's positive philosophy was predicated on the assumption that with the completion of the scientific mind, it had become possible to begin the process of rationally ordering society. Positivism and its methodology were therefore not practicable before the Hegelian demonstration of the rationality of the historical process.[13] But, once established, positivism would undermine the universal character of theology and metaphysics and subsequently displace the authority of both. In short, both philosophy and religion would come to be understood only *historically*, as relics of a prescientific past.

The State as Moral Organism: Reconciling Hegel and Christianity

The American Founders had attempted to derive the moral law from the laws of nature, or metaphysical reason. Freedom was therefore subordinate to the moral law; rational limits on human freedom were imposed by nature and the natural desire for happiness. But, as John Dewey later noted: "The earlier liberals lacked historic sense.... It blinded the eyes of liberals to the fact that their own special interpretations of liberty, individuality and intelligence were themselves historically conditioned, and relevant only to their own time. They put forward their ideas as immutable truths good at all times and places; they had no idea of historic relativity, either in general or in its application to themselves."[14] In the new Progressive view, freedom was not to be understood in terms of natural limitations, individual intelligence, or happiness, but in terms of "historic relativity" and the progress of social intelligence. It is mind, not nature, that reveals social reality as historically conditioned. Therefore, it is the progress of mind, or social intelligence, derived from the ongoing consciousness of its freedom, that establishes relative, or historic, truth.

The new disciplines of the social sciences were constructed on the assumption that evolving consciousness of freedom, or will, would determine the intellectual and moral foundations of each historical epoch. They accepted the views of Kant and Hegel that the ground of political rights originates in freedom, or will; not nature, or reason. And morality itself is to be determined by the uses of freedom, and the manner in which will becomes universalized and hence rational, or moral. Thus, the moral will would establish the ground of political legitimacy; rights and freedom are created, secured, and reconciled only within the state and its laws. When coupled with the method of positive science, the state and its government provide the possibility of the ongoing transformation of society and man.

At the beginning of the twentieth century, Charles Merriam, a young political scientist who helped organize the new discipline of political science, thought it necessary to characterize the difference between the new Progressive political science and that of the American Founding. He noted that the Founders were familiar with the works of the political philosophers, but "these leaders were not attempting to work out a science of politics." Until the Civil War, Merriam observed, "there was little energy expended in the study of systematic politics, in comparison with the contemporary English and Continental developments in social science, economics and politics, where the rise of the science of society under the inspiration of August Comte, and of Utopian and proletarian socialism, aroused general interest in social problems."[15] But, he noted, "in the last half of the nineteenth century, there appeared in the United States a group of political theorists differing from the earlier thinkers in respect to method and upon many important doctrines of political science. The new method was more systematic and scientific than that which preceded it, while the results reached showed a pronounced reaction from the individualistic philosophy of the early years of the century."[16]

The new Progressive political scientists accepted the European doctrines of *social* justice and a new science of society, which required government to provide political solutions to social and economic problems. The acceptance of the idea of the state as the framework to achieve social justice would result in the rejection of the theoretical and institutional framework of constitutionalism, or limited government. The American social compact had limited the power of government by separating church and state, government and civil society, politics and economics. It had established a defense of the autonomy of the private individual, based on an understanding of nature and the natural rights of individuals. With the acceptance of a philosophy of History and its practical embodiment, and the organic or rational state, the Progressives necessarily rejected the doctrine of natural right and the social compact, or constitutionalism. In addition, the authority of the new doctrines of History and the organic state were further legitimized by the scientific discoveries of the evolution of the living organism, man.

Consequently, Merriam noted that the new scientific theories derived from the study of biology were of great importance in legitimizing progressive doctrines based on an understanding of man as an evolving, or historical, being.[17] He noted that "in the general development of political thought many striking changes were made during this period. Overshadowing all others were those caused by the discoveries of Darwin and the development of modern science. The Darwinian theory of evolution not only transformed biological study, but profoundly affected all forms of thought. The social sciences were no exception, and history, economics, ethics and political science were all fundamentally altered by the new doctrine."[18]

But Merriam was well aware of the fact that the rejection of the American Founders' views had been derived from an earlier political theory: "the influence of the German school is most obvious in relation to the contract theory of the origin of the state and the idea of the function of the state. The theory that the state originates in an agreement between men was assailed by the German thinkers and the historical, organic, evolutionary idea substituted for it." Merriam, like many Progressive intellectuals, had been persuaded by the German thinkers before Darwin and had adopted the newly developed scholarship of the Comtean social sciences on the question of methodology. He noted: "the present tendency is to disregard the once dominant ideas of natural rights and the social contract.... The origin of the state is regarded, not as the result of a deliberate agreement among men, but as the result of historical development, instinctive rather than conscious; and rights are considered to have their source not in nature, but in law."[19]

The Darwinian theory, however, did serve to confirm, in a scientific or empirical way, the more abstract theoretical arguments that Rousseau and Hegel had made. By tracing the biological evolution of the various species, Darwin seemed to prove that in the natural world, the lower moves to the higher involuntarily, without apparent design. In the human world, it seemed to vindicate the view that if History is rational, the high (or perfection) will be achieved without, and in spite of, human choice. Indeed, the idea of progress assumes that History itself establishes the conditions that ensure the intellectual and moral advancement of mankind. Consequently, although the new discipline of political science (and the social sciences generally) accepted the authority of Darwinian theory as a ground of its legitimacy, it had already established its theoretical foundations based primarily on the earlier German thought.

In light of the historicist critique of natural right, it was not surprising that Progressive thought came to be characterized by its hostility to constitutionalism and limited government. As Merriam noted: "recent political theory in the United States shows a decided tendency away from many doctrines that were held by the men of 1776.... The Revolutionary doctrines of an original state of nature, natural rights, the social contract, the idea that the function of the government is limited to the protection of person and property—none of these finds wide acceptance among the leaders in the development of political science.... [T]he rejection of these doctrines is a scientific tendency rather than a popular movement."[20] Sociologist Lester Frank Ward observed, "Our Declaration of Independence, which recites that Government derives its just powers from the consent of the governed, has already been outgrown. It is no longer consent, but the positively known *will* of the governed, from which the government now derives its powers" (emphasis mine).[21]

In reflecting on the evolution of social and political thought in the last quarter of the nineteenth century, Charles Beard wrote in 1908:

[I]n comparing the political writings of the last twenty-five years with earlier treatises one is struck with decreasing reference to the doctrine of natural rights as a basis for political practice. The theory has been rejected for the reason that it really furnishes no guide to the problems of our time and because we have come to recognize since Darwin's day that the nature of things, once supposed to be eternal, is itself a stream of tendency. Along with decreasing references to natural rights there has gone an increasing hesitation to ascribe political events to providential causes. As in history, scholars are seeking natural and approximate causes; they treat politics as a branch of sociology.[22]

It is not surprising that within the ranks of the Progressive historians, sociology would replace politics as the queen of the new social sciences. After all, August Comte had invented the term sociology and had first called it social physics. It was meant to be the science that could begin the process of rationally ordering society.[23]

The social sciences were established in the American universities in the last decades of the nineteenth century. In the new disciplines of the social sciences, the state would come to be understood as the moral organism, the vehicle for the ongoing administration of progress by science-trained experts. The great political event that served as the text for the early interpretations of Progressive political thought was the American Civil War. In one of the first and most important books on that war, Elisha Mulford, a Pennsylvania pastor and supporter of Lincoln, interpreted the meaning of the Civil War as it had come to be understood in light of the new conception of the state.[24] In his book, *The Nation* (begun in 1865), Mulford insisted that the Civil War must be interpreted from the perspective of Hegel's *Philosophy of Right* and his concept of the state. Consequently, he denied what Lincoln had affirmed—that the war was fought over the issue of slavery and the meaning of equality and liberty. Mulford attempted to show that the historical significance of the war could not be understood simply in terms of equality, liberty, or the issue of slavery. He noted: "It cannot be too often repeated, that the War was not primarily between freedom and slavery. It was the war of the nation and the confederacy."[25]

As a result, Mulford understood the Civil War as having transformed the country from one of confederacy in terms of the old idea of a social compact, to a new nation understood in terms of the idea of the state.

As he noted:

> the aim of political science is the presentation of the nation, as it is in
> its necessary conception. Its object is to define it in that unity and law
> which alone is the condition of science. This necessitates an inner and
> critical justification of its representation. The nation is organic, and has
> therefore the unity of an organism, and in its continuity persists in and
> through the generation of men; it is a moral organism, it is formed of
> persons in the relations in which there is the realization of personality,
> it is not limited to the necessary sequence of a physical development,
> but transcends a merely physical condition, and in it there is the real-
> ization of freedom and the manifestation of rights; it consists in the
> moral order of the world, and its vocation is the fulfillment of the divine
> purpose in humanity in history. The nation as it exists in the necessary
> conception is the Christian nation.[26]

For Mulford, the historical development of the nation was rational
and inevitable. It was the fulfillment of an historic and divine destiny. In
acknowledging the Hegelian understanding of freedom and citizenship
within the state, he rejected the view that equality and the protection of
individual rights could establish the fundamental purpose of government. Rather, in his attempt to understand the nation scientifically as an
organic whole, he was convinced that the common good required a common will, and common will was represented in the moral organism: the
state. Moreover, the individual becomes free only when he participates in
establishing the moral will by universalizing or rationalizing the particular or individual will. Years later, Woodrow Wilson would observe that
he turned to Mulford's book when he desired some good "mental tonic."
He said it furnished him "with inspiration and philosophy."[27]

The state would become the conceptual framework for the understanding of politics in the newly organized discipline of political science
and the other social sciences as well. According to John Burgess, the
founder of the Department of Political Science at Columbia, the state was
"the product of the progressive revelation of the human reason through
history.... The gradual growth of the subjective into the objective, the
slow refinement of the clash of individual wills into a perfectly coordi-
nated form of human organization...the realization of the universal in

man."[28] In denying the importance of the principles of the Declaration of Independence, Burgess insisted that "a nation and a state did not spring into existence through that declaration. . . . The significance of the proclamation was this: a people testified thereby the consciousness of the fact that they had become, in the progressive development of History, one whole, separate, and adult nation, and a national state."[29] Thus, Burgess would insist that "the national popular state alone furnishes the objective reality upon which political science can rest in the construction of a truly scientific political system."[30]

It is not surprising that Columbia-trained Frank Goodnow, first president of the American Political Science Association, in his 1904 inaugural, would delineate the scope of the new discipline in the following manner: "Political science is that science which treats of the organization known as the State."[31] Moreover, it is the *will* of the people (not the *reason* of the constitutional doctrine of natural right) that would establish the moral foundation of the democratic state. "The State," said W. W. Willoughby, "is thus justified by its manifest potency as an agent for the progress of mankind." And E. L. Godkin, founder of *The Nation* magazine, although no defender of the socialist state, had high hopes for the new science of economics. He predicted that "the next great political revolution in the Western world" will give "scientific expression to the popular will."[32] The applied social sciences, working in the service of the people, would generate the objective knowledge necessary to carry out that will efficiently.

Politics would, in effect, become administration. Moreover, the end of politics would mean the end of partisan conflict over principles. Thus, for the first time, the power of government, like science, would be used only on behalf of the people. Once a democratic state is established, the unlimited power of government is no longer a danger, and science used in the service of government becomes the great human benefactor. As Walter Lippmann noted in 1914, "There is nothing accidental then in the fact that democracy in politics is the twin-brother of scientific thinking. They had to come together. As absolutism falls, science rises. It is self-government. For when the impulse which overthrows kings and priests and unquestioned creeds becomes self-conscious we call it science."[33] In the modern state, science would become an authority as absolute as monarchy, or religion, had ever been.

In its origins, a kind of religious fervor accompanied the birth of the modern state and the new social sciences.[34] In political and social thought, it seemed to require nothing less than a reconciliation of Christianity and Hegelianism. The young John Dewey attempted to make such a reconciliation. In his first job at the University of Michigan, where he was hired by his mentor at Johns Hopkins, George Sylvester Morris, Dewey was still an active Christian. He devoted much of his time to the Student Christian Association. He even conducted a Bible class on "The Life of Christ—with Special Reference to Its Importance as an Historical Event." In addition, Dewey published a paper, "Christianity and Democracy," in 1893. However, he was also very much affected by the thought of Hegel, a legacy of his teacher G. S. Morris and his days at Johns Hopkins. Moreover, he was confident of their compatibility. He went so far as to suggest that Hegelian philosophy "in its broad and essential features is identical with the theological teachings of Christianity."[35]

In an earlier work, *The Ethics of Democracy*, published in 1888, he provided his clearest statement concerning the reconciliation of Hegelian idealism and Christianity. Dewey noted:

> Democracy and the one, the ultimate, ethical ideal of humanity are to my mind synonyms. The idea of democracy, the ideas of liberty, equality and fraternity, represent a society in which the distinction between the spiritual and the secular has ceased, and as in Greek theory, as in the Christian theory of the Kingdom of God, the church and the state, the divine and the human organization of society are one. But this, you will say, is idealism. In reply, I can but quote James Russell Lowell once more and say that "it is indeed idealism, but that I am one of those who believe that the real will never find an irremovable basis till it rests upon the ideal"; and add that the best test of any form of society is the ideal which it proposes for the forms of its life, and the degree in which it realizes this ideal.[36]

This transcendence or reconciliation of the tension between politics and religion (theory and practice) on a higher plane had become possible on the foundation of the democratic state. For Dewey, this was confirmed historically in the coming into being of democratic society. As Dewey noted:

If democracy be a form of society, it not only does have, but must have, a common will; for it is this unity of will which makes it an organism. A State represents men so far as they have become organically related to one another, or are possessed of unity of purpose and interest.... But human society represents a more perfect organism. The whole lives truly in every member, and there is no longer the appearance of aggregation, or continuity. The organism manifests itself as what it truly is, an ideal or spiritual life, a unity of will. If, then, society and the individual are really organic to each other, then the individual is society concentrated. In conception, at least, democracy approaches most nearly the ideal of all social organization; that in which the individual and society are organic to each other. The organism must have its spiritual organs; having a common will, it must express it.[37]

His subsequent turning from idealism (religious or Hegelian) to the social ethic of democracy is already apparent at this time, as is its necessity in terms of human action. The need for social action, and the development of the methodology of the social sciences, would make metaphysics unnecessary and, indeed, irrelevant. Subsequently, Dewey and those who became pragmatists would reject any necessity of a foundation in metaphysics at all. The truth of God, or metaphysics, had become the truth of science. The aspirations of Christianity and idealist philosophy could be established on earth by science.[38]

In intellectual terms, it would become possible to reconcile the spirit of science and the new understanding of religion, one that had become secularized as the gospel of humanity in Comte's ethical teaching. Comte hoped to replace selfish individualism with another concept he coined in opposition to it—altruism.[39] As he noted: "the social point of view cannot tolerate the notion of rights, for such notion rests on individualism. We are born under a load of obligations of every kind, to our predecessors, to our successors, to our contemporaries. After our birth these obligations increase or accumulate, for it is some time before we can return any service.... Thus ['to live for others'], the definitive formula of human morality, gives a direct sanction exclusively to our instincts of benevolence, the common source of happiness and duty. [Man must serve] Humanity, whose we are entirely."[40] This moral teaching inspired the Progressives after the Civil War, especially those like David Croly, who would become the most important Comtean in America. Comte's ethical teaching, along with the Hegelian notion of the state, also provided the inspiration for the Progressives' understanding of the moral obligations of individuals to the nation, as well as the duty of public intellectuals in shaping popular opinion concerning politics. It is not surprising that his son, Herbert Croly, would write books that inspired Progressive politicians and would also become one of the founders of an intellectual journal: *The New Republic*.[41]

The new disciplines of the social sciences would derive much of their moral authority from the view that the theoretical pursuit of knowledge, when united with the scientific method, could supply the means by which to achieve *social justice*. Positivism had provided a perfect synthesis. It had reconciled the aspirations of religion and science on the new ground of social justice. Unlike justice, which had been understood metaphysically, or unscientifically, social justice is capable of genuine achievement and empirical measurement of that achievement. In the view of the positivists, theology and metaphysics had been abstractions; social science would make the promises of religion a reality. Thus, Christianity had been a religious abstraction; it would become real as the science of sociology. As a leading Progressive theologian, George D. Herron, noted in 1894, "Jesus Christ offers sociology, the only scientific ground of discovering all the facts and forces of life. That ground is his revelation of universal unity.... Sociology and theology will ultimately be one science."[42] The movement from religion to social science was a common one by the end of the nineteenth century.

The young social scientists, the children of the clergy, were quickly persuaded to the view that positivism had successfully united the spirit of science and the spirit of religion.[43] Moreover, that union would come to inspire great expectations concerning the use of technical rationality in solving every human problem. Such a transformation, however, would require an expanded or positive government and social control of economic organizations, as well as expanded and rationalized public bureaucracies. The expertise generated in the university would establish the conditions whereby organized intelligence, or knowledge derived from the scientific method, could begin the process of progressively transforming man, society, and nature itself. In the attempt to establish social justice as the fundamental condition of human justice on earth, positivism had transformed the concern for the eternal, or otherworldly, into a concern for man as he is on earth. Consequently, it had been necessary to destroy the authority of theology and metaphysics. In the future, the salvation of man and society could be found only in an earthly temple. In terms of authority, the university would become the closest thing to the sacred within the rational state.

Reconstructing Society: American Social Science and the Modern State

The modern American graduate research university, beginning with Johns Hopkins University in 1876, became an important intellectual force in the period after the Civil War. The social science disciplines established themselves as the preeminent authority in terms of defining the meaning of those newly evolving historical categories, *economy* and *society*. In doing so, they created the tangible, or concrete, measures of *class* (economy) and *race* (society) to establish the empirical and moral ground of what had been historical abstractions. The Progressive intellectuals, liberal and conservative, were in agreement in terms of denying the static natural right foundation of the social compact.[44]

They were convinced that the transformation of the economy and society (not the protection of political and religious liberty) was to be the primary purpose of a genuine political or social science. Although they disagreed as to whether government or a free market and society should determine the conditions of economic development, no one denied that the economy and society had replaced politics and religion in terms of public significance. As a result, the Progressives came to interpret the meaning of the Civil War not as Lincoln had, in terms of the social compact theory of the American Founders, but in light of the new developments in the understanding of History; more precisely, in terms of the economy and society (class and race). Those categories would provide the tools of measurement within the disciplines of the new social sciences.

The American Founders and Lincoln had understood equality and liberty as the fundamental theoretical ideas derived from the doctrines of natural right. From the Progressive point of view, both had failed to grasp the historical or evolutionary ground of the meaning of liberty and equality. That understanding was made intelligible only in the new social and economic disciplines that would give scientific meaning to those concepts.

Ironically, the Progressives were subsequently to support an opinion derived from the sciences that was remarkably close to the social theories that animated Southern opposition to the principles of the Declaration of Independence. That opposition to the American Founders had revealed itself nearly a generation prior to the Civil War. The Southerners had rejected the principle of natural equality, first, on the ground of modern historical philosophy, and, subsequently, on the ground of science and biology. The South had come to accept race, the superiority of the white race, as well as the necessity of a master class, as new discoveries of history that had established the empirical foundation of the new sciences. On those grounds, it had been possible for many, including John C. Calhoun, Henry Hughes, George Fitzhugh, and Alexander Stephens, to defend slavery as a positive good. Although the new social sciences, in the period after the Civil War, did not attempt to defend slavery itself, they did provide scientific authority for a view that legitimized white racial superiority and made it nearly impossible to incorporate former black slaves into the Union as equal American citizens.[45]

The modern trends in historical scholarship and social science research, both German and American, had helped transform the meaning of liberty and equality. As Merriam noted:

> The modern school has, indeed, formulated a new idea of liberty, widely different from that taught in the early years of the Republic. The "Fathers" believed that in the original state of nature all men enjoy perfect liberty, that they surrender a part of this liberty in order that the government may be organized, and that therefore the stronger the government, the less the liberty remaining to the individual. Liberty is, in short, the natural and inherent right of all men; government the necessary limitation of this liberty.

Merriam insisted, however, that:

> Calhoun and his school, as it has been shown, repudiated this idea, and maintained that liberty is not the natural right of all men, but only the reward of the races or individuals properly qualified for its possession.

Upon this basis, slavery was defended against the charge that it was inconsistent with human freedom, and in this sense and so applied; the theory was not accepted outside the South. The mistaken application of the idea had the effect of delaying recognition of the truth in what had been said until the controversy over slavery was at an end.[46]

In that remarkable assertion, Merriam acquiesced in the view that slavery obscured the truth of the historical and scientific fact that race, not nature, had established the fundamental conditions of political right and determined the meaning of human freedom and equality. Consequently, Merriam (and other leading Progressives) defended the view of Calhoun and the Southerners that racial superiority provided the moral foundation of a master class. Thus, he could state unequivocally, and in his own name, that: "not only are men created unequal ... but this very inequality must be regarded as one of the essential conditions of human progress. ... This fundamental fact that individuals or races are unequal is not an argument against, but rather in favor of, social and political advancement."[47] Merriam insisted therefore that "Liberty is not derived from the natural equality of all men, but is the reward of the races who have contributed most to human progress."

Herbert Croly, one of the most influential public intellectuals of the Progressive Era, agreed with Merriam and the Southern defenders of slavery concerning the question of race. "The slave holders may have been wrong in enslaving blacks, but they were right in their view that only certain races were capable of self-government." Croly was of the opinion that "negroes were a race possessed of moral and intellectual qualities inferior to those of white men"; therefore, they should not be enfranchised as fellow citizens.[48] In looking at the origins of the new disciplines of the social sciences, nearly all of them took the notion of racial superiority for granted. As a result, those disciplines were united in the rejection of the doctrine of natural right, natural human equality, and the Constitution understood as a social compact. Insofar as they rejected slavery, it was on the grounds that it had become an historical anachronism. Furthermore, they insisted that this view was confirmed by history itself, in the victory of the Union armies. With the passing of the institution of slavery, it had become possible to understand that political capacity, or the suitability for self-government and freedom, was dependent on the progress of the races. As Merriam had indicated in his assessment of Calhoun, it was "the mistaken application of the idea" (racial superiority) in the defense of slavery, that "had the effect of delaying recognition of the truth in what had been said until the controversy over slavery was at an end." In Merriam's view, Calhoun's theory could have been vindicated only after slavery had been ended. Until that time, it had not yet become possible to understand the historical and scientific truth "that only certain races are capable of self-government."

The historians' admiration of Lincoln rested on what they considered an historic achievement, the establishment of the modern nation, or state. Lincoln's own understanding of his actions in defense of the Union rested on the necessity of upholding the conditions of the social compact. It required, therefore, a reaffirmation of the founding principles of the regime. Yet the Progressive social scientists would interpret his role as that of establishing and vindicating the historical evolution of the state. The Civil War and the consolidation of the Union was thought to be historical proof of the fact that social compact theory (the foundation of constitutionalism) had been relegated to the dustbin of History. America, after the Civil War, had become a nation-state. The outcome of the war, as Merriam and the Progressives came to interpret it, was not to be understood in terms of the principles of the past, as Lincoln had tried to do, but in terms of the future.

In other words, Progressive social scientists had come to understand the Civil War as an historical progression that had brought about the establishment of a new nation, or the state. It was quite different from the one the "people" had established in the social compact. Merriam viewed the transformation in the following way: "In the new national school, the tendency was to disregard the doctrine of the social contract, and to emphasize strongly the instinctive forces whose action and interaction produces a state. This distinction was developed by (Francis) Lieber, who held that the great difference between 'people' and 'nation' lies in the fact that the latter possess organic unity. . . . In general, the new school thought of the Union as organic rather than contractual in nature." Thus, Merriam concluded: "the contract philosophy was in general disrepute, and the overwhelming tendency was to look upon the nation as an organic product, the result of an evolutionary process."[49] A living organism needs a state, or at least, as Woodrow Wilson came to see, a living constitution.

Merriam knew very well, however, that it was not the case that those who had fought for the Union had done so in repudiation of the social compact. In fact, he admitted that many had not yet become conscious of this historic transformation. Merriam was persuaded that "the supremacy of the Union repudiated the social-contract theory, but it is necessary to recognize the fact the nation was something different in the popular mind and in the philosophic mind from the 'people' of earlier days. Nation carried with it the idea of an ethnic and geographic unity, constituted without the consent of any one in particular; 'people' was understood to be a body formed by a contract between certain individuals. The very fact that the Union was 'pinned together with bayonets' was enough to show that the doctrine of voluntary consent had faded into the background."[50] Historical evolution (war) had established the new nation and destroyed the social compact. In Merriam's view, the popular mind was still held hostage to the old view of the Founders, a view that had culminated in a social compact. In other words, he was aware that the comprehension of the meaning of the new scientific view was yet to be established in the public mind. Although slavery had come to be seen as an historical anachronism, popular recognition of the fact that the social compact had also become obsolete was not yet fully apparent to most Americans.

In attempting to establish the meaning of the Civil War, many social scientists had concluded that the fundamental achievement of the war was the destruction of the social compact itself. Merriam insisted that "the general idea was that the United States, by virtue of the community of race, interest, and geographical location, ought to be and is a nation; and ought to be held together by force, if no other means would avail. This was the feeling that underlay the great national movement of 1861–1865, and could not fail to be reflected in the philosophy of that time and in the succeeding interpretations of that event."[51]

In short, the actual events of history had provided the interpretation for the new theory of the nation. The fact that force was necessary had shown that the doctrine of a voluntary compact of the people was no longer tenable. The South had destroyed the conditions of the social compact. Consequently, Lincoln had been (to use Hegelian language) the "world historic individual" whose will had established the nation. He had transformed the country from a "people," understood in terms of a social compact, into a modern nation, or state. Of course, Lincoln was unaware of his historic role.

In short, like the theory of evolution itself, success in the historical struggle had proved the rightness of the cause. Lincoln, who had tried to preserve a regime of civil and religious liberty based on the principle of human equality, was celebrated by Progressive social scientists and historians for having established a modern state. But the Progressive historians, who rejected slavery as a relic of the past, had also rejected the doctrine of natural right and human equality for historical reasons. It was possible, therefore, to embrace the theory of racial superiority as an evolving historical and scientific truth. In rejecting Lincoln's understanding of the principle of equality, the Progressives had come to understand equality historically, in the same manner in which they had understood slavery, as simply an historical anachronism. In assessing the Progressives' political project, equal citizenship would come to be understood in terms of membership in the state, and rights as citizens of the state would be bestowed by government.

In the aftermath of the Civil War, the meaning of nation, or state, and the understanding of equality and liberty came to dominate the political and intellectual discourse. It was not surprising that Southern politicians and Southern intellectuals would unite against the principle of equality as Lincoln and the Founders had understood it. However, it was not only the Southern intellectuals who had come to reject Lincoln's understanding of those principles. The defense of equality in terms of an abstract truth, as understood by the American Founders and Lincoln, had been systematically undermined by the growing and nearly universal acceptance among historians that History established the ground of social justice.

Moreover, the new social and biological sciences provided an intellectual defense of the inequality of the races. It is not surprising that the view of the Northern intellectuals who greatly admired Lincoln would not differ in any significant way from that of the Southerners. Many of the Northerners had become educated in the new graduate schools in America. But they, too, would come to reject Lincoln's defense of equality. Although they were opposed to slavery, they had come to understand equality and liberty in terms of the meaning that had been established in the new social and biological sciences.

Charles Merriam was typical of those who had rejected the natural right foundation of the meaning of equality and liberty. He insisted: "from the standpoint of modern political science the slave holders were right in declaring that liberty can be given only to those who have political capacity enough to use it, and they were also right in maintaining that two greatly unequal races cannot exist side by side on terms of perfect equality."[52] Furthermore, Merriam agreed with the Southerners that "rights do not belong to men simply as men, but because of the superior qualities, physical, intellectual, moral or political, which are characteristic of certain individuals or races."[53] The denial of the doctrine of natural right, as a standard for political rights, had made it nearly impossible, subsequently, to defend the original understanding of equality as the fundamental principle of union and citizenship. The new sciences had established race and class as the categories necessary to determine the capacity for political rights and as the ground of equal citizenship.

The failure of Reconstruction to establish a new ground of citizenship for the former slaves is widely viewed as a tragedy and a failure of politics in both the North and South. What has often been ignored is the near uniformity of intellectual opinion, North and South, on the question of equality and race. That solidarity of the intellectuals made it nearly impossible to solve the problem of citizenship in a manner consistent with the original meaning of equality and liberty. Much of the scholarly opinion in the newly developed social sciences following the Civil War criticized the North's attempt to enfranchise the former slaves as equal citizens. The North was condemned for extending the franchise, and the South was praised for obstructing Negro voting. The leading political scientist of the day, Columbia's John W. Burgess, observed that "it is the white man's mission, his duty and his right to hold the reins of political power in his own hands.... The claim that there is nothing in the color of the skin from the point of view of political ethics is a great sophism. A black skin means membership in a race of men which has never of itself succeeded to reason, has never, therefore created any civilization of any kind."[54]

In looking at the scholarship during Reconstruction, it is clear that historicist thought linked to science had prevailed. To take only one example, James Ford Rhodes, "who wrote the first detailed study of the Reconstruction period, fully subscribed to the idea that Negroes were innately inferior and incapable of citizenship." Rhodes thought it a great pity that the North had been unwilling to listen to such men of science as Louis Agassiz who could have told them that the Negroes were unqualified for citizenship. "What the whole country has only learned through years of costly and bitter experience," declared Rhodes, "was known to this leader of scientific thought before we ventured on the policy of trying to make negroes intelligent by legislative acts: and this knowledge was to be had for the asking by the men who were shaping the policy of the nation."[55] Rhodes had been an ardent opponent of slavery and a great admirer of Abraham Lincoln.

The learned opinion of the time was summed up in a single sentence by William A. Dunning, Charles Merriam's teacher and a prominent political theorist at Columbia University. He noted that "the whole difficulty of Reconstruction…stemmed from the fact that the 'antithesis and antipathy of race and color were crucial and ineradicable.'"[56] In looking back on that period, most social scientists and historians have considered Reconstruction a political failure. But given the intellectual opinion of the time, it is hard to see how it could have succeeded. Furthermore, it is not surprising that the country had great difficulty integrating the newly freed slaves as equal citizens even after the passage of the Civil War amendments to the Constitution. Nor is it surprising that Progressivism, in its origins as a political movement, was almost completely indifferent to the civil rights of black Americans.

Indeed, race theory had become so pervasive by the beginning of the twentieth century that Hannah Arendt, writing during World War II, noted:

> Few ideologies have won enough prominence to survive the hard competitive struggle of persuasion, and only two have come out on top and essentially defeated all others: the ideology which interprets History as an economic struggle of classes, and the other that interprets History as a natural fight of races. The appeal of both to large masses was so strong that they were able to enlist state support and establish themselves as official national doctrines. But far beyond the boundaries within which race-thinking and class-thinking have developed into obligatory patterns of thought, free public opinion has adopted them to such an extent that not only intellectuals but great masses of people

will no longer accept any presentation of past or present facts that is not in agreement with either of these views.[57]

Although the legitimacy of the opinion that justifies the superiority of the white race is no longer defensible, it is still difficult for social science not to think in terms of race or class.

It was not until after the Second World War, when Hitler and the Nazi Party had completely discredited race theory, that the equal rights of blacks would become a serious concern of the intellectuals and the politicians. Unfortunately, the demise of race theory as a justification of inequality of citizenship did not result in reestablishing the principled meaning of equality as it was understood in the natural right teaching of the Founders and Lincoln. Ironically, although Lincoln and the North had won the political battle of the Civil War, the political thought that animated his judgment and his public rhetoric, not to mention his principles, had not triumphed in its aftermath. Lincoln's memory was preserved, but his political thought, and that of the American Founders, did not survive the intellectual onslaught of Progressive thought. Consequently, the meaning of Lincoln's legacy and that of the Founding Fathers would be determined by an intellectual authority animated by the spirit of historicism that was established in the newly created graduate schools where the historians and social scientists received their training.

Conclusion: Natural Right and History

It was already clear by the end of the nineteenth century that the intellectual triumph of historicism and the growth of the authority of the social sciences had all but undermined the Founders' and Lincoln's legacy in defense of natural right and constitutional government. It was not restored in the twentieth century. In his book *Natural Right and History*, published in 1953, Leo Strauss traced the crisis of the West to the abandonment of the idea of natural right. In the America of the twenty-first century, it is still difficult, if not impossible, intellectually and politically to defend the philosophic doctrine of natural right. The self-evident truths that had provided the foundation for the public philosophy of constitutionalism are no longer thought to be self-evident or true. Lincoln's defense of the Constitution, which was simply a defense of the natural right doctrine that had established the meaning and purpose of constitutionalism, had been rejected even by his most ardent admirers in the immediate aftermath of the Civil War. Those philosophical truths and their political embodiment in a fundamental law have not been restored in a meaningful way.

The acceptance of a philosophy of History and its "historic sense," as well as science and its empirical method, had provided the theoretical foundations of the state and the social sciences. Intellectually, the meaning of constitutionalism, and the philosophic authority of natural right as its ground, had been successfully undermined by historicism and positivism in the newly established universities of the post–Civil War era. Politically, however, constitutionalism retained some of its vitality simply because of the institutional structure of the Constitution and the separation of powers in the American government itself. Thus, it always remained a possibility that prudent leadership in a branch of the government could help mobilize constituencies on behalf of limited government or in defense of the Constitution. Nonetheless, it has been very difficult to establish a theoretical defense of constitutionalism in the absence of a philosophic doctrine or a public philosophy derived from metaphysics and dependent on practical reason, or prudence. Moreover, the political virtue of prudence has little place in the rational state, where passion or will establishes the ground of morality, and technical expertise is established with the purpose of implementing that will.

When Leo Strauss wrote at mid-century, he was well aware of the need to restore the foundation of natural right. But he noted that "the seriousness of the need of natural right does not prove that the need can be satisfied." Strauss pointed to the reason for the difficulty in attempting to satisfy that need: "the problem of natural right is today a matter of recollection rather than of actual knowledge." Consequently, he insisted that "we are therefore in need of historical studies in order to familiarize ourselves with the whole complexity of the issue."[58] However strange it must seem, given the abundance of historical scholarship, Strauss demanded that we must, once again, become students of "the history of ideas." We need, he said, a "nonhistoricist understanding of nonhistoricist philosophy.... But we need no less urgently a nonhistoricist understanding of historicism, that is, an understanding of historicism that does not take for granted the soundness of historicism."[59] When Strauss wrote his book, those historical studies of American political thought that were open to the possibility of natural right had not been written. The intellectual triumph of historicism had precluded the kind of openness to the question of natural right necessary for its recovery. Consequently, the problem of natural right was merely a memory or recollection. In short, there was no meaningful knowledge of natural right. In the case of Lincoln, the scholarship of the historians and social scientists had made it nearly impossible to comprehend the doctrine of natural right, or, the theoretical perspective that had animated Lincoln's self-understanding.

However, in the past half century, historical scholarship has begun to reveal the contours of a natural right teaching. Many of Strauss's students have produced the kind of nonhistoricist historical studies that have shed light on this question. In terms of Lincoln scholarship, Harry V. Jaffa has provided an analysis of the Civil War in direct opposition to that of the Progressive historians after the Civil War. He has made the theoretical foundations of Lincoln's thought and political prudence intelligible for the first time in more than a century. He has enlightened a generation of scholars on the problem of natural right by revealing the limitation imposed on Progressive scholarship by historicism itself. Now, many other scholars are producing historical studies of a kind that open up the possibility of understanding the past as it understood itself. Such historical scholarship must be done in a nonhistoricist manner. It must be open to the problem of natural right.

The problem of natural right could not be made meaningful again as long as the reigning authority of historicism and social science remained unquestioned. The road to the recovery of natural right would provoke bitter debate. Strauss was well aware that such scholarship would ignite an intellectual war, which would be fueled by the passions of those whose careers had been achieved in defense of the status quo. Strauss indicated that difficulty by referring to a quotation of Lord Acton: "Few discoveries are more irritating than those which expose the pedigree of ideas. Sharp definitions and unsparing analysis would displace the veil beneath which society dissembles its divisions, would make political disputes too violent for compromise and political alliances too precarious for use, and would embitter politics with all the passions of social and religious strife."[60] What is true of political life is no less true when it comes to establishing the theoretical understanding by which meaningful knowledge of the factual or empirical world is made intelligible. Indeed, political life takes its shape and derives its intellectual and moral authority from those ideas that establish the foundation of human knowledge.

The recovery of the theoretical ground of natural right could not take place as long as the authority and methodology of the social sciences dictated the manner of inquiry and the determination of the substance of meaningful knowledge. The social sciences required impartial, objective, or neutral observation as the only source of genuine knowledge. Natural right was established as a philosophic ethics derived from metaphysics. It could not be indifferent to the questions of justice, or equality, or liberty. Indeed, the method, which mandated a distinction between facts and values, and insisted that only factual knowledge is meaningful, stood in the way of the possibility of such a recovery. The scientific method was an essential element of the empiricism sanctioned by the acceptance of the authority of philosophy of History.

Thus, the social sciences owed their theoretical coherence to a "historical sense" that denied the possibility of truth or trans-historical knowledge. That denial makes relative all claims of knowledge except empirical, or scientific, knowledge. But it rests on the authority of a philosophy of History, which purports to be true as a complete and final teaching. The recovery of the problem of natural right would require bringing into question the entire edifice of Progressive political thought. Nonetheless, there is no question that historicism and the authority of the social sciences are still dominant in the academic and intellectual world. But, given the new unhistorical studies of ideas, the problem of natural right can now begin to be understood as something more than simply "a matter of recollection."

The insurmountable problem posed by scientific political science is that the understanding of politics is no longer derived from practical observation of the conduct of political life itself. Modern political science had become wholly theoretical and scientific. It had separated itself from philosophy (or metaphysical reason) and had fallen under the authority of an ethically neutral, technically rational, methodology. In returning to Aristotelian political science, Strauss pointed the way back to a theoretical defense of prudential politics. He insisted that "prudence is always endangered by false doctrines about the whole of which man is a part;

prudence is therefore always in need of defense against such opinions, and that defense is necessarily theoretical." However, he knew that such a theory cannot be "taken to be the basis of prudence," because of "the fact that the sphere of prudence is, as it were, only de jure but not de facto wholly independent of theoretical science."[61] As a result, the defense of prudence itself, both theoretically and practically, had become nearly impossible.[62]

The reason for this, Strauss suggests, is because of

> the view underlying the new political science according to which no awareness inherent in practice, and in general no natural awareness, is genuine knowledge, or in other words only "scientific" knowledge is genuine knowledge. This view implies that there cannot be practical sciences proper, or that the distinction between practical and theoretical sciences must be replaced by the distinction between theoretical and applied sciences—applied sciences being sciences based on the theoretical sciences that precede the applied sciences in time and in order.[63]

In Strauss's opinion, it was necessary to reaffirm the dignity of the political by returning to a natural, or prescientific, understanding of the political. In doing so, prudence could once again be seen for what it is.

In establishing the theoretical ground of natural right, Strauss hoped to make it possible once again to illuminate the theoretical and prudential ground of constitutional or moderate government. The tyrannies of the twentieth century made it necessary to do so. In doing so, he made clear that "it would not be difficult to show that liberal or constitutional democracy comes closer to what the classics demanded than any alternative that is viable in our age."[64]

He noted, "According to the classics, the best constitution is a contrivance of reason, i.e., of conscious activity or of planning on the part of an individual or a few individuals. It is in accordance with nature, or it is a natural order, since it fulfills to the highest degree the requirements of the perfection of human nature, or since its structure imitates the pattern of nature."[65]

The defense of constitutionalism requires recognition of the necessity of philosophic reason (Socratic dialectic) as the theoretical means to illuminate the foundation of the distinction between nature and convention. In doing so, it becomes possible to establish a foundation for political right that is not derived from force or convention, but from nature, or in accordance with nature (i.e., natural right). Such a recognition makes it possible to understand that human nature itself establishes the necessity of limited government. It presupposes rational expectations regarding the ends of politics and prudential judgment concerning the means. The tyrannies and the immoderation of the totalitarian regimes of the twentieth century were a consequence of the ideological and utopian character of the political thought inspired by philosophy of History. The revival of constitutionalism was made more urgent by potential developments in science and technology that make possible the universal tyranny of the rational state. The political success of the universal homogenous state would open up the possibility of a global and perpetual tyranny. In attempting to elucidate the age-old problem of tyranny as it revealed itself in our time, Strauss saw the necessity of, once again, revitalizing the theoretical perspective of nature, or natural right.

Although natural right is now more than a memory, it has not established itself in any meaningful or influential way in our intellectual life or in our politics. This does not mean that there are no defenders of limited government. However, beneath the surface of the contemporary debate between defenders of limited government (and what is understood as constitutionalism) and those committed to the maintenance of the rational or administrative state, it is still necessary to confront the theoretical distinction that now animates partisan politics. And the ground of this distinction still rests on a philosophy of History—the acceptance of which has already helped to shape the outcome of the political struggle.

The moral foundations of constitutionalism, and the principled distinctions derived from them, have been undercut. The ground of political morality was established on an understanding of those permanent human problems made intelligible by nature through reason. The social compact was the political expression of that philosophic tradition. Consequently, it was primarily differences of opinion over the practical meaning of the Constitution and the limitations implicit within the social contract that were meant to animate political life. The moral foundations of society were established within the philosophical and religious traditions. Most importantly, philosophy and religion were in agreement concerning the content of morality and the traditional distinctions between good and evil or good and bad.[66]

However, with the establishment of the modern rational state, the moral foundation of constitutional government has been eroded by the Progressive understanding of the meaning of freedom and rights as constantly evolving in accordance with historical conditions. Those permanent truths embodied in the constitutional tradition have become less meaningful and far less important than the ideological differences that exist between Progressives and Reactionaries, or liberals and conservatives. Consequently, in the absence of a philosophic defense of natural right, politics cannot be understood prudentially, in terms of practical reason, or theoretically, in terms of the principles that established the moral foundation of constitutionalism. Furthermore, the ground of traditional morality, derived from that philosophic tradition and religion, which had established a nonpartisan consensus on cultural issues, has itself been undermined. As Strauss noted, "The substitution of the distinction between progressive and reactionary for the distinction between good and bad is another aspect of the discovery of History. The discovery of History...is identical with the substitution of the past or the future for the eternal—the substitution of the temporal for the eternal."[67]

The American Founding had been established on the theoretical ground that reason and nature were meaningful and intelligible categories of human understanding. Furthermore, the Founders were confident that the principles of natural right derived therefrom are eternal, or trans-historical. Those who have embraced History, whether they look to a glorious future (Progressives or liberals) or—disillusioned with the future—demand that the experience of the past must be our only guide (Reactionaries or conservatives); both deny theoretical metaphysics, or natural right. As Strauss has observed, "historicism...stands or falls by the denial of the possibility of theoretical metaphysics and of philosophic ethics or natural right."[68] Until the authority of natural right, or philosophy (and religion), can become meaningful again, contemporary politics will continue to be dominated by an intellectual authority derived from the understanding of History, which has become legitimized by the rational empirical methodology of the social sciences. The doctrine of History has established the measure and meaning of Western man in the twentieth century. In the twenty-first century, postmodernism may pose the most direct threat to the authority of History, understood in terms of its rationality. In addition, it may pose the greatest danger to social science, because it undermines the objective authority of science and the scientific method itself.

14

Wisdom and Moderation: Leo Strauss's *On Tyranny*: Modern Thought and Its "Unmanly Contempt for Politics"

THE PARTICIPANTS ON THIS PANEL have had access to four good and thoughtful papers on the Strauss-Kojève debate.[1] They range from analysis of the philosophic and theological dimensions of the debate, to the hidden influence of Heidegger. There is even an attempt to make the case that Kojève won the debate. All of the papers are quite abstract and theoretical. Yet, the experience of tyranny is not an abstraction but a political reality, which manifests itself in enormous human suffering. Modern historicist political thought, and the social sciences that accompanied it, have failed to recognize tyranny, because they have failed to understand it. Tyranny is a danger that accompanies all political life and can be understood only on the basis of a political science capable of *evaluating politics* and making sound moral judgments concerning opinion about right and wrong, or good and evil. I will limit myself to a few questions and observations concerning the papers of Professor Murray Bessette and Professor Bryan Frost. Nonetheless, my observations and questions were raised in response to themes common to all of the papers and may apply generally to dilemmas posed by the debate itself.

In Professor Bessette's paper, we are given a philosophic critique of Kojève's understanding of tyranny, which is dependent upon and requires Kojève's interpretation of Hegel's *Phenomenology of Spirit*. As

Bessette notes: "Granting the Hegelian assumptions that there is meaning to History and historical progress, Kojève sees the coming completion of History in the gradual conquest, through the political action of reforming tyrants, of the Socratic idea of a common essence of man (i.e., logos) and its synthesis with the secularized Christian idea of the equality of believers before god." That is, History is seen to be "the continuous succession of political actions guided more or less by the evolution of philosophy. This historical-philosophical process issues forth in the universal and homogeneous state wherein the quest for wisdom finally can be transformed into Wisdom simply." What are we to make of this? Can tyranny reveal itself as a practical phenomenon, if the actions of tyrants are justified theoretically as necessary for historical progress? Are those who experience tyranny ever aware that they suffer for a good cause? Leo Strauss was certain that the actual *experience* of tyranny, understood simply in terms of common sense, was what it had always been. It was modern political science's understanding of tyranny that had changed and obscured the reality of tyranny. The most extreme formulation of the new thought rested on the assumption that the end of History was also the end of philosophy (because wisdom had been actualized) and the end of politics (because in the absence of principled quarrels, politics could be rationalized and understood as a merely technological phenomenon). Politics would be transformed into an ongoing administrative process organized and operated by scientific and technologically trained elites.

Strauss rejected the historicist assumptions of modern philosophy. He denied that philosophy, as the quest for wisdom in its Socratic form, had ended, or could end. And, he denied that politics as a human problem could be transcended. On the contrary, he insisted that "tyranny is a danger coeval with political life. The analysis of tyranny is therefore as old as political science itself. The analysis of tyranny that was made by the first political scientists was so clear, so comprehensive, and so unforgettably expressed that it was remembered and understood by generations which did not have any direct experience of actual tyranny. On the other hand, when we were brought face to face with tyranny—with a kind of tyranny that surpassed the boldest imagination of the powerful thinkers of the past—our political science failed to recognize it."[2] Although the massive destruction unleashed by those tyrannies, animated by the triumph of will in the service of History, resulted in totally undermining the racial superiority theories of Hitler, and partially discrediting the class analysis of the Marxist regimes; the social sciences emerged unscathed with their racial and class theories still an integral part of their theoretical perspective and their methodology.

The constitutional democracies had triumphed on the basis of the defense of principles and practices of government that predated the discovery of History. Nonetheless, the social sciences, in the very heart of those regimes, had denied the possibility of natural right and were unable to profit from the great lessons presented by the evils of the twentieth century. Strauss has noted: "Natural right must be mutable in order to be able to cope with the inventiveness of wickedness. What cannot be decided in advance by universal rules, what can be decided in the critical moment by the most competent and most conscientious statesman on the spot, can be made visible as just, in retrospect, to all; the objective discrimination between extreme actions which were just and extreme actions which were unjust is one of the noblest duties of the historian."[3] The historians, under the spell of History and animated by social science methodology, not only failed in their duty to reveal the injustice of those tyrannies, they continued to understand political phenomena in terms of the theoretical perspective of those defeated on the battlefield.

In his *Thoughts on Machiavelli*, Leo Strauss suggested that "contemporary tyranny has its roots in Machiavelli's thought, in the Machiavellian principle that the *good end justifies every means*" (emphasis mine).[4] Since Machiavelli, all specifically modern political thought, including modern science and social science, has justified itself in terms of its practice, or its ability to approximate or realize its goals or ends made good by success, or the rationality of the historical process itself. As a result, the actual experience of tyranny could not be understood from the perspective of a political thought that had become ideological and scientifically technological. Therefore, Strauss insisted:

> that there is an essential difference between the tyranny analyzed by the classics and that of our age. In contradistinction to classical tyranny present day tyranny has at its disposal "technology" as well as "ideologies"; more generally expressed, it presupposes the existence of "science", i.e. of a particular interpretation, or kind, of science. Conversely, classical tyranny, unlike modern tyranny, was confronted ... by a science

which was not meant to be applied to the 'conquest of nature' or to be popularized and diffused. But in noting this one implicitly grants that one cannot understand modern tyranny in its specific character before one has understood the elementary and in a sense *natural* form of tyranny which is pre-modern tyranny. This basic stratum of modern tyranny remains, for all practical purposes, *unintelligible* to us if we do not have recourse to the political science of the classics.[5] (emphasis mine)

In returning to the classics, Strauss denied that the "issue has been finally settled by historicism." Rather, "the 'experience of history' and the less ambiguous experience of the complexity of human affairs may blur, but they cannot extinguish, the evidence of those simple experiences regarding right and wrong which are at the bottom of the philosophic contention that there is a natural right. Historicism either ignores or else distorts these experiences."[6] Strauss insisted that

> the existence and even the possibility of natural right must remain an open question as long as the issue between historicism and nonhistoricist philosophy is not settled. The issue is not understood if it is seen merely in the way in which it presents itself from the point of view of historicist philosophy. This means, for all practical purposes, that the problem of historicism must first be considered from the point of view of classical philosophy, which is nonhistoricist thought in its pure form.

Thus, Strauss further insisted that "our most urgent need can then be satisfied only by means of historical studies which would enable us to understand classical philosophy exactly as it understood itself, and not in the way in which it presents itself on the basis of historicism." We need, he said, a "nonhistoricist understanding of nonhistoricist philosophy. But we need no less urgently a nonhistoricist understanding of historicism, that is, an understanding of historicism that does not take for granted the soundness of historicism."[7]

In other words, Strauss contended that we need an adequate interpretation of "the experience of history"; one that

> does not make doubtful the view that the fundamental problems, such as the problems of justice, persist or retain their identity in all historical

change, however much they may be obscured by the temporary denial of their relevance and however variable or provisional all human solutions to these problems may be. In grasping these problems as problems, *the human mind liberates itself from its historical limitations*. No more is needed to legitimize philosophy in its original, Socratic sense: philosophy is knowledge that one does not know; that is to say, it is knowledge of what one does not know, or awareness of the fundamental problems and, therewith, of the fundamental alternatives regarding their solution that are coeval with human thought.[8] (emphasis mine)

In turning away from contemporary philosophy to its Socratic original, Strauss returns to *political* philosophy, one which recognizes the importance of *politics* and *opinion* to the understanding of human things. In doing so, he sides with Socrates against the pre-Socratics. As Strauss noted,

Socrates seems to have regarded the change which he brought about as a return to "sobriety" and "moderation" from the "madness" of his predecessors. In contradistinction to his predecessors, he did not separate wisdom from moderation. In present-day parlance one can describe the change in question as a return to "common sense" or to "the world of common sense." That to which the question "What is?" points is the *eidos* of a thing, the shape or form or character or "idea" of a thing. It is no accident that the term *eidos* signifies primarily that which is visible to all without any particular effort or what one might call the "surface" of the things. Socrates started not from what is first in itself or first by nature but from what is first for us, from what comes to sight first, from the phenomena. But the being of things, their What, comes first to sight, not in what we see of them, but in what is said about them or in opinions about them. Accordingly, Socrates started in his understanding of the natures of things from the opinions about their natures. For every opinion is based on some awareness, on some perception with the mind's eye, of something. Socrates implied that disregarding the opinions about the natures of things would amount to abandoning the most important access to reality which we have or the most important vestiges of the truth which are within our reach.[9]

The return to Socratic political philosophy is a return to the world of common sense, of opinion derived from convention as the first access to an understanding of *nature*, which makes the dialectic or the quest for wisdom or knowledge both possible and necessary.

Strauss, therefore, attempted to provide a philosophic critique which would make it possible to recover an understanding of the theoretical roots of Socratic rationality and prudential politics, which had been undermined by the victory of historicism. He knew better than most that the immoderate political practice of the twentieth century was a consequence of the utopian, scientific, and ideological character of its political thought. In turning to classical political thought, he showed that Socratic rationality provided a political solution to the problem of reconciling wisdom and moderation. He noted:

> the political problem consists in reconciling the requirement for wisdom with the requirement for consent. But whereas, from the point of view of egalitarian natural right, consent takes precedence over wisdom; from the point of view of classic natural right, wisdom takes precedence over consent. According to the classics, the best way of meeting these two entirely different requirements—that for wisdom and that for consent or for freedom—would be that a wise legislator frame a code which the citizen body, duly persuaded, freely adopts. That code, which is, as it were, the embodiment of wisdom, must be as little subject to alteration as possible; *the rule of law* is to take the place of the rule of men, however wise.[10]

In the modern or post-Christian world, Strauss believed that the political manifestation of egalitarian natural right, or the rule of law established in a constitutional regime, would provide the best foundation for moderate or reasonable government.

The problem of reconciling wisdom and moderation had been impossible in terms of pre-Socratic thought. Moreover, it had become increasingly difficult to maintain moderate governments in modern times as a consequence of the victory of historicist thought and the scientific methodology of the social sciences. But, insofar as modern natural right retained its authority in the political practice and institutional structures of constitutionalism, constitutional government and the rule of law remained the best defense of wisdom and moderation. Strauss noted, "It would not be difficult to show that…liberal or constitutional democracy comes closer to what the classics demanded than any alternative that is viable in our age."[11] In providing a defense of constitutionalism, and in laying bare the tyranny implicit in the modern rational state, or its manifestation in the universal homogeneous state, Strauss provided the foundations for an analysis of modern political thought that could reveal its failure to understand "the actual experience of tyranny."[12]

In Strauss's view, modern historicist philosophy had corrupted the theory and practice of politics, undermining the possibility of understanding and therefore providing a defense of moderation and prudence as essential to good government. Moreover, the social science, which accompanied the modern state, showed itself to be incapable of making reasonable—or prudent—judgments concerning politics. It could not understand nor identify politics at its worst; it could not identify *tyranny*. Most importantly, however, the modern administrative state and its science, although incapable of recognizing tyranny, opened up the prospect of the greatest tyranny of all. "We are now brought face to face with a tyranny which holds out the threat of becoming, thanks to 'the conquest of nature' and in particular human nature, what no earlier tyranny ever became: perpetual and universal."[13]

Why was this so? Modern political thought had so corrupted the relationship of theory and practice as to make it nearly impossible to understand the proper ground of either theory or practice. Strauss notes that:

> Political theory became understanding of what practice has produced or of the actual and ceased to be the quest for what ought to be; political theory ceased to be "theoretically practical" (i.e., deliberative at a second remove) and became purely theoretical in the way in which metaphysics (and physics) were traditionally understood to be purely theoretical. There came into being a new type of theory, of metaphysics, having as its highest theme human action and its product rather than the whole, which is in no way the object of human action. With the whole and the metaphysic that is oriented upon it, human action occupies a high but subordinate place. When metaphysics came, as it now did, to regard human action and its product as the end toward which all other beings or processes are directed, *metaphysics became*

philosophy of history [emphasis mine]. Philosophy of history was primarily theory, i.e., contemplation, of human practice; it presupposed that significant human action, History, was completed. By becoming the highest theme of philosophy, practice ceased to be practice proper, i.e., concern with *agenda*.[14]

But the end of philosophy created its own crisis, a crisis of meaning that was animated by the deadening effect of the recognition that History, as meaningful practice, had ended. Strauss insisted that the rebellion of the Right Hegelians was in the direction of reviving meaningful *political* and *religious* experience. It consisted in an attempt to make History compatible with *life* and human *aspiration*. He suggested that:

> The revolts against Hegelianism on the part of Kierkegaard and Nietzsche, in so far as they now exercise a strong influence on public opinion, thus appear as attempts to recover the possibility of practice, i.e., of a human life which has a significant and undetermined future. But these attempts increased the confusion, since they destroyed, as far as in them lay, the very possibility of theory. "Doctrinairism" and "existentialism" appear to us as the two faulty extremes. While being opposed to each other, they agree with each other in the decisive respect—they agree in ignoring prudence, "the god of this lower world." Prudence and "this lower world" cannot be seen properly without some knowledge of "the higher world"—without genuine *theoria*.[15]

It would seem that modern historicist political theory had returned to the "madness" of pre-Socratic thought, in terms of separating wisdom and moderation. The second and third waves of modern political thought had so distorted the relationship between theory and practice that it undercut the autonomy of prudence and deprived politics of its dignity.

The great thinkers of the nineteenth century, Strauss showed, had rejected nature as a standard. They had all, in one form or another, embraced the idea of History. In pointing specifically to the failures of Marx and Nietzsche, Strauss noted the importance of prudence and moderation in political life: "But perhaps one can say that their grandiose failures make it easier for us who have experienced those failures to understand again the old saying that wisdom cannot be separated from moderation and hence to understand that wisdom requires unhesitating loyalty to a decent constitution and even to the cause of constitutionalism. Moderation will protect us against the twin dangers of visionary expectations from politics and unmanly contempt for politics."[16] In the twentieth century, the rational administrative structures, which have become dominant in the modern state, are the product of "visionary expectations from politics." At the same time, they reflect in their neutral bureaucracies an "unmanly contempt for politics," an indulgence which accompanies the belief that partisanship has ended and rational rule has begun.

In his paper on the Strauss-Kojève debate, Professor Frost seeks to prove that Kojève had won the debate. That might be so if the debate is judged in terms of modern intellectual history, or contemporary political practice. There is no question that Hegelians of the Left or Right have dominated the political and social thought of the twentieth century. They have influenced the practical conduct of modern governments, when those institutions are animated by the theory of the rational or universal state. As a result, Frost assumes that there is an area of agreement between Strauss and Kojève concerning contemporary theory, if not concerning practice. Professor Frost noted that "both Strauss and Kojève strongly imply that theirs are the only two tenable philosophic understandings available, the rest being either contradictory or subsumed by their own." He notes that "Kojève conceded that if 'there is something like human nature, then you (Strauss) are surely right in everything'"; Strauss, similarly, states that "no one had made the case for modern thought in our time as brilliantly as you." Does this constitute an area of agreement concerning the terms of the debate?

Professor Frost assumes that the "two tenable philosophic understandings" constitute a common ground that would enable a comparison of the two. However, Kojève's theoretical view would be right only if an affirmation, or possible refutation of Hegelianism, is of necessity judged *historically* by contemporary intellectuals or theorists. Strauss, however brilliant he thought Kojève's analysis was, would not agree that his (Strauss's) own thought could be judged by any historical standards whatsoever. Moreover, Kojève agreed that Strauss would be right if something like human nature exists. Consequently, it appears that the debate itself was dependent upon a proper understanding of philosophy—that is, natural right (Socratic) or History (Hegel). Kojève denied philosophy, understood in terms of natural right. And Strauss denied History, understood in terms of the end of philosophy and its culmination into wisdom or knowledge. Indeed, Kojève himself admitted subsequently that he would have never understood philosophy (in its Socratic form) if he had not known Leo Strauss. Although he appears to have been charmed, nonetheless, he was not persuaded by Strauss.

On the other hand, Strauss would not agree that the coming into being of the universal homogeneous state could vindicate Kojève's position, either in theory or practice. Strauss's theoretical position cannot be understood historically, nor could it be judged by historicist standards. Likewise, his practical or political conclusions could not be dependent upon any actual historical current or force, however popular or powerful. Unlike Edmund Burke, Strauss did not think "that to oppose a thoroughly evil current in human affairs is *perverse* if that current is sufficiently powerful." Strauss insisted that Burke

> is oblivious of the nobility of last-ditch resistance. He does not consider that, in a way which no man can foresee, resistance in a forlorn position to the enemies of mankind, "going down with guns blazing and flags flying," may contribute greatly toward keeping awake the recollection of the immense loss sustained by mankind, may inspire and strengthen the desire and the hope for its recovery, and may become a beacon for those who humbly carry on the works of humanity in a seemingly endless valley of darkness and destruction. He does not consider this because he is too certain that man can know whether a cause lost now is lost forever or that man can understand sufficiently the meaning of a providential dispensation as distinguished from the moral law.[17]

In his failure to oppose an historical force he knew to be evil, it was "only a short step from this thought of Burke to the supersession of the distinction between good and bad by the distinction between the progressive and the retrograde (reactionary), or between what is and what is not in harmony with the historical process" (emphasis and addition mine).[18] If philosophy, or natural right, is possible, it cannot be evaluated in terms of the conditions established by any understanding of the rationality of History, or historicist thought.

Strauss noted that Kojève's position depended upon the truth of the supposition that the universal and homogeneous state is the best social order. The universal homogeneous state presupposed the conquest of nature, as well as the end of work and fighting. But Strauss denied the assertion that the end state could be the best social order. "The simply best social order," as Kojève conceived of it, Strauss noted, "is the state in which every human being finds his full satisfaction." A human being is satisfied, "if his human dignity is universally recognized and if he enjoys 'equality of opportunity,' i.e., the opportunity, corresponding to his capacities, of deserving well of the state or of the whole."[19] However, Strauss wondered if humans could be satisfied in such circumstances. Strauss noted that Kojève's position depended upon the assumption that "there is no longer fight nor work. History has come to its end. There is nothing more to do." In response, Strauss observed that the "end of History would be most exhilarating but for the fact that, according to Kojève, it is the participation in bloody political struggles as well as in real work or, generally expressed, the negating action, which raises man above the brutes. The state, through which man is said to become reasonably satisfied, is, then, the state in which the basis of man's humanity withers away or, in which man loses his humanity."[20]

Strauss was of the opinion that "perhaps it is not war nor work but thinking that constitutes the humanity of man. Perhaps it is not recognition (which for many men may lose in its power to satisfy what it gains in universality) but wisdom that is the end of man." Strauss insisted that "if the final state is to satisfy the deepest longing of the human soul, every human being must be capable of becoming wise. The most relevant difference among human beings must have practically disappeared."[21] But Strauss asks: "if not all human beings become wise, then it follows that for almost all human beings the end state is identical with the loss of their humanity, . . . and they can therefore not be rationally satisfied with it."[22] Strauss was certain Kojève's utopia would require the use of force, and a tyrant, to enforce the satisfaction that all supposedly desired. Strauss maintained that "the actual satisfaction of all human beings, which allegedly is the goal of History, is impossible. It is for this reason, I suppose, that the final social order, as Kojève conceives of it, is a *State* and not a stateless society: the State, or coercive government, cannot wither away because it is impossible that all human beings should ever become actually satisfied" (emphasis mine).[23] The final state is and must be a tyranny.

Moreover, the "Universal and Final Tyrant" would not be wise. Strauss notes that

> to retain his power, he will be forced to suppress every activity which might lead people into doubt of the essential soundness of the universal and homogeneous state: he must suppress philosophy as an attempt to corrupt the young. In particular he must in the interest of the homogeneity of his universal state forbid every teaching, every suggestion, that there are politically relevant *natural* differences among men which cannot be abolished or neutralized by progressing scientifically technology.[24] (emphasis mine)

In short, the universal state would be a tyranny, which if successful, would result in the "end of philosophy on earth." Strauss insisted that "from the Universal Tyrant however there is no escape. Thanks to the conquest of nature and to the completely unabashed substitution of suspicion and terror for law, the Universal and Final Tyrant has at his disposal practically unlimited means for ferreting out, and for extinguishing, the most modest efforts in the direction of thought."[25]

Kojève confirmed Strauss's doubt concerning the goodness, or even the possibility, of satisfying all in a manner compatible with man's humanity. In a letter written to Strauss, Kojève described the actual character of "satisfaction" in the end state. Kojève noted:

> the universal and homogeneous state is "good" only because it is the *last* (because neither war nor revolution are conceivable in it: mere "dissatisfaction" is not enough, it also takes weapons!) Besides, "not human" can mean "animal" (or better—automaton) as well as "God." In the final state there naturally are no more "human beings" in our sense of an *historical* human being. The "healthy" automata are "satisfied" (sports, art, eroticism, etc.), and the "sick" ones get locked up. As for those who are not satisfied with their "purposeless activity" (art, etc.), they are the philosophers (who can attain wisdom if they "contemplate" enough). By doing so they become "gods." The tyrant becomes an administrator,

a cog in the "machine" fashioned by automata for automata.[26] (Kojève's emphasis)

However, Strauss was confident that Kojève had overestimated the tameness of man and from that he remained hopeful. Strauss suggests: "There will always be men (*andres*) who will revolt against a state which is destructive of humanity or in which there is no longer a possibility of noble action and of great deeds."[27] In his view, nature and politics cannot be easily expunged from the earth. The very real tyrannies of the twentieth century made it possible to understand the practical or political character of tyranny that was made intelligible theoretically by reviving Socratic rationalism, or political thought in its original meaning. It also made it necessary to reestablish a theoretical perspective capable of relating politics to the reality of human experience. In establishing a nonhistoricist philosophy and a nonhistoricist account of history, a realistic understanding of politics had revealed the danger of tyranny in our time; the universal homogeneous state in the form of a universal tyrant. Strauss does not doubt that it is possible, and necessary, to inspirit man on behalf of noble action in defense of his own humanity. Moreover, even if it is not possible now, it may become possible in the future to revive the understanding of, and the aspiration for justice that would rekindle an awareness of the danger of tyranny by revealing its essential character. In doing so, we may, as Strauss suggested, "contribute greatly toward keeping awake the recollection of the immense loss sustained by mankind, [and] may inspire and strengthen the desire and hope for its recovery."[28]

15

Trump and the Future of American Politics

AMERICAN PARTISANSHIP has come to be understood in terms of History, or progress, as establishing the moral ground of politics and society. The desire for change, the widespread expectation that change is itself a good, had animated politics throughout much of the nineteenth and twentieth centuries. That understanding of the meaning of progress was realized and justified by the transformation of social life brought about by the benevolent use of science and its method in the service of social and political change. Humans everywhere have benefited from progress in science, technology, and medicine. But political science, as well as economics, has not yet established a universal, or objective, science that has delivered benefits that are universally recognized as a common good in the eyes of its citizens.

Nonetheless, Progressivism has created a partisanship on behalf of change as the ground of establishing the measure of a political good. Understood historically, those who view the future as a better guide than the past have embraced progress as the ground and goal of political and social well-being. Those who are doubtful of change, or who seek to preserve some past good, are thought to be Reactionaries. In terms of political partisanship, liberals are thought to be on the right side of History. Conservatives, wary of an unknown future good, are thought to be impediments to the progressive transformation of social life. They insist on clinging to an outmoded past. But both have become necessary to the political existence of the other. And there seems to be no political alternative to those two choices seemingly imposed by the demands of History itself.

In American politics, the election of 2008 established what appeared to be the high point of twenty-first-century Progressivism. But its very success produced a crisis of liberalism that threatened a Progressive legacy that had been established over much of the last century. Barack Obama won the most decisive presidential election of any Democrat since Lyndon Baines Johnson. His party gained control of both houses of Congress. His campaign slogan said it all: *Hope and Change*. Hope is established and animated by an awareness of an abstract and future good. And the purpose of government is to bring about social change on behalf of that vision. In his first term, Obama sought to achieve the dream of every Progressive president since Teddy Roosevelt and Woodrow Wilson. In FDR's memorable phrase, "necessitous men cannot be free," the purpose of government is to establish universal security against natural necessity, relief from those very exigencies established by life itself. In short, an enlightened administration must establish the guarantees of universal security against those necessities that have made it impossible to be free outside of the confines of a rational, or administrative, state.

The election of Donald Trump changed the landscape of American politics. The 2016 election could be seen as a repudiation of those past progressive policies that had dominated both parties in domestic and foreign affairs since the end of the Cold War. Unlike the intellectuals, liberal and conservative, Trump did not appear to understand change or progress historically, in terms of a future good. Nor did he understand the past in terms of those quarrels between the intellectuals who disagreed practically over current policies, but agreed theoretically on the meaning of past and future—on history. Trump's campaign slogan revealed much: *Make America Great Again*. In other words, he did not understand politics, or the past, from what had been the perspective of the intellectuals, liberal or conservative. In Trump's view, America was great in the past, and that greatness could be restored.

In political practice, liberals and conservatives had established a kind of symbiotic relationship that made them appear as opposite sides of the same coin. The contemporary meaning of those terms had been derived from the theories and policies that had become embodied within the administrative state. There were disagreements over how certain domestic or foreign policies should be promulgated, or when they should take effect, or how much they should cost. However, there was little partisan disagreement as to whether those policies should have been pursued, or abandoned, because there was no *political* standard by which to judge results in terms of success or failure. Those decisions were put in the hands of experts, or bureaucrats, whose knowledge established their authority. But the outcome of the decisions based on that supposed knowledge, whether successful or not, remained unquestioned by those who had political power.

The authority of the intellectuals had established a theoretical, or socially constructed, reality that appeared indifferent to reality as it revealed itself in practical or political life. It seemed as though liberal and conservative intellectuals could disagree when it came to practical means, but they were in apparent agreement concerning technical ends. But it was the ends—the results or failures—that brought about the political turmoil that led to the questioning of their authority. Much of official Washington rested on the authority of the knowledge that had been invested in those technical administrative positions. And nearly all concerned had a stake in maintaining the status quo. It seemed that the whole of Washington, Republican or Democrat, liberal or conservative, was opposed to Trump. Their interests as stakeholders within the administrative state required a defense of the Washington establishment.

At the same time, Trump, in his political appeals, had also challenged, and depreciated, the intellectual authority of the leaders of organized conservatism. In short, he succeeded in separating parts of the political constituencies of both parties from their organizational and ideological leadership. This caused a civil war between numerous conservative opinion leaders who opposed Trump and their many followers who embraced him. It is not surprising that the whole of the Washington intellectual establishment, liberal and conservative opinion leaders alike, have objected to the manner in which he has removed the political discourse from their hands and placed it directly in the hands of the electorate itself.

For the last twenty-five years or more, American elections have been framed not by political partisans on behalf of the people, but by professionals on behalf of the Washington establishment. As a result, it is not the varied constituencies of the national electorate but the spokesmen for the centralized organized interests in Washington—the economic, social, political, and intellectual elites—who have determined not only what was acceptable in terms of policy, but in terms of political debate as well.

That centralization of politics, economics, administration, and public opinion had empowered the Washington elites. But it had also impoverished the political and economic lives of those people with little access to Washington. Despite all the talk of diversity, genuine political diversity would require real power and genuine politics at the state and local levels of government. As it stands, only the organized interests, and the issue networks allied to them, were able to exercise real influence in the centralized administrative state that had been erected in Washington over the past half century. Genuine diversity would require reestablishing the ground of politics in the nation as a whole. It would necessitate reanimating the distinction between the social and the political, the public and the private, as essential to a revival of the institutions of civil society. Political communities, established and represented within civil society institutions, would reflect the diverse economic, social, demographic, and geographic interests that are necessary to define the political authority of the people. Moreover, it would require a decentralization of political and rational authority that now resides in Washington, and a restoration of political and administrative authority in state and local governments.

Trump mobilized a political constituency by recognizing a political reality that was still visible to a large segment of the American people. It was a reality they experienced in their own lives in their own communities. But it was in opposition to the socially constructed public world, a self-proclaimed narrative established by, and on behalf of, the elites. That narrative, which they themselves have explicitly distinguished from factual reality, is a product of the intellectuals. It is authorized and legitimized by the political, social, economic, and media elites. It has dictated what constituted the morally defensible in the political and social world. Although Trump has mobilized the constituency that has propelled him to the forefront of American politics, it remains to be seen whether the political authority of the people can be restored.

Trump was not the first to argue against a narrative that was rooted in an abstract theoretical vision inspired by a future good. When Ludwig von Mises analyzed this phenomena in his book *Bureaucracy,* he attacked the various forms of Progressivism on the ground of their denigration of reason and common sense. He noted that "the champions of socialism call themselves progressives, but they recommend a system which is characterized by rigid observance of routine and a resistance to every kind of improvement. They call themselves liberals, but they are intent upon abolishing liberty.... They promise the blessings of the Garden of Eden, but they plan to transform the world into a gigantic post office. Every man but one a subordinate clerk in a bureau, what an alluring utopia! What a noble cause to fight for! Against all this frenzy of agitation there is but one weapon available: *reason.* Just *common sense* is needed to prevent man from falling prey to illusory fantasies and empty catchwords."[1] Where would common sense come from?

Since the end of the Cold War, American leaders have understood their offices in terms of global and administrative rule, rather than political rule on behalf of the American people and the sovereignty of the American nation. Yet those offices were established on the foundation of the moral authority of the people and their Constitution. Once elected or appointed, politicians and bureaucrats have utilized their will, in both domestic and foreign policy, in an unrestrained manner on behalf of bureaucratic rule and organized-interest privilege. They govern on the implicit premise of elections as plebiscites, but it is no longer clear who confers the legitimacy of an electoral mandate. Bureaucratic rule has become so pervasive that it has undermined the ability of the people to establish their consent as the ground of legitimate government. Rather it is the will of the various national—and often international—social, economic, political, and cultural interest groups that determine the outcome of elections.

Trump established his candidacy on the basis of an implicit understanding that America was the midst of a crisis. Those who opposed him denied the seriousness of the crisis and saw Trump himself as the greatest danger. And here again, Trump's success will likely be dependent upon his ability to articulate the ground of a common good that is still rooted in the past—a common good established by a government that protects the rights of its citizens in a constitutional manner and establishes limits on the authority of government by demanding that the rule of law replace that of political privilege and bureaucratic patronage.

Almost from the start, Donald Trump defined the political contours of the election. He did so by attempting to defy and delegitimize the Washington establishment and its moral defense of diversity and interest-group liberalism. In doing so, he challenged an orthodoxy that had been embraced by both political parties. That orthodoxy, defended as diversity, was made politically unassailable by imposing a monolithic political correctness as the only intellectual and moral standard of public discourse. And that moral and political standard was legitimized and reinforced by the authority of nearly all of the national political elites. It was made politically viable by dividing and appealing to the electorate as discrete groups understood in terms of economic and social interests. It was defined in terms of class, race, ethnicity, gender, and other measurable and controllable demographic categories. Diversity was to become the moral substitute for what had always established unity in any nation or polity: the necessity of pursuing a common good, or justice.

Trump attempted to sever the connection between the governing establishment and those electorally decisive minority groups. Those groups have consistently supported the Democratic Party. But they have served the interests of both parties within the Washington establishment for decades. They have provided both parties with reliable voters who have established the margins of victory in many of the most important states. Trump has insisted from the beginning that he wanted to unify America. Consequently, he made an appeal for the votes of the many minorities who had been long written off by the Republican Party. But he appealed to them as American citizens and offered to secure their rights as citizens, not as members of interest groups. Thus, he avoided, as much as possible, making his appeal to their political leaders and their organizations—those who claim to represent and attempt to speak for them but seem to benefit only themselves or their organized interests.

Of course, it is not easy to appeal to a common good when public discourse, and so much of the country, had come to be defined in terms of its diversity. When political identity is established on the ground of interests, whether economic, social, ethnic, gender, or religious group difference, it is nearly impossible to pursue a common good. Nor is it easy to distinguish residents and aliens, or citizens and noncitizens. In such a time, an appeal to American citizenship is itself almost a revolutionary act because it requires the ability to determine what is common among citizens, while at the same time making a distinction between citizens and all others.

In looking at the people as sovereign, and the country as requiring borders, he made the American nation and its people his primary concern. Along the same lines, Trump has appealed to the rule of law and has attacked bureaucratic rule as the rule of privilege and patronage on behalf of social, economic, foreign policy, and political interest groups. Nonetheless, this appeal on behalf of citizenship is made difficult by the fact that the administrative state has fragmented and isolated the people by undermining or destroying the institutions of civil society. Those institutions include the family, church, professional, and other private associations. In these terms, the success of Trump's campaign will depend upon the American people's ability to still recognize the existence of a common or public good.

The problem of revitalizing the political in an administrative state is extraordinarily difficult. At first glance, it would seem to be necessary to return to the political parties as the place to begin. But Trump appeared to have understood that the political parties no longer establish a meaningful link between the people and the government. Party patronage has been replaced by political and bureaucratic patronage, and a professional elite has established itself as the vital center between the people and the government. The authority of that elite cannot be understood simply in terms of social, economic, or even political power. What unites the vital center—what establishes their prominence and legitimizes their public authority—is knowledge. They understand the world through their attachment to their professions: academia, science, economics, business, media, entertainment, and even religion. They often lack political consciousness of themselves as a class. Many of them do not even think of themselves as political. Their interest and loyalty is to what they profess to study and what they think they know, and what establishes their intellectual and political authority is their production of what is seen as useful knowledge in the administrative state.

It is the technical requirements of the modern administrative state that have made it possible to politicize the elites in a manner that disguises their political role. When nearly every social, economic, scientific, religious, and political problem is decided in a bureaucratic or legal way—and always from a central authority; usually Washington, but sometimes New York or one or two other places—the professional elites are given a stake in the political and bureaucratic world. Trump has apparently refused to acknowledge the authority of this policymaking establishment and in doing so has perplexed nearly all of the public intellectuals, both liberal and conservative. In refusing to allow the established vital center to mediate the political debate, he has gone directly to the people. And so doing, he has made it nearly impossible for the vital center to condone or even attempt to understand, let alone praise, his candidacy.

It is not surprising that American elections have also been placed in the hands of the Washington professionals. Social scientists, media pundits, and policy professionals may tilt liberal or conservative and may differ in their party preferences, but they are united in their dependence upon intellectual authority, derived from empirical science and its methodology, in their understanding of politics and economics. Moreover, the latest progressive theories have established themselves as the closest thing to a public philosophy. And they are institutionalized, legitimized, and enforced by all of the powers of the bureaucratic state.

Progressive, or postmodern, critical theory had established personal autonomy and group diversity as central to what is now morally defensible in terms of public policy and private behavior. As a result, political partisanship and analysis has focused on race, class, gender, and other such demographics to provide the kind of information that has become central to the shaping and predicting of elections. Moreover, it has served to legitimize dividing the electorate into racial and demographic categories that have come to be understood in moral terms.

Consequently, political campaigns have made a science of dividing the electorate into groups and reassembling them as voting blocs committed to specific policies and issues denominated by the demographic categories themselves. This strategy requires the systematic mobilization of animosity to ensure participation by identifying and magnifying what it is that must be opposed. Appeals to the electorate are strategically controlled by the experts. The kinds of issues that are allowed to be raised are thought to be more important than the manner in which they are packaged and sold to the electorate. Understood in this way, what is central to politics and elections is the elevation of the status of personal and group identity to something approaching a new kind of civil religion.

Individual social behavior, once dependent on traditional morality and understood in terms of traditional virtues and vices, had become almost indefensible when judged in light of the authority established by social science and postmodernism. Public figures have come to be judged not as morally culpable individuals, but by the moral standing established by their political, or partisan, group identity. When coupled with the politicization of civil society and its institutions, the distinction between the public and the private, the personal and the political, has almost disappeared. The destruction of the moral authority of civil society institutions has marginalized the family and the church and has placed the public and private character of American culture in the hands of the intellectuals.

Many conservatives have rejected Trump on the ground that he is not a conservative. But what is conservatism? Is it merely a doctrine, or even a dogma, to be upheld intellectually, as the antidote to liberalism? Or is it the political defense of a certain way of life that derives much of its authority from the past? If conservatism means anything, it must require a defense of the good as established by a tradition that has preserved the best of the past. At its political peak, it came to be understood in terms of the traditional defense of civil and religious liberty. That is what the American Founders and Lincoln understood constitutionalism to be. Yet modern Progressivism is established upon a rejection of the good of the past. And it has established the intellectual and political ground of both liberalism and conservativism.

It is not surprising that many now wonder if they can conserve anything meaningful from the past, including constitutional government itself. They have experienced the wholesale destruction of the regime of civil and religious liberty; one that was built upon a moral tradition that was established in the course of a two-thousand-year-old civilization. It may still be possible to preserve a conservative doctrine, but it is not unreasonable to ask whether it is possible to live a traditional or conservative life. In reality, it is the traditional moral and political defense of civil and religious liberty that has been undermined by liberalism. American citizens, who want to live by the virtues established by that tradition, have no real public means of defending their way of life. The Washington elites have succeeded in transforming the moral foundations of contemporary political and social life behind the backs of the American people, and without their consent.

By mobilizing a constituency outside of and against the Washington establishment, Trump seized the opportunity to revitalize politics in a manner that may, at least potentially, make a revival of the political separation of powers possible. The administrative state had concentrated all economic, social, and political power in the central institutions of government. Trump sought to bypass the organized interests in order to make a direct political appeal to the electorate—one that would have been difficult for anyone from within the Washington policymaking establishment to make. Politicians have had to appeal indirectly to the organized interests, and to the centralized media, not to or on behalf of the political constituencies themselves. The representatives of organized and centralized interests, and the media, had become the mediators between government and the people—but the brusque Trump cut through that layer.

Because the political representatives have represented organized public and private interests *en masse*, it has been difficult to establish a governing coalition on behalf of a public interest. Modern professional elections have exacerbated the problem by dividing the electorate and appealing to discrete demographic groups. Nonetheless, the officeholders have alienated themselves from the political electorate. Under these circumstances, the Washington establishment itself became a political target. Only an outsider could have benefited from the hostility of the American electorate and their acute awareness that the federal government was no longer able to pursue, let alone establish, a political common good.

Trump was unable to unite his party after the nomination. And he was unable to do so after the election. Indeed, after nearly a year in office, his support within his own party remained lukewarm at best. That has made it difficult for Republican candidates to embrace Trump, thereby depriving them of the energy of potential Trump voters. And it has made it difficult to expand his own base. In addition, that lost year makes the midterm election more difficult than what is normally a difficult first appeal to the electorate after being elected. Will candidates embrace Trump? Will Trump campaign on behalf of those bold enough to support him? Must he recruit wholly new candidates in states that are sympathetic to Trump but have representatives who are not? Are there still forces in society and the electorate that remain hidden or unforeseen? If so, he has the opportunity to establish a new political landscape, one that is not yet recognizable. There is little question that the new partisanship he has brought to bear will be at odds with many of the organized interests in Washington. It goes without saying that those interests will defend themselves and their alliances with the old political elites, the organized interests, and the bureaucracy.

Nonetheless, Trump must establish a governing coalition, and this requires the cooperation of a legislature that has been the anchor of the administrative state. He does benefit from one major asset: the political electorate he has mobilized. He will likely enjoy greater flexibility in dealing with Congress if his policies begin to work and are recognized as beneficial. He cannot count on establishment generosity in terms of mobilizing public opinion on his behalf. That hostility will cease only if he succeeds politically. If that happens, he may well bargain with members of Congress in both parties, establishing a governing coalition on a new ground of partisanship not yet visible. The field is open for him to lay the groundwork for a political realignment, perhaps of a magnitude not seen since FDR. On the other hand, there is no guarantee that Donald Trump can or will prevail against the organized forces that inhabit the administrative state.

The great difficulty Trump faces is the lack of respectable intellectual defenders, those who help shape and inform public opinion. As a Republican, he could have expected support from leading conservative intellectuals. It has not been forthcoming. Before he was elected, many conservatives attacked Trump because he was not a conservative. Yet, after nearly a year in office, he seems to have done what conservatives have advocated for years. Despite this accomplishment, many conservative pundits have failed to acknowledge this success. It is as though the fake, unqualified Trump is still more real in the minds of those who oppose him than the real Trump and his actual accomplishments. If he is not judged by what he has done, it is almost impossible to assess factual reality as it relates to Trump. It is not surprising that those who see Trump in terms of his personality, rather than his politics, judge him personally and not politically. Even after a year in office, many of the opinion leaders, liberal and conservative, have denied the legitimacy of Trump's election despite the judgment of the electorate. Although they have not sought to undermine the election by turning from ballots to bullets, they have substituted words, or volatile rhetoric, as a means to accomplish that task.

Trump may or may not succeed in transforming the landscape of American politics in a manner that makes it possible to reestablish political rule once again. All of those who have a stake in preserving Washington as it now exists are his enemies. The public that is drawn to him is almost wholly unorganized. The ability of the established order to manipulate and control public opinion rests on the authority and respectability of the social, economic, and political elites, nearly all of whom oppose Trump. Trump has built his constituency in opposition to those elites who have denied his legitimacy as president. He has denied that the press and media, which establishes the medium that links the government to its people, fairly and accurately portrays the reality of Washington to those outside of it. He is the first president to vigorously contest the motives and the objectivity of the press, even in terms of presenting simple factual information without bias. He decries fake news and creates his own method of communicating with his constituency.

His success thus far has revealed the need to restore the political rule of the people as a whole. To do so, American public opinion must be reflected in the creation and mobilization of national political majorities. Constitutional government is not possible in the absence of the mobilization of such majorities. They are indispensable for establishing the legitimacy of law in a manner compatible with the rule of law and the common good. That requires revitalizing the meaning of citizenship and reaffirming the sovereignty of the people and the nation. It also requires restoring the link between the people and the political branches of the government, so that both can become the defenders of the Constitution as well as the country that has made it essential to its political existence.

Trump assumed the presidency directly after Barack Obama had succeeded in strengthening the power and reach of the administrative state. Trump questioned not only the legacy of Obama, but the whole of the Washington establishment that had arisen since the end of the Cold War. It seems that at every important juncture in the growth of the modern state, there have been those who have questioned the expansion of the powers of the administrative or regulatory state. In those perilous days of the 1930s, when contending ideologies "were fighting for the mastery of the modern world," Walter Lippmann, in *The Good Society*, expressed his fear of the growing concentration of power in government.

He focused his criticism on those Progressive intellectuals who had developed great contempt for the achievements of the past. In that time, he noted, "Most men had forgotten the labors that had made them prosperous, the struggles that had made them free, the victories that had given them peace. They took for granted, like the oxygen they breathed and the solid ground beneath their feet, the first and last things of Western civilization."[2] In the aftermath of the Cold War, the victorious nations of the West seemed also to have forgotten the struggles of the past. They embarked upon a new, wholly self-created world oblivious of history and political reality itself.

That intellectual turmoil, Lippmann thought, "reflected the fact that in the modern world there is a great schism: those who seek to improve the lot of mankind believe they must undo the work of their predecessors. Everywhere the movements which bid for men's allegiance are hostile to the movements in which men struggled to be free."[3] In such circumstances, the practice of politics soon succumbed to the delusions of the intellectuals. In Lippmann's words, "With man degraded to a bundle of conditioned reflexes, there was no measure of anything in human affairs: all the landmarks of judgment were gone and there remained only an aimless and turbulent moral relativity.... All the diverse prophets who knew the noble plan of realized reason in world history developed a magnificent contempt for any idea which, because it respected the inviolability of the individual, might justify resistance to these missions."[4] All that remains is the triumph of will.

Amid the moral confusion and intellectual chaos of that day, all that remained was contempt for "the inviolability of the individual." Lippmann insisted that "these are the choices offered by the influential doctrines of the contemporary world. Those who would be loyal to the achievements of the past are in general disposed to be fatally complacent about the present, and those who have plans for the future are prepared to disown the heroic past."[5] He was aware that the defense of freedom was indistinguishable from the defense of constitutionalism, which required the protection of individual rights and the rule of law. In the end, Lippmann understood the fateful choice of Western man in the following way: "But still the question remained as to where, at what final rampart, a man must stand when he fights for human freedom. I could see that in the polity of a free society the regulation of human affairs was achieved by the definition and the adjudication of personal rights and duties, whereas in all unfree societies it was done by administration from above."[6] Is it possible to retain individual freedom in the absence of political, or constitutional, rule?

If the people are to understand themselves as sovereign, they must reestablish the political authority of the Constitution in a manner that makes it possible to restore the moral ground of civil and religious liberty. A government that does not recognize the sovereignty of the people cannot defend the rights of individuals in a constitutional manner. A constitution is a compact of the people, and the government is created on its behalf. The people grant it power, but only the constitution can establish limits on the power of government. In the modern administrative state, the power of government is unlimited, and the rights of citizens, and the rule of law itself, rests on a precarious ground. For if the government alone creates and confers rights, the Constitution can no longer limit the power of government, nor can it protect the civil and religious liberty of its citizens. It is still possible to reestablish limits on government, but only by restoring the political conditions of constitutionalism.

Replies to Symposium Participants, "Abandoning the Constitution"

I ATTEMPTED TO SHOW that Progressivism as an intellectual movement had triumphed even before the beginning of the twentieth century.
It dominated political thought and established the ground of all partisanship by the election of 1912. Theodore Roosevelt, Woodrow Wilson,
and Eugene Debs were not the only ones who described themselves as
Progressives; even William Howard Taft called himself a progressive
conservative. In my attempt to elucidate the difference between constitutionalism and the administrative state, I tried to make clear that it is the
theoretical character of the American Founding that no longer resonates
and has been replaced by another theoretical perspective.

I chose Thomas Paine as the best representative of the earlier view
because he was the most influential theoretical politician of the revolutionary era. And Washington, Jefferson, and nearly all of the American
Founders subscribed to Paine's principles, derived from theoretical reason. Agreement on theoretical principles, however, does not preclude
disagreement on prudential grounds, or concerning politics, which is
derived from practical reason and rests upon opinion. Surely, Paine's
political opinions, as opposed to his principles, were not so widely shared
when the political science of the Constitution came to be understood
by the Federalists as "inventions of prudence." The *theoretical* character

of the American Founding was dependent upon both theoretical and practical reason, not to mention nature or natural right. When theoretical reason resonated, it was possible to distinguish principles from political practice, which rested upon opinion. It was possible, therefore, to distinguish a constitution from government. Subsequently, historians, oblivious to the principled agreement derived from metaphysical reason, could see only political disagreement among the Founders and came to conclude that it lacked any theoretical coherence, or unity of purpose. In denying the authority of nature as well as theoretical and practical reason, Progressive thought was constructed upon an understanding of freedom, or will; human action establishes the ground of morality and becomes the animating force of historical progress. Consequently, there is no further need to distinguish theoretical reason (principles derived from nature) from practical reason, or prudence (application of those principles in concrete circumstances). The moral will is derived from practical reason, making prudence superfluous. Thus, the problem of politics becomes one of establishing scientific or technical rationality (eventually, it became social science), which would practically and efficiently ensure that the will is made actual. That historical transformation requires moral leadership, or vision, as they now say. As with Paine, in terms of theory, I looked to the single most successful progressive practitioner, or politician, of our time. As important as Theodore Roosevelt was in the early century, I focused on Franklin Roosevelt because he was the one who transformed what had been primarily a powerful intellectual movement, Progressivism, into the most successful political movement of the twentieth century: *liberalism.*

Yarborough gently reminds me that not all the blame for the ills of Progressivism can be laid at the feet of Hegel. I agree. She suggests that Tocqueville foresaw some of those problems in the "tendency of democratic societies to love *equality* more than *liberty.*" Tocqueville was persuaded that the passion for equality of conditions arises from the acceptance of the general idea of equality, which derives from Christianity. The demand for equality requires ever-greater uniformity, rationality, and centralization of administration. In his view, equality then becomes the closest thing to a principle of democracy. Thus, he insists that all democratic regimes are characterized by a commitment to equality, and all modern regimes will become democratic.

The problem that concerned Tocqueville was the status of liberty in democratic societies.

Tocqueville's Limitations

I...am a great admirer of Tocqueville's analysis of centralized administration as the "kind of despotism democratic nations have to fear." Yet, I did not think he was helpful in establishing the theoretical character of a constitutional regime based upon principles of natural right. Nor, do I think that Hegel was any less concerned with liberty than Tocqueville. And, although Hegel understood equality in terms of citizenship in the *state* and Tocqueville in terms of democratic *society*, both understood theory from a perspective of History, not nature. Tocqueville accepted the practical implications of what Hegel had made explicit theoretically; that the historical process is purposeful without regard for human choice. If providence had mandated the triumph of democracy and equality, the defense of freedom rested upon the preservation of those pre-democratic institutions (aristocratic traditions, religion, free townships) where "communal liberty" existed before democratic equality was established.

Tocqueville's new political science, therefore, was an attempt to fathom a new world made intelligible by History, not nature. Consequently, his view of equality comes to be understood in historical terms, as a general idea that shapes, and is shaped, in democratic society. If the democratization of society leads inevitably to equality of conditions or administrative centralization, no natural beneficial order of human society, which must be made intelligible through the use of human reason, is attainable. Rather, democracy and equality of conditions leads inevitably to despotism. In Tocqueville's view, equality was not to be understood in terms of reason or metaphysics, nor is it derived from philosophical principles established on the grounds of nature, or natural right. Not surprisingly, Tocqueville did not attempt to defend the American Founders' understanding of the principle of equality, because he did he not think that equality could serve as the grounds of political right or justice. For Tocqueville, the closest thing to a universal principle of political right is not equality, but liberty. Equality was fated; the problem that concerned him was the fate of human freedom in democratic times, something which was still within human control. The problem of democratic despotism arises because of an inability to harmonize equality and liberty once society is democratized. Although equality is compatible with freedom or despotism, it moves almost inexorably toward democratic despotism. Freedom, therefore, must be preserved against the growing demands for greater equality, which originate in democratic society.

Unlike Tocqueville, the American Founders had argued that equality and liberty were not only compatible but necessary concomitants. Neither was fated, but both were understood to be objects of political choice derived from reflection. Both could be lost if not properly understood and nurtured. A proper understanding of the equality and liberty is akin to a proper understanding of theory and practice. They are opposite sides of the same coin. The political problem requires a reconciliation of theoretical and practical reason, of principle and prudence, of constitutionalism and government. In the Founders' view, both equality and liberty were wholly necessary and only compatible when established within a constitutional or political regime in which a limited government and an autonomous civil society serve to protect individual natural rights. When constitutionalism was undermined and came to be understood in terms of the administrative state, the meaning of equality and liberty was transformed by political necessity. Equality was no longer understood in terms of a defense of individual natural rights, nor was liberty understood in terms of preserving the autonomy of civil society. Rather, equal citizenship required that government becomes the arbiter of all political rights, based upon the unity of the state itself. Indeed, the state was meant to transcend the distinction between government and civil society, church and state, and the individual and the social or communal. In John Dewey's view, progressive liberalism was meant to replace the Founders', or John Locke's, liberalism.

Group Rights versus Individual Rights

It is not surprising that the Progressives like John Dewey and Mary Parker Follett came to understand political freedom in terms of social, or group, rights and individual freedom not in terms of self-government but of self-expression, or creative self-discovery. When government established the grounds of right in the state, freedom comes to be understood in terms of equality of rights, or equal citizenship. Individual rights and civil society become unintelligible theoretically, and eventually politically as well. Is it possible then to understand equality and liberty as having both a theoretical unity and a practical separation, as it was understood by the Founders? Furthermore, are not the various twentieth-century social and cultural movements (what came to be called identity politics, whether of blacks, women, ethnic, religious, minorities, gays, etc.) made on behalf of liberation, or evolving consciousness of freedom? And, always, it seems that these demands for equality have been made on behalf of liberty. I don't doubt that the Progressive intellectuals, like the theorists who inspired them (including Rousseau, Kant, Hegel, and Marx), loved liberty as much as equality. It was the meaning of equality and liberty that had changed. Tocqueville was right about the meaning of equality as it came to be understood historically. At the same time, he refused to understand liberty in the way it came to be understood in the Hegelian conception of freedom as equal citizenship within the state.

Finally, I can only agree with Brad Watson that "our problem runs even deeper than Marini shows." Watson points to a crisis of historicism itself that was revealed most clearly by Nietzsche. To achieve some clarity on that subject would require what Nietzsche described as a kind of knowledge about man derived from physio-psychology. I did not want to descend to those kinds of subjective depths. I preferred to remain on the surface. Consequently, I tried to give a political and theoretical account of the transformation of the American regime. And perhaps I succeeded somewhat. Professor Watson himself concluded that my analysis offered, in his words, "concrete grounds for hope." In political philosophy, as well as reasonable religious belief, there is always ground for hope. That is because the desire for justice and happiness, or salvation, offers human possibilities that force individuals to look outside of their subjective world. The optimistic Progressives had hoped that politics and religion could be replaced by a free, or uncoerced, rational or scientific democratic society. That hope came to be viewed as more akin to a dream, rather than as an objective analysis. The pessimism of twentieth-century liberalism grows out of a loss of confidence in the rationality of the historical process and science itself. In denying any objective or meaningful reality, it has revealed itself as a kind of nihilism. It is for this reason that I wanted to remain on the level of a theoretical and political, or commonsense, analysis of our problem.

The Political Conditions of Legislative-Bureaucratic Supremacy

IT WOULD BE A MISTAKE for American conservatives to rely heavily on the performance of judges—or the judiciary—to achieve victory in the policy arena. The contemporary role of the Supreme Court becomes intelligible only upon recognition of the fact that the judiciary has become an indispensable tool in the growth and legitimation of the administrative state. However, the administrative state was a creature of the Democratic Party. Its evolution required an activist judiciary in alliance with a liberal and apparently passive legislative body. It was the wholesale delegation of authority to the bureaucracy by its architect, the congressional majority, which in effect forced the judiciary to enter the policymaking arena. (Of course, judges have not been immune to the temptation of reveling in their newly gained power and defending it as heaven-sent.) It will be much more difficult for Republicans to utilize the least democratic branch for its political purposes precisely for this reason: the policymaking power of the courts is predicated on the assumption that the judiciary will serve as the linchpin of the bureaucratic state. Proponents of this state recognize no principled limitation upon the power of government; in practice, they insist upon limiting the power of the majority—now especially with the national majority represented by the president—while at the same time denying any limitation upon the power of the unelected minority institution, the judiciary. But constitutional government presupposes a limitation upon the power of government in all its parts.

The constitutional separation of powers reflects the primary necessity of preventing the legislative branch from undermining the Constitution, due to its supremacy as the ongoing lawmaking body. Judicial review of legislation inhibits that supremacy and thus ensures the supremacy of the constitutional order, assuming that the court will defend the Constitution in its judicial role. What we have seen in recent years, however, is the participation of the two political branches in enlarging the court's role. They have deferred to the judiciary in nearly all matters, political as well as judicial, and have failed to insist that it limit its power to its constitutional role of judging as opposed to making law. Thereby the court has been allowed to undermine not only the separation of powers, but the Constitution itself, by judicial interpretation. Judicial review has given way to judicial supremacy.

This change is widely remarked upon, not so the specific and revolutionary purpose for which it was accomplished. In recent years, the Democratic Party in Congress has utilized the judiciary to overcome the limitations placed upon the power of all government. For by aggrandizing the judiciary while at the same time ignoring its constitutional role, the legislative branch gained legitimacy for the bureaucratic state. The court, freed from constitutional restraints, legitimized the prevailing legislative–bureaucratic relationship, which liberated Congress from the necessity of making general laws. And as Congress's function of overseeing the bureaus eclipsed that of deliberating and making laws, its power moved from the body as a whole to committees, subcommittees, and the offices and staffs of individual members who control them.

The situation today is this: Congress controls the administrative details of politics through the bureaucracy it created, and the judiciary reigns supreme in the realm of politics or regarding general policy matters. In terms of constitutional government, this arrangement has prevented the true sovereign—the American people—from exercising its decisive political role.

The greatest practical task faced by contemporary conservatism, therefore, is to sever the link between the judiciary and the administrative state. But this should not—nor can it—be done by means of the judiciary. A results-oriented court, whether it favors liberal or conservative results, represents, at the most fundamental level, a denial of the consent of the governed. The conservative agenda then requires a return to a proper working of the constitutional separation of powers. And, judges themselves are unlikely to relinquish power under prevailing conditions; indeed, it may be nearly impossible for them to do so. Any fundamental change must be made rather in the political branches of government.

In the latter regard, it is important to realize that Democrats are not responsible for the contemporary court majority. Republican presidents have appointed seven of the last nine justices who have served most recently on the Supreme Court. Those justices have responded to the political environment of the administrative state—a product forged by the Democratic majority in the 1964 election—and no subsequent Republican president has been able to resist the most powerful trends of subsequent Democratic majorities in Congress. Thus, the most important fact of recent American politics is that the Democrats have controlled the legislative branch for nearly all of the past six decades. While it is true that they have been unable to dominate presidential politics for much of the same period, presidential leadership is not required for the successful operation of the administrative state as outlined above. In fact, strong presidential leadership becomes a positive annoyance to that operation.

Democrats have maintained firm control of the House of Representatives since the 1950s, and in 1986 their brief tenure as a minority in the Senate became an aberrant historical footnote. Most importantly, the Democrats in Congress have been able to control the domestic policy agenda by strategic control of the bureaucracy and skillful manipulation of the judiciary. The reason the latter is so crucial has been the failure of the political branches of government and of the political parties to create a partisan consensus on issues of great political or moral significance. The court has stepped in to settle those divisive issues—to the satisfaction of very few, one might add. Thus, from the perspective of congressional Democrats, control of an ideological Supreme Court majority has precluded the necessity of having to win the presidency in order to shape policy on even the most controversial issues. A change in the court majority of the sort Reagan conservatives desire, however, will not result in a similar kind of conservative alliance with the court. At best, a court majority animated by a philosophy of judicial restraint could do no more than prevent the expansion of the administrative state; it would likely only be able to maintain the status quo. For the Republicans, ultimately, the battle for the future will be the battle to shape public opinion, and victory will hinge upon their ability to ratify such public opinion as they have shaped in partisan political elections. This victory would and could only be legitimized by a democratic majority animated by a consensus on fundamental principles.

The massive mobilization of organized groups against the Bork confirmation made clear that what conservatives are up against today is the most widely accepted public philosophy among American elites: interest-group liberalism, or pluralism. At issue was the question of whether the rights of Americans ought to be protected as members of the various groups or classes that make up the nation or whether rights adhere to individuals and ought to be protected as such by the courts. At a more fundamental level, this involves the necessity of determining whether rights are derived from historical circumstances or whether they exist by nature. At stake is the question of who will determine, in an authoritative way, the meaning, or the philosophy, of the Constitution.

Those opposed to Robert Bork were animated by a philosophy of History and an evolutionary theory of law. In their view, the Constitution is a "living document" that must incorporate the changing ideas and mores of each generation. In practice, this means that contemporary elites—or leading intellectuals—will determine the meaning of the Constitution, because they will articulate the leading ideas—or ideology—of each period. The contemporary ideology most acceptable to our elites today, however, rests upon a radical interpretation of the meaning of equality. Indeed, the understanding of equality that animates leading contemporary intellectuals is not different from that of the "economists" described by Tocqueville in the Old Regime and the French Revolution. Tocqueville noted of these eighteenth-century intellectuals that their writings had the democratic-revolutionary tenor characteristic of so much modern thought, for they attacked not only specific forms of privilege but any kind of diversity whatsoever. To their thinking, all men should be equal even if equality spelled servitude, and every obstacle to the achievement of this end should be done away with immediately. For contractual engagements, they had no respect and no concern for private rights.

Similarly, in the view of contemporary intellectuals, it has become necessary to abandon the principle of political equality, not to mention individual liberty, in order to achieve what is for them the only legitimate equality—social and economic equality, equality of outcome or what might be called communal equality.

Originally, the American regime was committed to the protection of the equal political rights of all individuals, based on the assumption that all men were created equal. As a consequence, government encouraged the greatest possible political, economic, and religious liberty as well as social diversity. Although government was supposed to protect rights, it was not to take sides regarding interests, whether of individuals or of groups within society. The significant exception to this rule, one which has plagued America throughout its history, was the protection of the slaveholders' property interest in fellow human beings. And, it is as a consequence of the fact that this was incompatible with the principle of human equality—and with those principles of constitutional government that flow from it—that the Constitution cannot be defended in terms of its language alone or as simply a legal document. Rather, such a defense must be grounded in the principles underlying constitutionalism itself, which are the essential objects of the enmity revealed by those who attacked Mr. Bork.

Liberal governments, in their origins, were characterized by a fundamental distinction between the state and society, or the public and the private sphere. Because the state, or government, rests on the necessity of using force and society on voluntary actions or private contracts, the sphere of government or state activity was limited. However, this protection of the private sphere necessarily led to economic and social heterogeneity in society. Therefore, those who have come to posit communal equality as the only legitimate form have had to undermine the distinction between the public and the private theoretically and to place their confidence in the state as it operates through the bureaucracy and the courts practically. Subsequently, it came to be believed that all rights are a product of government or the courts. Even the right of privacy, which was originally thought to be secured by limiting the power of government in the private sphere, is now said to exist only when it is enforced by government. What this means as a practical matter is that government's powers must be essentially unlimited in the private as well as the public sphere. Moreover, "communalists" hold that it must use its powers to benefit those social groups or individuals who are most disadvantaged.

These groups must be given special status within the law and protected by the public bureaucracies in order to remedy advantages achieved by others, politically or naturally. In short, only a bureaucratic state can ensure the achievement of equality as they define it.

Ronald Dworkin has designated homosexuals, along with any group or "lifestyle" that suffers opprobrium at the hands of society or of a majority, a "moral minority" and, as such, entitled to the greatest protection by government and the courts. In opposing Bork, he cited "the idea of constitutional integrity—that the freedom and dignity recognized for one set of Americans, in one set of decisions, must be available to all other groups with equal moral claim." He would not suggest, however, that all groups have "equal moral claims." It is unlikely, for instance, that the Ku Klux Klan is of equal moral worth in his eyes with homosexuals, AIDS victims, or the homeless. But there is no nonarbitrary way to determine the moral worth of groups. It is wholly dependent upon their status within the ideology of the most authoritative elites. There is no reason, in principle, why the most powerful groups, as opposed to the most oppressed, ought not rule in their own interest if they can claim historical or scientific legitimacy. In principle, then, the Dworkin view is not unlike that which animated Nazi Germany or which animates communist regimes today.

When the rights of individuals are not understood as rooted in nature, it is merely the arbitrary will of the most powerful group, ideologically or politically, that determines the rights or moral worth of groups in society. And, by extension, the rights of individuals are only as secure as the status of the group to which they belong. This case demands the attention of the American people. But, while Bork and most of his supporters rallied around the banner of the original intention of the Constitution, their defense of that intention was sapped of its rhetorical and political force because it was merely a defense of the Constitution's language, not its principles.

Bork has stated: "The effort to create individual rights out of a general, abstract, moral philosophy is doomed to failure from the beginning, because I don't think there is any version of moral philosophy that can claim to be absolutely superior to all others." But the framers believed, without a doubt, that the principles of civil and religious liberty, derived from the equality of all men, comprised a moral philosophy that was so superior. Moreover, they thought their arguments for the superiority of constitutionalism, or moderate and limited government, over arguments for government based on force, superstition, religious belief, or the arbitrary will of any individual or group or class of men could be justified in terms of nature and reason and were not dependent upon mere preferences.

By interpreting and explicating an understanding of the Constitution as essentially "positive law," Bork was unable to make a principled defense of the constitutional order—against those who oppose him only because they oppose it—as fundamentally just. Furthermore, he undermined the most powerful argument in defense of individual rights: the view that those rights depend upon no government, nor upon positive law, for their legitimacy, because they are rooted in the laws of nature. The question then arises: In the absence of reasonable argument, or of any claim to justice, why ought it be preferable for the American people to be ruled by a founding elite, or even a founding majority, rather than a contemporary elite or a contemporary majority?

Bork's supporters defended him as an advocate of judicial restraint; and as a policy matter, Bork is surely right in his opinion that the Founders intended for the majority to prevail in policy matters. Practically speaking, this means that the legislative branch rather than judges ought to be predominant in the political arena. When it comes to rights, however, as opposed to policy, the Constitution itself is a denial of the view that the legitimacy of law derives from the fact that it reflects the majority's will. The whole constitutional order, with its separation of powers, is an attempt to prevent domination by the unreasonable will of the legislature as well as of the majority itself. Jefferson made clear what this meant in his first inaugural: "All, too, will bear in mind this sacred principle, that though the will of the majority is in all cases to prevail, that will to be rightful must be reasonable; that the minority possess their equal rights, which equal law must protect, and to violate would be oppression."

Bork's critics understood that the majority is not always mindful of the rights of individuals or minorities, and they look to the judiciary to protect the interests of groups, including minorities. Bork should have insisted that courts must protect the rights, not the interests, of minorities and individuals; that it is only because the court is impartial as it regards interests that an enlightened people are willing to entrust their rights to an independent, unelected judiciary.

Bork needlessly allowed his critics the moral high ground and, on top of that, failed to show that their notion of right or justice is little more than the prevailing ideology of contemporary elites. But, his failure provides a lesson that modern American conservatism itself, and not just Mr. Bork, must draw upon in the future: One need not deny the existence of justice, moral principles, and natural rights merely because one's opponents cloak misguided arguments in terms of justice, morality, and minority rights. Indeed, doing so is a sure ticket to defeat in our nation. Rather, it is necessary to show that such arguments as were leveled against Bork—arguments of which we have not heard the last by any means—have no basis in reason or nature and thus no legitimate claim to being just; they are rooted in passion—or compassion—and will, rather than reason, and therefore lack the essential element of constitutionalism as our Founders understood and defended it.

The Reagan administration has not tried to hide the fact that it had hoped to leave its longest-lasting legacy through the process of judicial appointments. This is little more than a tacit admission that it has been unable to change the political landscape through the electoral process. Its failure to do so—and its failure in a sense even to attempt to do so, which has given some the impression that the Republican Party has grown accustomed to, if not fond of, its minority status—has in turn proved extremely costly in the waning years of the Reagan presidency. The president's inability to get confirmation of his leading nominees to the Supreme Court is but one case in point.

In terms of ensuring an enduring legacy, Reagan would have done better to follow the example of Franklin Roosevelt, who, following the election of 1932, created an electoral coalition that proved to be irresistible. A recalcitrant court bucked the Roosevelt tide for a short time after his extremely partisan reelection in 1936. But this presented only a temporary obstacle to the long-term goals of the Roosevelt administration, which set the agenda of American politics for the next half century. Moreover, every Republican president since has had to contend with that legacy in the form of Democratic Congresses and particularly Democratic Houses of Representatives. Viewed in this light, Reagan's electoral victory in 1980 was but half a victory and short-lived to boot. Reagan was able to help Republicans gain control of the Senate but failed to dislodge the Democrats in the House. And, after the 1982 midterm election—and to a considerable degree even before it—he and his administration backed away from the partisanship, not to mention the animating principles, which had led to 1980s success.

Reagan strategists ran the 1984 election as a rerun of 1972. The goal was to win a huge electoral victory for the incumbent in the White House at the expense of a partisan battle designed to continue the electoral realignment barely begun in 1980. Such an election would have resulted in a necessary polarization of the country, much in the way FDR divided the electorate in 1936. In that election, Roosevelt went so far as to brand the opponents of the Democratic Party as enemies of democracy and of the people themselves. He wanted his party to win all branches of government at every level, and he wanted the great majority of voters to abandon their allegiance to the opposition party.

In 1984, however, the Reagan campaign invited Democrats to remain Democrats while asking them to join in voting for the president. Unlike the partisan appeal of FDR, Reagan did not ask voters to join his party because it had the best principles, or insist that voters abandon their allegiance to the disloyal opposition. Thus, the electoral debacle of 1986 should have surprised no one; likewise, the Iran-Contra controversy, and all that it entails, and the fate of the Bork nomination.

There is an aura of tragedy about contemporary American politics. The Democratic Party can no longer openly win a national majority in order to legitimately pursue its policies in the partisan political arena. Rather, it has succeeded in nationalizing what are essentially local concerns, creating in the process a massive executive apparatus to administer those concerns. As a consequence, the interests of the legislature and those of the executive have diverged, regardless of party. Presidents are elected and are expected to govern on the basis of an appeal to general or national issues. Members of Congress are elected on their perceived capacity to satisfy local and particular interests. Furthermore, incumbents of either party in the legislature are able to win reelection by appealing to local or organized constituencies on particular issues, now administered at the national level. At the same time, members have become skilled at obscuring controversial or partisan stands, which are of a general character and of national importance (e.g., their stands on

Central American communism). As a result, Congress has the ability to prevent the president from governing on the basis of an appeal to general or national issues. Thus, the national majority has been rendered politically impotent, and the court has stepped in to fill the vacuum with the blessing of Congress. Recent Republican presidents have been successful only when they have been able to mobilize national sentiment sufficiently to force members of Congress to refrain from bucking the will of the national majority. Only in this circumstance is it politically difficult for members of Congress to ignore the president in order to satisfy organized or local constituencies. But, of course, it is difficult to mobilize national sentiment, and it can be done only on a few occasions involving select issues. Ordinarily, the organized interests and the issue networks, in alliance with the bureaucracy, the legislature, and the courts, dominate in the normal affairs of government.

It is clear, after several decades of experience, that control of the presidency has not resulted in the conservative transformation of American politics. Nor will such a change occur through the judiciary. In the final analysis, it requires the transformation of the legislature. There is little doubt, however, that the presidential office remains the critical catalyst that can create the kind of partisan consensus—animated by the original principles of the Republican Party and of America—that is necessary to bring about such an electoral realignment and to save the Constitution.

Notes

PART 1: THE TRIUMPH OF THE ADMINISTRATIVE STATE OVER THE CONSTITUTION

1　John Marini, *The Politics of Budget Control: Congress, the Presidency, and the Growth of the Administrative State* (New York: Taylor & Francis, 1992).

2　Gordon S. Jones and John A. Marini, eds., *The Imperial Congress: Crisis in the Separation of Powers* (New York: Pharos Books, 1988).

3　John Marini and Ken Masugi, eds., *The Progressive Revolution in Politics and Political Science: Transforming the American Regime* (Lanham, MD: Rowman & Littlefield, 2005).

4　John Marini, "Trump and Conservatism" (lecture, Hillsdale College Kirby Center Constitution Day Celebration, Washington, DC, September 16, 2016). https://www.youtube.com/watch?v=M3maovSNm8M.

CHAPTER 1: HUNTING THE ADMINISTRATIVE STATE

1　Alexis de Tocqueville, *Democracy in America*, ed. and trans. Harvey Mansfield and Delba Winthrop (Chicago: University of Chicago Press, 2000), 664–65.

2　Leo Strauss, *On Tyranny*, ed. Victor Gourevitch and Michael S. Roth, corrected and expanded edition (Chicago: University of Chicago Press, 2013), 27.

3　Ibid., 194–95.

4　Leo Strauss, *Natural Right and History* (Chicago, University of Chicago Press, 1953), 314.

5　G. W. F. Hegel, *Philosophy of Right,* trans. T. M. Knox (London: Oxford University Press, 1977), 10.

6　G. W. F. Hegel, *Lectures on Natural Right and Political Science*, trans. J. Michael Stewart and Peter C. Hodgson (Berkeley: University of California Press, 1995), 242. See also Hegel, *Philosophy of Right*, 170–73, infra.

7　Leo Strauss, *Liberalism Ancient and Modern* (New York: Basic Books, 1968), 24.

8　George Washington, "Circular to the States" (1783), in *George Washington: A Collection*, ed. W. B. Allen (Indianapolis: Liberty Fund), 240–41.

CHAPTER 2: OUR ABANDONED CONSTITUTION

1　This article originally appeared as "Abandoning the Constitution," *Claremont Review of Books* XII:2, Spring 2012. https://www.claremont.org/crb/article/abandoning-the-constitution/. Marini responded to commentators in "On Further Review," December 12, 2012, http://www.claremont.org/crb/basicpage/42/. *See Appendix I.*

2 Thomas Paine, "Rights of Man" in *The Political Works of Thomas Paine in Two Volumes*, vol. 1, ed. Richard Carlile (London: W. T. Sherwin, 1817), 29.

3 Ibid.

4 Ibid.

5 Thomas Paine, "Rights of Man" in *The Political Works of Thomas Paine in Two Volumes*, vol. 1, ed. Richard Carlile (London: W. T. Sherwin, 1817), 29–30.

6 Franklin D. Roosevelt, *The Public Papers and Addresses of Franklin D. Roosevelt*, vol. 1 (New York: Random House, 1938).

7 US Declaration of Independence, 1776.

8 Ibid.

9 Franklin D. Roosevelt, *Public Papers*.

10 Mary Parker Follet, *The New State: Group Organization the Solution of Popular Government* (Mansfield Ctr., CT: Martino Publishing, 2016; originally published Longmans, 1916), 137–38.

11 John Dewey, "Liberalism and Social Action," in *The Later Works*, vol. 11, ed. Jo Ann Boydston (Carbondale: University of Southern Illinois Press, 1987), 25–26.

12 Ibid., 48.

13 Roscoe Pound, *Introduction to the Philosophy of Law* (New Jersey: Lawbook Exchange, Ltd., 2003; originally published New Haven: Yale University Press, 1922), 84–85.

14 Harry V. Jaffa, "Judicial Conscience and Natural Rights," in *Original Intent and the Framers of the Constitution: A Disputed Question* (Washington, DC: Regnery Gateway, 1994), 238–39.

15 Roscoe Pound, "Justice According to Law," *Midwest Quarterly* 1 (1959): 226.

16 Roscoe Pound, "Juristic Problems of National Progress," *American Journal of Sociology* 22, no. 6 (May 1917): 721–33, https://www.jstor.org/stable/2764004.

17 Roscoe Pound, "Justice According to Law," *Midwest Quarterly* 1 (1959): 226.

18 Samuel P. Huntington, "Congressional Responses to the Twentieth Century," in David B. Truman, ed. *The Congress and America's Future* (Englewood Cliffs, NJ: Prentice-Hall, 1965), 6.

19 James L. Sundquist, *The Decline and Resurgence of Congress* (Washington, DC: The Brookings Institution, 1981), 411.

20 Charles R. Kesler, "The Tea Party Spirit," *Claremont Review of Books* 10, no. 1 (Winter 2009/10). http://www.claremont.org/crb/article/the-tea-party-spirit/.

21 Ibid.

22 Ibid.

23 John Marini, *The Politics of Budget Control: Congress, the Presidency, and the Growth of the Administrative State* (New York: Taylor & Francis, 1992), xiii.

CHAPTER 3: DONALD TRUMP AND THE AMERICAN CRISIS

1 This article appeared online in *CRB Digital*, July 22, 2016, https://www.claremont.org/crb/basicpage/donald-trump-and-the-american-crisis/.

2 Friedrich Nietzsche, *On the Advantage and Disadvantage of History for Life*, trans. Peter Preuss (Indianapolis: Hackett Publishing Company, 1980), 62.

CHAPTER 4: CONGRESS: RELUCTANT DEFENDER OF THE ADMINISTRATIVE STATE

1 This chapter was first presented as a paper at the Annual Meeting of the American Political Science Association, 2016, Philadelphia, Pennsylvania.

2 I have provided examples of Congress adapting itself to the requirements of

the administrative state from Samuel Huntington and James Sundquist in an earlier chapter, "Our Abandoned Constitution."

CHAPTER 5: STATE OR CONSTITUTION? THE POLITICAL CONDITIONS OF BUREAUCRATIC RULE: THE EXECUTIVE, CONGRESS, AND THE COURTS UNDER THE ADMINISTRATIVE STATE

1 The theoretical origins of the administrative state rest upon the Hegelian assumption of the rationality of the historical process. This philosophy of History established the intellectual and political foundations of *Progressivism*. The Progressives sought to achieve a complete break with the American Founding that resulted in a rejection of constitutionalism. It was animated by the necessity of transcending nature and entailed a rejection of philosophic reason as the ground of human understanding. The rational state itself, the culmination of the historical process, would become the vehicle for the *administration of progress*. Hegel had insisted that "the science of the state is to be nothing other than the endeavor to apprehend and portray the state as something inherently rational." Within the state, the rational would be made real. The Progressives accepted the Hegelian assumption that "the general dividing line between constitutions is between those that are based on nature and those based on freedom of the will." It is in the exercise of freedom, or will, that man establishes his morality, indeed his humanity. There can be no higher moral authority than that derived from will, or freedom. Nature, or reason, no longer imposes limits on human choice. Consequently, the modern state was meant to create the rational structures capable of generating the technical means of carrying out *will* by making it real, or practicable. It required unlimited power in the government of the *state* and was meant to replace limited government, or constitutionalism.

2 What is at stake in this quarrel becomes clear in light of the disagreement concerning a comprehensive understanding of the meaning of justice. This can be made intelligible only in terms of those political theories that have given meaning to human experience. In the past two centuries, those theories were established on the foundation of *nature* or *History*. The modern doctrine of natural right had created the theoretical ground of limited government and constitutionalism. The doctrine of philosophy of History had culminated in the concept of the rational state. It provided the theoretical foundations of Progressivism. Although the doctrine of History has prevailed, and although its theoretical claims are taken for granted, it is no longer well understood. However, the doctrine of natural right has been revived in historical memory, but its meaning is almost wholly obscure. In short, the partisans of both views defend a theory of justice and a practice of politics of which they have little understanding.

3 There seems to be little doubt that the American Founders considered the legislative branch to be the first branch of government. It was thought to be the branch with the most power and therefore the most difficult to rein in. It armed the other two branches with significant powers, but they were confident that the legislative branch had ample power to defend itself. It was assumed that each branch would exercise its power from an institutional perspective, but on behalf of a constitutional purpose. Although the institutional perspective was fundamental, that was only the starting point. It was also necessary to recognize the constitutional purpose of its power within a regime

of separated powers—that is, each branch must pursue a public good from the perspective of its own institution and unique power. It is thinking about the whole from the perspective of the parts that would allow each of the branches to participate in defining a public good. It would also serve the useful purpose of allowing ambition to counteract ambition.

4   See John Marini, "Can Congress Survive?" *Law and Liberty Blog*, May 21, 2012. http://www.libertylawsite.org/liberty-forum/can-congress-survive/. James Burnham, *Congress and the American Tradition* (Chicago: Henry Regnery, 1959).

5   See John Samples, "First Among Equals: Reconsidering Congressional Power in James Burnham's *Congress and the American Tradition*," Law and Liberty (blog), May 21, 2012, http://www.libertylawsite.org/liberty-forum/first-among-equals-reconsidering-congressional-power-in-james-burnhams-congress-and-the-american-tradition.

6   "House Appropriations after the Republican Revolution," John H. Aldrich, Brittany N. Perry, David W. Rohde, *Congress & the Presidency* 39:229–53, 2012.

7   Ibid., 234.

8   The Constitution established a way of structuring political conflict in a manner most conducive to the establishment of justice and the avoidance of tyranny. The separation of powers was thought to be the best way of ensuring that practical reason, or prudence, rather than unbridled will, would moderate that inevitable conflict in a manner compatible with the defense of human freedom. Consequently, all of the branches of government were meant to understand their powers in light of their constitutional purpose. The two political branches have different constituencies that provide for an electoral base that establishes their independence. That independence requires, first of all, that those who hold office under the Constitution must understand their duties in terms of the institution to which they have been elected or appointed. Secondly, they must pursue the national or common good, as it is understood from the perspective of that institution. Moreover, each branch of government must participate in defining a common good, one that satisfies the interests of the various constituencies as well as the national interest. As a result, there arises a different perspective on the meaning of the public interest.

9   Moreover, Madison's political science, derived from prudence or practical reason becomes unintelligible. Prudence was meant to negotiate the terrain between theoretical and practical reason by establishing the moral conditions of free government through distinguishing what is possible, or doable, from what is knowable. The moral law is understood in terms of the natural law, or reason. It can be made intelligible through practical reason, and approximated prudentially, but it cannot be promulgated. However, if morality is established by will, or practical reason, it establishes the ground of what is *known* and what is *right*. The moral *will* must be promulgated. The fundamental practical problem becomes one of making the will actual. That requires not prudence but technical, or scientifically rational, or expert knowledge. It is not surprising, therefore, that for Wilson and the Progressives, the actual power of modern government resides in the realm of administration.

10 Adrian Vermeule, "The Administrative State: Law, Democracy, and Knowledge," in *Oxford Handbook of the U.S. Constitution*, ed. Mark Tushnet, Mark A. Graber, and Sanford Levinson (New York: Oxford University Press, 2015).

11 Perhaps, because of the importance of public opinion, it is still the case that the administrative state can gain legitimacy only in light of the *authority* of the Constitution. In that case, the importance of constitutional law derives from the necessity of legitimizing the policies of the administrative state as an ongoing process. Or, because the administrative state is an inevitability of modernity, it must be made palatable to the unenlightened electorate through the judiciary. Therefore, the Constitution can only be defended as a legal document.

12 William J. Novak, "The Legal Origins of the Modern American State" (essay), 1, http://www.constitution.org/ad_state/novak.htm.

13 Ibid, 3.

14 Nor is that surprising when you consider that nearly all of the personnel of modern governments comes out of the institution that was meant to be the real heart of the administrative state, the *university*. It was not without reason that Hegel had called the state a *rational* state, a much more comprehensive term than administrative state (just one element of the state). He understood it as the *rule of organized intelligence*. In other words, those trained in its disciplines and the positive tradition of law, all meant to be the applied sciences of the state, had already been shaped by a theoretical tradition that had repudiated constitutionalism. It is nearly impossible to defend constitutionalism in a meaningful way from within an intellectual tradition established by a philosophy of History.

15 This is quite apparent in a unanimous decision of the Supreme Court in 1984. In *Block v. Community Nutrition Institute,* Justice Sandra Day O'Connor rejected consumer claims that the Agriculture Department had used its statutory authority to keep milk prices high. In her opinion, she noted: "Congress intended that judicial review of market orders ordinarily be confined to suits by dairy handlers.... Allowing consumers to sue the secretary would severely disrupt the Act's complex and delicate administrative scheme.... [T]he congressional intent to preclude consumer suits is 'fairly discernible' in the detail of the legislative scheme. The Act contemplates a cooperative venture among the Secretary, producers, and handlers; consumer participation is not provided for or desired under that scheme." The court's purpose was to defend the administrative nexus created by the legislature. There seems to be no consideration for the rights of those harmed by the legislation or the administrative action. Moreover, the judiciary does not seem to consider its own independence in such cases arising out of the administrative process. In other words, the policy–administration nexus, established by the political branches of government and defended by the court in the legal arena, must of necessity determine the ground of the judgment of all of the branches. It is the necessity to defend the policy of the legislature, and it is not judicial independence that predetermines the outcome of decisions arising from the actions of the administrative bureaucracy.

16 Consequently, the American political institutions, primarily Congress and the presidency, are animated by political necessities imposed by the requirements of an administrative state. Although the Supreme Court still takes the Constitution seriously, it has become the arbiter of the meaning of the Constitution primarily because the other branches do not take their constitutional powers seriously enough to defend their own constitutional prerogatives. Indeed, the political branches only question the authority of the

Supreme Court when the court threatens the use of powers that are essential to the operation of the administrative state. Nonetheless, it seems the political branches need not worry about the ongoing support of the courts. The courts have become major players in the policy arena.

17 See *Appendix II* for how the different parties' view of the role of the Supreme Court was revealed in the Robert Bork confirmation struggle.

CHAPTER 6: BUDGETS, SEPARATION OF POWERS, AND THE RISE OF THE ADMINISTRATIVE STATE

1 I refer to other critics of the administrative state and their conceptions of Congress in "Congress in Search of Itself," *Law and Liberty* (blog), March 1, 2017, http://www.libertylawsite.org/liberty-forum/congress-in-search-of-itself/.

CHAPTER 7: PROGRESSIVISM, IMMIGRATION, AND THE TRANSFORMATION OF AMERICAN CITIZENSHIP

1 Joseph Cropsey, "Karl Marx," in *History of Political Philosophy*, ed. Leo Strauss and Joseph Cropsey (Chicago: Rand McNally, 1963), 722.

2 The scientific method would subsequently replace the faculty of reason as the means by which to make that knowledge useful to man. The social sciences, then, would become the applied science of the rational state. The crucial condition of philosophy of History, or historicism, was the abandonment of the doctrine of natural right. Thus, the new sciences rejected not only religion but metaphysical reason—as well as prudence, or practical reason—in exchange for a scientific methodology. As Leo Strauss has observed, historicism "stands or falls by the denial of the possibility of theoretical metaphysics and of philosophic ethics or natural right." *Natural Right and History* (Chicago: University of Chicago Press, 1953), 29.

3 Georg Wilhelm Hegel had established the philosophic ground of the world view that informed Progressivism. He did so in his comprehensive defense of the rational state, in which it would become possible to reconcile the particular and general will, or freedom and necessity. In Hegel's view, "the state is the mind on earth and consciously realizing itself there." It had replaced nature and nature's God. He observed that "the State is the divine Idea, as it exists on earth. In this perspective, the State is the precise object of world history in general. It is in the State that freedom attains its objectivity, and lives in the enjoyment of this objectivity. For the law of the State is the objectification of Spirit; it is will in its true form. Only the will that is obedient to the law is free.... Insofar as the State, our country, constitutes a community of existence, and insofar as the subjective will of human beings submits to laws, the antithesis between freedom and necessity disappears. The rational is the necessary, the substantiality of a shared existence; and we are free to the extent that we acknowledge it as law, and follow it as the very substance of our being. The objective and subjective will are then reconciled, as one and the same serene whole." G. W. F. Hegel, *Introduction to the Philosophy of History*, trans. Leo Rauch (Indianapolis, IN: Hackett Publishing Company, 1988), 42. Accordingly, Hegel insisted that "man must therefore venerate the state as a secular deity." First and last quotations are from *Philosophy of Right*, trans. T. M. Knox (London: Oxford University Press, 1942), 279, 285.

4 Hannah Arendt, "Race-Thinking Before Racism" in *The Origins of Totalitarianism* (San Diego, CA: Harcourt, 1976), 159.

5 Henry Adams, *The Education of Henry Adams*, ed. Henry Cabot Lodge (Boston: Houghton Mifflin, 1918), 411–12.

6 Thomas Paine, himself an immigrant, called America "the asylum for the persecuted lovers of civil and religious liberty from every part of Europe." George Washington, in a letter to Lucretia Van Winter, noted, "At best I have only been an instrument in the hands of Providence, to effect a revolution which is interesting to the general liberties of mankind, and to the emancipation of a country which may afford an Asylum, if we are wise enough to pursue the paths wch. lead to virtue and happiness, to the oppressed and needy of the Earth. Our region is extensive, our plains productive, and if they are cultivated with liberality and good sense, we may be happy ourselves, and diffuse happiness to all who wish to participate." Paine and Washington quotes are in *Immigration and the American Tradition*, ed. Moses Rischin (Indianapolis, IN: Bobbs-Merrill Company, 1976), 34, 43–44. George Washington noted his reason for fighting the British: "The establishment of Civil and Religious Liberty was the motive which induced me to the Field." Quoted in Charles Kesler, "The Promise of American Citizenship," in *Immigration and Citizenship in the Twenty-First Century*, ed. Noah M. J. Pickus (Lanham, MD: Rowman & Littlefield Publishers, 1998), 12.

7 Alexis de Tocqueville, too, had grasped the importance of the ability of Americans to reconcile "the spirit of Religion and the spirit of Liberty." He pointed to the reason why it had become possible to reconcile religion and politics, and morality and liberty. He observed that "religion perceives that civil liberty affords a noble exercise to the faculties of man, and that the political world is a field prepared by the Creator for the efforts of mind. Free and powerful in its own sphere, satisfied with the place reserved for it, religion never more surely establishes its empire than when it reigns in the hearts of men unsupported by aught beside its native strength. Liberty regards religion as its companion in all its battles and its triumphs,—as the cradle of its infancy, and the divine source of its claims. It considers religion as the safeguard of morality, and morality as the best security of law, and the surest pledge of the duration of freedom." *Democracy in America Vol. I*, trans. Henry Reeve (New York: Barnes & Noble Publishing, 2003; originally published in Boston: Ticknor and Fields, 1862), 27–28.

8 Religion, consequently, always played an important role in civil society, even after it had ceased to establish the ground of citizenship. As John Higham has noted, "By far the oldest and—in early America—the most powerful of the anti-foreign traditions came out of the shock of the Reformation. Protestant hatred of Rome played so large a part in pre-Civil War nativist thinking that historians have sometimes regarded nativism and anti-Catholicism as more or less synonymous." *Strangers in the Land* (New Brunswick, NJ: Rutgers University Press, 1955), 5.

9 Kesler, "The Promise of American Citizenship," in *Immigration and Citizenship in the Twenty-First Century*, 13.

10 Ibid., 14.

11 Quoted in Thomas G. West, *Vindicating the Founders* (Lanham, MD: Rowman & Littlefield Publishers, 1997), 149.

12 Kesler, 13.

13 Quoted in West, *Vindicating the Founders*, 147.

14 John Quincy Adams, quoted in *Immigration and the American Tradition*, ed. Moses Rischin (Indianapolis, IN: Bobbs-Merrill Company, 1976), 46.

15 It is in the notion of self-perfection, or perfectibility, that the prospect of a glorious future finds its justification. Charles Beard provides an example of the extravagant hope placed upon a new understanding of the future and its vehicle, the rational state. Beard insisted that "the highest type of modern citizen [is one] who surrenders the hope of private gain that he may serve the state.... The eighteenth century philosophers were wrong. We have not been driven from a political paradise; we have not fallen from a high estate, nor is there any final mold into which society is to be cast. On the contrary, society has come from crude and formless associations beginning in a dim and dateless past and moves outward into an illimitable future, which many of us believe will not be hideous and mean, but beautiful and magnificent. In this dynamic society, the citizen becomes the co-worker in that great and indivisible natural process which draws down granite hills and upbuilds great nations." Charles A. Beard, *Politics: A Lecture Delivered at Columbia University in the Series on Science, Philosophy and Art, February 12, 1908* (New York: Columbia University Press, 1908), 9. Woodrow Wilson, too, believed that the idea of progress was a modern discovery. Unlike previous generations, Wilson noted, "We think of the future, not the past, as the more glorious time in comparison with which the present is nothing." "What Is Progress?," in *The New Freedom* (Garden City, NY: Doubleday, Page & Company, 1913), 42.

16 Jean-Jacques Rousseau, *Second Discourse*, ed. and trans. Roger Masters (New York: St. Martin's Press, 1964), 114.

17 Herbert Croly, *The Promise of American Life* (New York: The Macmillan Company, 1911), 400.

18 Ibid, 418.

19 Ibid.

20 Mary Parker Follett, "Democracy Not 'Liberty' and 'Equality': Our Political Dualism," in *The New State: Group Organization the Solution of Popular Government,* (New York: Longmans, Green and Co., 1923 [originally published in 1918]), 137–38.

21 Ibid, 138.

22 John Dewey, *The Ethics of Democracy* (Ann Arbor: Andrews and Company, 1888), 6, 7, 13–14, 15.

23 Follett, 60.

24 Quoted in John G. Gunnell, *The Descent of Political Theory* (Chicago: University of Chicago Press, 1993), 99.

25 See Daniel J. Tichenor, *Dividing Lines: The Politics of Immigration Control in America* (Princeton, NJ: Princeton University Press, 2002), 75–97.

26 Charles Edward Merriam, *A History of American Political Theories* (New York: The Macmillan Company, 1910), 339.

27 Ibid., 346.

28 Herbert Croly, 81.

29 Merriam, *A History of American Political Theories*, 311.

30 Ibid., 311–12.

31 Ibid., 230.

32 Ibid., 312.

33 Ibid., 296–97.

34 Ibid., 297–98.

35 Ibid.

36 Ibid., 250–51.

37 Ibid., 248.

38 John William Burgess, *Reconstruction and the Constitution, 1866–1876* (New York: Charles Scribner's Sons, 1902), ix.

39 Ibid., 133.

40 Thomas F. Gossett, *Race: The History of an Idea in America* (New York: Oxford University Press, 1997), 284. Quotations are from James Ford Rhodes, *History of the United States from the Compromise of 1850 to the Final Restoration of Home Rule at the South in 1877* (New York: Harper & Brothers, 1893, 1906), seven volumes.

41 William Archibald Dunning, *Reconstruction: Political and Economic, 1865–1877* in *The American Nation: A History*, vol. 22 (New York: Harper & Brothers, 1907), 213.

42 Hannah Franziska Augstein, *Race: The Origins of an Idea, 1760–1850* (Bristol: Thoemmes Press, 1996), xxx.

43 Quoted in Gunnell, *The Descent of Political Theory*, 54.

44 Tichenor, 78.

45 Walker, "Immigration and Degradation," quoted in Tichenor, *Dividing Lines*, 78.

46 Ibid.

47 Jay K. Varma, "Eugenics and Immigration Restriction: Lessons for Tomorrow," *Journal of the American Medical Association* 275, no. 9 (March 6, 1996): 734, doi:10.1001/jama.1996.03530330075045.

48 Tichenor, 115.

49 Quoted in Higham, *Strangers in the Land*, 273.

50 Tichenor, 87–88.

51 Before the Progressive understanding of immigration and citizenship had been established on the ground of race, national and state laws had pursued prudential policies, which restricted immigration and citizenship on moral grounds. In 1882, the national government had tried to simplify the task of making prudential judgments by focusing on race. If race had not been taken into account as decisive, and if a restrictive immigration policy was desirable—as it would come to be in a few years—it would have been necessary to establish immigration policy on other grounds. In that case, immigration and citizenship laws could have restricted those whose morals—using opium, pimping, maintaining allegiance to the Emperor or a foreign sovereign— were incompatible with the character necessary for good citizenship. Indeed, some states had attempted to pass legislation on similar moral grounds. The fundamental necessity of any immigration policy is that of preserving and perpetuating the social compact of free and equal citizens. It is possible to exclude anyone from immigration into a sovereign country. Indeed, the borders may be closed. But it is not possible to deny the principle of the regime—equality—without undermining the conditions of the social compact itself.

52 Frank Julian Warne, *The Tide of Immigration* (New York: D. Appleton and Company, 1916), 135.

53 Tichenor, 114.

54 Quoted in Ibid.

55 Quoted in Ibid., 146–47.

56 Quoted in Stephen Jay Gould, *The Mismeasure of Man* (New York: W. W. Norton & Co., 1981), 231.

57 Quoted in Gossett, *Race*, 377.

58 Quoted in Tichenor, 144.

59 Ibid.

60 Abba Schwartz, *The Open Society* (New York: Simon & Schuster, 1968), 105–6.

61 Tichenor, 129.

62 See Tichenor, 143.

63 Mae M. Ngai, "The Architecture of Race in American Immigration Law: A Reexamination of the Immigration Act of 1924," *Journal of American History* 86, no. 1 (1999): 71, https://www.jstor.org/stable/2567407.

64 Tichenor, 143.

65 Quoted in Peter H. Wang, *Legislating Normalcy: The Immigration Act of 1924* (San Francisco: R and E Research Associates, 1975), 9.

66 Ibid., 126.

67 Ibid., 9, 91.

68 Quoted in Moses Rischin, *Immigration and the American Tradition*, 431.

69 Quoted in Ibid., 449.

70 Quoted in Ibid.

71 Tichenor, 220.

72 Peter Schuck and Rogers Smith, *Citizenship Without Consent: Illegal Aliens in the American Polity* (New Haven, CT: Yale University Press, 1985), 106–8.

73 Tichenor, 215.

74 Arendt, "Race-Thinking Before Racism," 159.

CHAPTER 8: POLITICS, RHETORIC, AND LEGITIMACY: THE ROLE OF BUREAUCRACY IN THE WATERGATE AFFAIR

1 This chapter, containing minimal updates, was published in *Political Communication* 9, no. 1 (1992): 1–13, https://doi.org/10.1080/10584609.1992.996 2930. See the author's Afterword at the end of this chapter from the original.

2 Douglas Yates, *Bureaucratic Democracy: The Search for Democracy and Efficiency* (Cambridge: Harvard University Press, 1982), 54.

3 John Wettergreen, "The American Voter and His Surveyors," *Political Science Reviewer* 7 (Fall 1977): 223.

4 Walter Dean Burnham, "Insulation and Responsiveness in Congressional Elections," *Political Science Quarterly* 90, no. 3 (Autumn 1975): 411–35, https://www.jstor.org/stable/2148294.

5 Henry Kissinger, *Years of Upheaval* (Boston: Little Brown, 1982), 1209.

6 Colin Seymour-Ure, *The American President: Power and Communication* (London: Macmillan Press Ltd, 1982), 134, doi:10.1007/978-1-349-04113-8.

7 Nelson Polsby, "A Critical Introduction," *Law and Contemporary Problems* 40, no. 2 (Spring 1976): 6, https://scholarship.law.duke/edu/lcp/vol40/iss2/2.

8 Ibid.

9 Aaron Wildaysky wrote just after Watergate, "Nixon, especially at the start of

his second term, apparently set out to alienate every national elite—the press, Congress, the Republican National Committee—the fact that he had long been attacking his own federal bureaucracy has escaped notice." "Government and the People," in *Watergate and the American Political Process*, ed. Ronald E. Pynn (New York: Praeger, 1975), 36.

10 Theodore White, *The Making of the President 1972* (New York: Atheneum, 1973), 107.

11 *Public Papers of the Presidents of the United States, Richard M. Nixon, 1972* (Washington: GPO, 1974), 1088.

12 *Public Papers of the Presidents of the United States, Richard M. Nixon, 1973* (Washington, 1975), vi.

13 James L. Sundquist, "Whither the American Party System?," *Political Science Quarterly* 88, no. 3 (December 1973): 580.

14 White, *Making of the President 1972*, 107.

15 Ibid.

16 Ibid., xvii.

17 Ibid., 108.

18 Ibid.

19 Ibid., xvii.

20 *Public Papers 1973*, 6.

21 Ibid.

21 Ibid.

23 Richard Nixon, *A New Road for America: Major Policy Statements* (Garden City: Doubleday, 1972), 7.

24 *Federal Reorganization: The Executive Branch, Public Documents Series*, ed. Tyrrus G. Fain (New York: R. R. Bowker, 1977), 23.

25 Ibid., 31.

26 John Hart, "Presidential Power Revisited," *Political Studies*, vol. 25 (March 1977): 58.

27 Nixon, *Memoirs*, 761–62.

28 Ibid., 762.

29 Ibid., 767.

30 Richard Nathan, *The Plot That Failed: Nixon and the Administrative Presidency* (New York: Wiley, 1975), 61.

31 Nixon, *Memoirs*, 768.

32 Ibid., 769.

33 Ibid., 761.

34 Nixon had set the tone in his second inaugural. He noted, "I offer no solutions of a purely governmental kind for every problem. We have lived too long with that false hope." *Historic Documents* (Washington: Congressional Quarterly, Inc., 1974), 83.

35 Nathan, *The Plot That Failed*, 70.

36 *Public Papers 1973*, 33.

37 Ibid.

38 Nixon, *Memoirs*, 769.

39 Ibid., 767.

40 Ibid.

41 Ibid., 771.

42 Ibid.

43 Ibid.

44 Ibid., 772.

45 Quoted in Larry Berman, *The Office of Management and Budget and the Presidency* (Princeton, NJ: Princeton University Press, 1979), 123.

46 Nixon, *Memoirs*, 772.

47 Philip Kurland, "The Watergate Inquiry, 1973," in *Congress Investigates*, vol. 5, ed. Arthur Schlesinger, Jr. (New York: Chelsea House, 1975), 3926.

48 Nixon, *Memoirs*, 773.

49 *Congressional Quarterly Report*, vol. 23 (December 28, 1974).

50 White, *Making of the President*, 367.

51 Harold Seidman, *Politics, Position, and Power* (New York: Oxford University Press, 1975), 118.

52 Henry Kissinger, *Years of Upheaval* (Boston: Little Brown, 1982), 1209.

CHAPTER 9: TOCQUEVILLE'S CENTRALIZED ADMINISTRATION AND THE "NEW DESPOTISM"

1 Edward T. Gargan, *De Tocqueville* (London: Bowes & Bowes, 1965), 28.

2 Ibid., 27.

3 François Guizot, *Historical Essays and Lectures*, ed. Stanley Mellon and Leonard Krieger (Chicago: University of Chicago Press, 1972), 257.

4 Gargan, *De Tocqueville*, 29.

5 Alexis de Tocqueville, *Democracy in America*, trans. Harvey Mansfield and Delba Winthrop (Chicago: University of Chicago Press, 2000), 52. Hereinafter cited as *Democracy*.

6 Ibid., 663.

7 Seymour Drescher, "Tocqueville's Two Democracies," *Journal of the History of Ideas* 25 (April–June 1964): 249.

8 Alexis de Tocqueville, *The Old Regime and the French Revolution*, trans. Stuart Gilbert (Garden City, NY: Doubleday, Anchor Books, 1955), 158. Hereinafter cited as *Old Regime*.

9 Ibid.

10 Ibid., 159.

11 Ibid., 163.

12 Ibid., 164.

13 *Democracy*, 84.

14 Ibid., 90.

15 Ibid., 88.

16 Henry Steele Commager, "Tocqueville's Mistake," *Harper's* (August 1984), 71.

17 Ibid., 72.

18 Ibid.

19 Ibid.

20 *Democracy*, 83.

21 John Stuart Mill, "Centralisation," *Collected Works*, ed. John M. Robson (Toronto: University of Toronto Press, 1977), 19:581. Hereinafter cited as Mill, "Centralisation."

22 Ibid.

23 Ibid.

24 John Stuart Mill, *Autobiography* (New York: Liberal Arts Press, 1957), 124.

25 Ibid., 124–25.

26 Ibid., 125.

27 Mill, "Centralisation," 582.

28 James T. Schleifer, *The Making of Tocqueville's "Democracy in America"* (Chapel Hill: University of North Carolina Press, 1980).

29 Alexis de Tocqueville, *Journeys to England and Ireland*, ed. J. P. Mayer (Garden City, NY: Doubleday, Anchor Books, 1968), 63. Hereinafter cited as *Journeys*.

30 Schleifer, *Making of Tocqueville's "Democracy in America"*, 177.

31 *Democracy*, 645.

32 Ibid., 650.

33 Ibid., 666.

34 Ibid., 646.

35 Quoted in Schleifer, *Making of Tocqueville's "Democracy in America"*, 135. Schleifer is quoting manuscript drafts of *Democracy*. Yale, CV b, Paquet 13, 57–58.

36 Ibid., 87.

37 Ibid.

38 Ibid., 90.

39 Marvin Zetterbaum, *Tocqueville and the Problem of Democracy* (Stanford, CA: Stanford University Press, 1967), 99. Hereinafter cited as Zetterbaum, *Problem*.

40 John C. Koritansky, "Decentralization and Civic Virtue in Tocqueville's 'New Science of Politics,'" *Publius* 5 (Summer 1975), 68.

41 *Democracy*, 107.

42 Ibid., 145.

43 Koritansky, "Decentralization," 68n39.

44 Ibid., 68.

45 Ibid., 68–69.

46 Martin Diamond, "The Ends of Federalism," *The Federal Polity*, ed. Daniel J. Elazar (New Brunswick, NJ: Transaction Books, 1974), 139.

47 Roger Boesche, "Tocqueville and *Le Commerce*: A Newspaper Expressing His Unusual Liberalism," *Journal of the History of Ideas* 44 (April–June 1983).

48 Zetterbaum, *Problem*, 118.

49 *Democracy*, 57.

50 Quoted in J. P. Mayer, *Alexis de Tocqueville: A Biographical Essay in Political Science* (New York: Viking Press, 1940), 26. Hereinafter cited as Mayer, *Biographical Essay*.

51 *Democracy*, 301.

52 Rousseau, *The Social Contract* (New York: Hafner, 1947), 38.

53 John Stuart Mill, *Essays on Politics and Culture*, ed. Gertrude Himmelfarb (Garden City, NY: Doubleday, Anchor Books, 1963), 238.

54 Zetterbaum, *Problem*, 86.

55 Mayer, *Biographical Essay*, 149.

56 Ibid., 37–38.

57 Ibid., 110.

58 Ibid., 111.

59 Alexis de Tocqueville, "The Art and Science of Politics," trans. J. P. Mayer, *Encounter* 36 (January 1971): 29–30. Hereinafter cited as "Politics."

60 *Democracy*, 405.

61 Ibid., 10–11.

62 "Politics," 32.

63 *Democracy*, 428.

64　Ibid., 426–27.

65　Ibid, 427.

66　Ibid.

67　Ibid.

68　Ibid., 426.

69　*Journeys*, 66–67.

70　Ibid., 67.

71　Delba Winthrop, "Tocqueville's *Old Regime*: Political History," *The Review of Politics* 43 (January 1981), 98.

72　Irving M. Zeitlin, *Liberty, Equality, and Revolution in Alexis de Tocqueville* (Boston: Little, Brown, 1971), 126.

73　*Old Regime*, 98–99.

74　Ibid., 160.

75　Ibid., 60.

76　Alexis de Tocqueville, *"The European Revolution" and Correspondence with Gobineau*, trans. John Lukacs (Gloucester, MA: Peter Smith, 1968), 103. Hereinafter cited as *European Revolution*.

77　*Old Regime*, 60.

78　*European Revolution*, 101.

79　Ibid., 101–2.

80　*Democracy*, 647.

81　Ibid.

82　Ibid., 648.

83　Ibid., 412.

84　Ibid., 413.

85　Ibid., 413–14.

86　Ibid., 411.

87　Ibid., 86.

88　Ibid., 703.

89　Ibid., 640.

90　Ibid.

91　Ibid., 641.

92　Ibid., 482.

93　Ibid.

94　Ibid., 515.

95　Ibid., 654, footnote 3.

96　Ibid., 485.

97　Quoted in Harry D. Gideonse, "De Tocqueville, Liberal of a New Type," *American Journal of Economics* 19 (July 1960): 412.

98　Roger Boesche, "The Prison: Tocqueville's Model for Despotism," *Western Political Quarterly* 33 (December 1980): 553.

99　Ibid., 556.

100　*Old Regime*, xiv.

101　*Democracy*, 645.

102　Gargan, *De Tocqueville*, 65.

CHAPTER 10: ON HARVEY MANSFIELD'S JEFFERSON LECTURE: HOW TO UNDERSTAND POLITICS

1　The text of the Jefferson Lecture, "How to Understand Politics: What the Humanities Can Say to Science", delivered May 8, 2007, at the Warner Theatre in Washington, DC, can be found here: https://www.neh.gov/about/awards/ jefferson-lecture/harvey-mansfield-lecture.

2   Tocqueville used the term "centralized administration" to describe a phenomenon that we now call "bureaucracy." The term was not yet in use in Tocqueville's time. Bureaucratization grows out of the attempt to rationalize every aspect of human life. The most important philosopher of what came to be known as bureaucracy was G. F. W. Hegel. He attempted to establish the rule of organized intelligence as the fundamental requirement of the rational state.

3   Tocqueville insisted that "as I studied American society, more and more I saw in equality of conditions the generative fact from which each particular fact seemed to issue, and I found it before me constantly as a central point at which all my observations came to an end." *Democracy in America*, trans. Harvey Mansfield and Delba Winthrop (Chicago: University of Chicago Press, 2000), 3.

4   In *The Old Regime and the French Revolution*, trans. Stuart Gilbert (Garden City, NY: Anchor Books, 1955), Tocqueville insisted that "freedom and freedom alone can extirpate these vices"—he is speaking of the process of centralization that isolates the individual and leads to despotism—"which, indeed, are innate in communities of this order; it alone can call a halt to their pernicious influence. For only freedom can deliver the members of a community from that isolation which is the lot of the individual left to his own devices and, compelling them to get in touch with each other, promote an active sense of fellowship. In a community of free citizens every man is daily reminded of the need of meeting his fellow men, of hearing what they have to say, of exchanging ideas, and coming to an agreement as to the conduct of their common interests." xiv. In his view, local freedom makes it possible to reconcile the individual and the general will.

5   The American Founders would have agreed with Edmund Burke's observation that "men of intemperate minds cannot be free. Their passions forge their fetters."

6   Strauss has suggested that "it became ever more clear that man's freedom is inseparable from a radical dependence. Yet this dependence was understood as itself a product of human freedom, and the name for that is history. The so-called discovery of history consists in the realization, or in the alleged realization, that man's freedom is radically limited by his earlier use of his freedom, and not by his nature or by the whole order of nature or creation." "Progress or Return?" in *The Rebirth of Classical Political Rationalism*, ed. Thomas L. Pangle (Chicago: University of Chicago Press, 1989), 245.

7   In the thinkers who came after Rousseau, this understanding of will was to become the foundation of the moral law. One of those thinkers, Immanuel Kant, made it clear that Rousseau had set him right. Kant's expression of this understanding of Rousseau resulted in the elevation or primacy of practical reason, or moral reason, as the only thing of absolute worth. In Kant, will and practical reason had become identical. There was no longer a possibility of apprehending the moral law, which was not but the willing of it. At the same time, the old understanding of prudence, or practical reason, is left without any reason for being. Kant consequently undermined the authority or primacy of theoretical reason and the autonomy of prudence, or practical reason. Neither physics nor metaphysics could supply knowledge of the absolute; the only knowledge of the absolute is knowledge of the moral law, which originates

solely in the will. Tocqueville's view of morality also presupposes such a defense of the sovereignty of the will, even when he believes the people may be wrong. Like Rousseau and Kant, Tocqueville thinks there is no appeal—to nature or God—from an unjust law. In such a case, Tocqueville says, "I only appeal from the sovereignty of the people to the sovereignty of the human race." *Democracy in America*, 240.

8 Leo Strauss, *Natural Right and History* (Chicago, University of Chicago Press, 1953), 278–79.

9 Tocqueville insisted that "freedom alone is capable of lifting men's minds above mere mammon worship and the petty personal worries which crop up in the course of everyday life, and of making them aware at every moment that they belong each and all to a vaster entity, above and around them—their native land. It alone replaces at certain critical moments their natural love of material welfare by a loftier, more virile ideal; offers other objectives than that of getting rich; and sheds a light enabling all to see and appraise men's vices and their virtues as they truly are." *Old Regime*, xiv.

10 Strauss, *Natural Right and History*, 281.

11 Ibid., 274.

12 Thus Rousseau's social contract is not the same as that of John Locke, or the American Founders. It is not nature, but the general will of the sovereign— the people—which establishes the ground of morality and legitimacy. The political problem requires a reconciliation of the particular and general; the individual will become moral by being generalized. To be free after he has become a social, or dependent, being, every individual must participate in his own governance; he must be a self-legislator on behalf of the community. This is why a democracy must be small, or, as Tocqueville insisted, liberty must be local liberty.

13 The theoretical dilemma posed by this change of orientation, as it was interpreted by Rousseau's successors, goes to the heart of the transformation of the understanding of the meaning of nature, and natural right, and its displacement, first by a philosophy of freedom (Rousseau), and subsequently by a philosophy of History (Hegel).

14 Although Tocqueville feared centralization, he understood it as a concomitant of a process of rationalization, or the taste for general ideas. Therefore, his understanding of centralization as a kind of inevitable process indicated his agreement with Rousseau that nature and the faculty of reason does not provide the ground for understanding man and his capacity for choice. It was free *will*, not reason, that legitimized choice. Rousseau had been partly persuaded by the new science of politics of Hobbes, which incorporated Galileo's physics. (Hobbes incorporated the discovery of the laws of motion to help explain the passions that drive humans; man is matter in motion.) But Rousseau insisted that science and the laws of motion only explain physical man, not what is truly unique or important about man. "For physics explains in some way the mechanism of the senses and the formation of ideas; but in the power of willing, or rather of choosing, and in the sentiment of this power are found only purely spiritual acts about which the laws of mechanics explain nothing." He concluded, "Therefore it is not so much understanding which constitutes the distinction of man among the animals as it is his being a free agent.... It is above all in the *consciousness of this freedom that the spirituality of*

his soul is shown" (emphasis mine). Rousseau, *The First and Second Discourses*, ed. Roger D. Masters (New York: St. Martin's Press, 1964), 2:114. It is here that Rousseau introduced what he thought was indisputable in terms of distinguishing man and animal, the faculty of self-perfection, or perfectibility. Tocqueville agrees: "Perfectibility is therefore as old as the world; equality did not give birth to it, but it gives it a new character." *Democracy in America,* 427.

15 Strauss has suggested that "Rousseau's concept of the general will, which as such cannot err—which by merely being is what it ought to be—showed how the gulf between the is and ought can be overcome." Nonetheless, Strauss insisted that, "strictly speaking, Rousseau showed this only under the condition that his doctrine of the general will, his political doctrine proper, is linked with his doctrine of the historical process, and this linking was the work of Rousseau's great successors, Kant and Hegel, rather than of Rousseau himself. According to this view, the rational or just society, the society characterized by the existence of a general will known to be the general will, i.e., the ideal, is necessarily actualized by the historical process without men's intending to actualize it. Why can the general will not err? Why is the general will necessarily good? The answer is: it is good because it is rational, and it is rational because it is general; it emerges through the generalization of the particular will, of the will which as such is not good." Strauss, "The Three Waves of Modernity," in *An Introduction to Political Philosophy: Ten Essays by Leo Strauss,* ed. Hilail Gildin (Detroit: Wayne State University Press, 1989), 91.

16 Strauss, *Natural Right and History,* 276.

17 Ibid., 276–77.

18 Marvin Zetterbaum, *Tocqueville and the Problem of Democracy* (Stanford, CA: Stanford University Press, 1967), 86. Interestingly, in his review of *Democracy in America* in 1840, John Stuart Mill concluded the opposite. "It is perhaps the greatest defect of M. de Tocqueville's book, that... his propositions, even when derived from observation, have the air of mere abstract speculations." *Essays on Politics and Culture,* ed. Gertrude Himmelfarb (Garden City, NY: Doubleday, Anchor Books, 1963), 238. Paradoxically, both Mill and Zetterbaum might be right. Tocqueville was concerned with placing politics within a proper historical framework, but he was aware that every society is animated by certain ideas. Indeed, Tocqueville believed that it was the science of politics itself that gave "birth or at least form to those general concepts whence emerge the facts with which politicians have to deal, and the laws of which they believe themselves the inventors. They form a kind of atmosphere surrounding each society in which both rulers and governed have to draw intellectual breath, and whence—often without realizing it—both groups derive the principles of action. Only among barbarians does the practical side of politics exist alone." Tocqueville, quoted in J. P. Mayer, *Alexis de Tocqueville: A Biographical Essay in Political Science* (New York: Viking Press, 1940), 149. The question arises, however: Where does the science of politics originate? Zetterbaum seems to deny that Tocqueville understood politics in a philosophical way. If so, does it mean that Tocqueville was primarily concerned with placing politics within a proper historical framework? Even if that is so, Tocqueville, as Mill understood, was aware that every society is animated by certain general ideas. Did Mill believe that Tocqueville's observations were too dependent upon mere abstract speculation? Tocqueville, himself, insisted upon what he called "the

mingling of history proper with historical philosophy. I do not yet see how I can mix the two things (and it is most important that this should be done, for one can put it that the former is the canvas, the latter the color—and both these are necessary to make a picture)." Quoted in Mayer, 111.

19 Indeed, the political science that came after Tocqueville—certain that history had revealed itself as intelligible and that theory was rationalized will—abandoned prudence in exchange for a scientific or empirical methodology.

20 Strauss, *Natural Right and History*, 274.

21 It was Hegel, who purportedly solved the political and the human problem, which required uniting true knowledge of public right with perfect knowledge of the end or purpose of the historical process. As a result, it was possible to transcend all those distinctions that the earlier liberalism (particularly that of John Locke) had thought to be rooted in nature, or human nature. It was those natural distinctions that brought about the necessity of separating church and state, government and civil society, the public and private sphere. Those sources of factionalism could not be transcended or ameliorated, except in a regime of civil and religious liberty. Consequently, constitutional or limited government is necessary to preserve a kind of liberty that is compatible with equality and human nature. A rational solution to the political-theological problem is possible, but no such solution to the human problem is possible, unless man becomes fully wise. The philosophy and end of History made such knowledge accessible to man. Strauss notes that "Hegel's time was the absolute moment, the end of meaningful time; the absolute religion, Christianity, had become completely reconciled with the world; it had become completely secularized or the *saeculum* had become completely Christian in and through the post-revolutionary State; history as meaningful change had come to its end; all theoretical and practical problems had in principle been solved; hence, the historical process was demonstrably rational." Leo Strauss, "Relativism," in *The Rebirth of Classical Political Rationalism*, ed. Thomas L. Pangle (Chicago: University of Chicago Press, 1989), 24–25. Tocqueville, unlike his friend Gobineau, was never persuaded by Hegel or the Germans.

22 However, Tocqueville did not believe that the individual and general will could be reconciled on the level of the rational state, but only under conditions of local liberty. Therefore, Hegel insisted, "this essential being is itself the union of two wills: the subjective will and the rational will. This is an ethical totality, the *state* [Hegel's italics]. It is the reality wherein the individual has and enjoys his freedom—but only insofar as he knows, believes, and wills the universal.... As against this negative concept of freedom, it is rather law, ethical life, the state (and they alone) that comprise the positive reality and satisfaction of freedom. The freedom which is limited in the state is that of caprice, the freedom that relates to the particularity of individual needs.... For we must understand that the State is the realization of freedom, i.e., of the absolute end-goal, and that it exists for its own sake." *Introduction to the Philosophy of History*, trans. Leo Rauch (Indianapolis: Hackett Books, 1988), 41. Tocqueville still understood human freedom, in terms of the private, or individual, capacity for self-government.

23 In the nineteenth century, Abraham Lincoln provided a political defense of the idea of natural right in his attempt to ground the principle of equality, and the regime based upon it, in the "abstract truths" of the Declaration of

Independence, or the laws of nature and nature's God. Lincoln's defense of the Union and the Constitution required a defense of natural right, or the grounding of the Constitution in the principle of equality. But after the Civil War, particularly in the American university, the victory of historicism and positivism undermined the theoretical and intellectual ground of natural right. Consequently, many of the new social scientists, even those who admired Lincoln, and who had fought for the Union, became Progressives and embraced the historical understanding of man, made scientifically respectable by Darwinism. Subsequently, they became enemies of constitutional government. That was so because they had accepted the view of Rousseau, Kant, and Hegel—that nature, natural right, and metaphysical reason could provide no moral guidance for human life. Instead, the Kantian view of practical reason had created the foundation for the primacy of moral will. That view would establish the theoretical framework that provided the grounds for positivism and, after Nietzsche, moral relativism and nihilism. In the absence of a theoretical or metaphysical defense of nature and reason, it is nearly impossible to make a defense of limited or constitutional government.

24 Strauss, *Natural Right and History*, 7.

CHAPTER 11: ROOSEVELT'S OR REAGAN'S AMERICA? A TIME FOR CHOOSING

1 Franklin D. Roosevelt, 1944 State of the Union Address, http://www.presidency.ucsb.edu/ws/?pid=16518.

2 Cass Sunstein, *The Second Bill of Rights: FDR's Unfinished Revolution* (New York: Basic Books, 2004).

3 Ronald Reagan, First Inaugural Address, http://www.presidency.ucsb.edu/ws/?pid=43130.

4 Franklin D. Roosevelt, *The Public Papers and Addresses of Franklin D. Roosevelt*, vol. 1 (New York: Random House, 1938), 782.

5 Franklin D. Roosevelt, "Campaign Address on Progressive Government at the Commonwealth Club in San Francisco, California," September 23, 1932. Online by Gerhard Peters and John T. Woolley, *The American Presidency Project*, http://www.presidency.ucsb.edu/ws/?pid=88391.

6 Ronald Reagan, "A Time for Choosing," October 27, 1964, Los Angeles, California, http://www.americanrhetoric.com/speeches/ronaldreaganatimeforchoosing.htm.

CHAPTER 12: THEORIES OF THE LEGISLATURE: THE CHANGING CHARACTER OF THE AMERICAN CONGRESS

1 See John L. Jackley, "U.S. Congress: A Sick Body Getting Sicker," *The Wall Street Journal*, January 3, 1991.

2 Roger Davidson, "The Two Congresses and How They Are Changing," in *The Role of the Legislature in Western Democracies*, ed. Norman J. Ornstein (Washington: American Enterprise Institute Symposium, 1981), 3–4.

3 See Richard Fenno, "If, As Ralph Nader Says, Congress Is 'the Broken Branch,' How Come We Love Our Congressmen So Much?" *Congress in Change*, ed. Norman Ornstein (New York: Praeger Publishers, 1975), 277–78.

4 Morris Fiorina, "Congressional Control of the Bureaucracy: A Mismatch of Incentives and Capabilities," in *Congress Reconsidered*, ed. Lawrence Dodd and

Bruce Oppenheimer, 2nd ed. (Washington: Congressional Quarterly Inc., 1981), 345.

5　Alexis de Tocqueville, *Democracy in America*, ed. and trans. Harvey Mansfield and Delba Winthrop (Chicago: University of Chicago Press, 2000), 91.

6　John Wettergreen, "Bureaucracy in America," presented at the annual meeting of the American Political Science Association, Chicago, Illinois, 1983, 5.

7　John Wettergreen, "Constitutional Problems of American Bureaucracy in *I.N.S. v. Chada*." A paper presented at the annual meeting of the American Political Science Association, New Orleans, Louisiana, 1985, 13.

8　Ibid.

9　Ibid., 14.

10　Ibid., 31.

11　Ibid., 5.

12　Harold Seidman and Robert Gilmour, *Politics, Position, and Power* (New York: Oxford University Press, 1986), 136–37.

13　Ibid., 312.

14　Ibid., 313.

15　Wettergreen, "Constitutional Problems of American Bureaucracy," 22–23.

16　Seidman and Gilmour, *Politics, Position, and Power*, 278.

17　Wettergreen, "Constitutional Problems of American Bureaucracy," 5.

18　Walter Lippmann, *The Public Philosophy* (New York: Mentor Books, 1955), 44.

19　Wettergreen, "Constitutional Problems of American Bureaucracy," 44.

20　Ibid., 44–45.

21　Ibid., 45.

22　Ibid., 26.

23　Ibid., 25.

24　Randall B. Ripley and Grace A. Franklin, *Congress, the Bureaucracy, and Public Policy* (Chicago: The Dorsey Press, 1987), 78–79.

25　Harvey C. Mansfield, "The Constitution and Modern Social Science," *The Center Magazine* 19 (September/October l986): 52.

26　Wettergreen, "Constitutional Problems of American Bureaucracy," 26.

27　Ibid., 32.

28　Fiorina, "Congressional Control of the Bureaucracy," 343.

29　Seidman and Gilmore, *Politics, Position, and Power*, 340.

30　Cited in Lester M. Salamon, "Federal Regulation: A New Arena for Presidential Power?" in *The Illusion of Presidential Government*, ed. Hugh Heclo and Lester Salamon (Boulder, CO: Westview Press, 1981), 157.

31　Harvey C. Mansfield Jr., "Republicanizing the Executive," in *Saving the Revolution*, ed. Charles R. Kesler (New York: Free Press, 1987).

32　Ibid., 9.

33　Edward S. Corwin, "The Impact of the Idea of Evolution on the American Political and Constitutional Tradition," in *Corwin on the Constitution*, vol. 1, ed. Richard Loss (Ithaca, NY: Cornell University Press, 1981), 191–92.

34　Paul Eidelberg, *The Philosophy of the American Constitution* (New York: Free Press, 1968), 231.

35　Carl Schmitt, *The Crisis of Parliamentary Democracy*, trans. Ellen Kennedy (Cambridge: Massachusetts Institute of Technology Press, 1985), 48.

36　Ibid., 49.

37　Ibid., 24.

38　Ibid., 23.

39 Harry McPherson, *A Political Education* (Boston: Atlantic Monthly Press, 1972), 301–2.

40 James W. Ceaser, "The Theory of Governance of the Reagan Administration," in *The Reagan Presidency and the Governing of America*, ed. Lester M. Salamon and Michael S. Lund (Washington: Urban Institute Press, 1984), 70.

41 Theodore Lowi, "Ronald Reagan—Revolutionary," in *The Reagan Presidency and the Governing of America*, 51.

42 "380 of 393 House members (97%), 27 of 29 senators (93%) won another term." Kyle Kondik and Geoffrey Skelley, "Incumbent Reelection Rates Higher Than Average in *Larry J. Sabato's Crystal Ball*," December 15, 2016, http://www.centerforpolitics.org/crystalball/articles/incumbent-reelection-rates-higher-than-average-in-2016/.

43 John Locke, *Second Treatise of Government*, bk 12, para. 144.

44 Ibid., bk 13, para. 151.

45 Carl Schmitt, *The Crisis of Parliamentary Democracy*, 42–43.

46 John Locke, *Second Treatise of Government*, bk 12, 12.

47 Schmitt, *The Crisis of Parliamentary Democracy*, 43.

48 Baron de Montesquieu, *The Spirit of the Laws*, trans. Thomas Nugent (London: Colonial Press, l900), 154.

49 Schmitt, *The Crisis of Parliamentary Democracy*, 45.

50 Ibid., 42.

51 *Federalist,* no. 51 (Madison).

52 Ibid.

53 Montesquieu, *Spirit of the Laws*, 157.

54 Ibid., 156.

55 Schmitt, *The Crisis of Parliamentary Democracy*, 41.

56 Ibid., 49–50.

57 Montesquieu, *Spirit of the Laws*, 161–62.

CHAPTER 13: PROGRESSIVISM, THE SOCIAL SCIENCES, AND THE RATIONAL STATE

1 This chapter was originally published in Bradley C. S. Watson, ed., *Progressive Challenges to the American Constitution* (New York: Cambridge University Press, 2017).

2 Wilson believed that the Founders' political science had been based on a misunderstanding of man and nature. He thought that the laws of politics, though dependent on the laws of science, are historical laws, derived from the evolution of organic life, not natural laws of physics. He insisted: "In our own day, whenever we discuss the structure or development of a thing, whether in nature or in society, we consciously follow Mr. Darwin; but before Mr. Darwin they followed Newton." Thus, Wilson criticized the *Federalist* writings because "they are full of the theory of checks and balances. . . . Politics is turned into mechanics under his touch. The theory of gravitation is supreme." Wilson contended that "the trouble with the theory is that government is not a machine but a living thing. It falls, not under the theory of the universe, but the theory of organic life. It is accountable to Darwin, not to Newton." *The New Freedom* (New York: Doubleday, Page & Co., 1913), 41. Wilson accepted the Kantian view that natural laws are scientific laws and cannot be the foundation of the moral law. In short, he either rejected, or was unaware of, the view that theoretical metaphysics, or philosophical ethics (natural right), could have established the foundations of the Founders' political science.

3   Wilson is surely wrong in his assumption that the American Founders derived
    their moral and political understanding from theoretical foundations provided
    by Newtonian physics. The Founders did not deny that Newton's theories
    are an accurate description of the natural or physical universe. However,
    their political science and their principles were thought to be derived from
    theoretical or metaphysical reason. And they believed practical politics must be
    understood from the perspective of practical reason or prudence. Madison, in
    Federalist 37, made very clear the lack of an exact science and the dependence
    of political science on prudence. In terms of political science, he notes: "when
    we pass from the works of nature, in which all the delineations are perfectly
    accurate, and appear to be otherwise only from the imperfection of the eye
    which surveys them, to the institutions of man, in which the obscurity arises
    as well from the object itself as from the organ by which it is contemplated,
    we must perceive the necessity of moderating still further our expectations
    and hopes from the efforts of human sagacity." The institutional structure of
    constitutional government (separation of powers) is not based on mechanical
    laws, but on prudential necessity derived from an understanding of human
    nature. As Madison notes: "experience has instructed us that no skill in the
    science of government has yet been able to discriminate and define, with
    sufficient certainty, its three great provinces—the legislative, executive, and
    judiciary." "Questions daily occur in the course of practice, which prove the
    obscurity which reigns in these subjects, and which puzzle the greatest adepts
    in political science" (*Federalist* 37). Madison's understanding of prudence in his
    political science is a far cry from a mechanical political science based on the
    theory of the universe of "graviton" or a "machine," as Wilson suggested.

4   In bringing government into conformity with the proper science, Wilson
    suggested that it was necessary to unify what the Founders had divided. "The
    object of constitutional government," Wilson observed, "is to bring the active,
    planning will of each part of the government into accord with the prevailing
    popular will, thought and need, and thus make it an impartial instrument
    of symmetrical national development; and to give to the operation of the
    government thus shaped under the influence of opinion and adjusted to the
    general interest both stability and an incorruptible efficiency" (emphasis
    mine). *The New Freedom*, 41. In unifying government on behalf of will,
    Wilson assumed that Darwinian science provided support for democratic
    government, as opposed to constitutional government. It is not surprising
    that any impediment to carrying out the will of the people is undemocratic.
    It is not the separation of powers (Newtonian), but the separation of politics
    and administration (Darwinian), that is compatible with the idea of progress
    in human affairs. Politics is the organic expression of the will (or spirit) of the
    people; administration is the technical, rational means by which it is made
    adaptable and put into practice.

5   Woodrow Wilson provides insight into the link between the new discipline
    of political science and its use in the transformation of the politics of the
    American regime. Wilson, with a PhD in political science from Johns
    Hopkins, helped undermine the natural right foundation of the American
    regime. He hoped to replace it with the newer Hegelian concept of the state.
    He understood that his adversary was the Constitution and the old political
    science of *The Federalist* that had created it.

6   Leo Strauss, *The Rebirth of Classical Political Rationalism*, ed. Thomas L. Pangle (Chicago: University of Chicago Press, 1989), 24–25.

7   G. F. W. Hegel, *Lectures on Natural Right and Political Science* (Heidelberg Lectures, 1817–1819), trans. M. Stewart and P. C. Hodgson (Berkeley: University of California Press, 1996), 242.

8   Ibid.

9   G. W. F. Hegel, *Introduction to the Philosophy of History*, trans. Leo Rauch (Indianapolis, IN: Hackett Press, 1988), 41.

10 Ibid.

11 Mary Parker Follett, *The New State: Group Organization the Solution of Popular Government* (New York: Longmans, Green & Co., 1918), 138.

12 August Comte, *Introduction to Positive Philosophy*, trans. Frederick Ferre (Indianapolis, IN: Library of Liberal Arts, 1970), 13–14.

13 As Comte noted: "All competent thinkers will agree with Bacon that there can be no real knowledge except that which rests upon observed facts. This fundamental maxim is evidently indisputable if it is applied as it ought to be, to the mature state of our intelligence. But, if we consider the origin of our knowledge, it is no less certain that the primitive human mind could not and, indeed, ought not to have thought in that way. For if, on the one hand, every positive theory must necessarily be founded upon observations, it is, on the other hand, no less true that, in order to observe, our mind has need of some theory or other. If in contemplating phenomena we did not immediately connect that with some principles, not only would it be impossible for us to combine these isolated observations and, therefore, to derive any profit from them, but we should even be entirely incapable of remembering the facts, which would for the most part remain unnoted by us." *Introduction to Positive Philosophy*, 5–6.

14 John Dewey, *Liberalism and Social Action* (Amherst, NY: Prometheus Books, 2000), 40–41.

15 Charles E. Merriam, *American Political Ideas: Studies in the Development of American Political Thought 1865–1917* (New York: The Macmillan Company, 1923), 371.

16 Lester Frank Ward, *The Psychic Factors of Civilization* (Boston: Ginn & Company, 1893), 30.

17 What is sometimes considered a distinctively American philosophy, pragmatism, nonetheless rests on the same theoretical foundation—that of philosophy of History and social evolution. In recognizing the importance of John Dewey's contribution to social thought, Charles Merriam noted: "pragmatism is a tentative philosophy of developing life. Its basis lies in the broad historical background of modern life, in the central place of evolution in the scheme of modern thought, in the social character of consciousness—'in short, it bears many of the resemblances of the general theory of things adapted to a democratic era.' In ethics its followers applied it to the evolutionary theory of morality, although they did not originate this point of view." *American Political Ideas: Studies in the Development of American Political Thought 1865–1917* (New York: The MacMillan Company, 1923), 424.

18 Merriam, *American Political Ideas*, 371.

19 Charles E. Merriam, *A History of American Political Theories* (New York: The Macmillan Company, 1910), 346.

20 Merriam, *A History of American Political Theories*, 332.

21 Ward, *The Psychic Factors of Civilization*, 304.

22 Charles A. Beard, "Politics," *Columbia University Lectures on Science, Philosophy and Art, 1907–1908* (New York: Columbia University Press, 1908).

23 Interestingly, the very first books on sociology written in the English language were defenses of slavery: Henry Hughes, *Treatise on Sociology, Theoretical and Practical* (1854), and George Fitzhugh, *Sociology for the South*. Both attempted to defend slavery using Comte's new science of sociology. See L. L. Bernard, "Henry Hughes, First American Sociologist," *Social Forces* 15, no. 2 (December 1936): 154–74.

24 At Johns Hopkins University, George Sylvester Morris referred to Hegel's *Philosophy of Right* "as representing the high-water mark...in the treatment of the philosophical conception of the state." "The Philosophy of the State and of History," in *Methods of Teaching History*, vol. 1, 2nd ed., ed. G. Stanley Hall (Boston: Ginn, Heath, & Co., 1885), 163. Morris was the teacher of Dewey and Wilson, and he had studied in Berlin. To those students who were not able to read German, he recommended Elisha Mulford's *The Nation*. In Heidelberg, Mulford, too, had come to appreciate the concept of the state as derived from Hegel.

25 Elisha Mulford, *The Nation: The Foundation of Civil Order and Political Life in the United States* (New York: Hurd & Houghton, 1870), 340.

26 Ibid., 382.

27 Quoted in Mark E. Neely Jr., "Romanticism, Nationalism, and the New Economics: Elisha Mulford and the Organic Theory of the State," *American Quarterly* 29, no. 4 (Autumn 1977): 421.

28 John W. Burgess, *Political Science and Comparative Constitutional Law*, vol. 1 (Boston: Ginn & Company, 1890), 67.

29 Ibid., 100.

30 Ibid., 58. In a similar vein, Woodrow Wilson, in his 1894 lecture on public law, thought it necessary to incorporate constitutionalism into the doctrine of the state. He noted: "[W]e have adopted the theory of the 'Constitutional State.' This involves an 'organic' conception of the nature of the State. Every State is the historical form of the organic common life of a particular people...(the) expression of a form of life higher than that of the individual: that common life which gives leave and opportunity to individual life, makes it possible and makes it full and complete." *The Papers of Woodrow Wilson*, Vol. 7: 1890–1892, ed. Arthur S. Link (Princeton: Princeton University Press), 13.

31 Frank J. Goodnow, "The Work of the American Political Science Association: Presidential Address by Frank J. Goodnow," *Proceedings of the American Political Science Association* 1 (1904): 37.

32 Westel Woodbury Willoughby, *An Examination of the Nature of the State: A Study in Political Philosophy*, and Godkin, both cited in Dennis J. Mahoney, "A Newer Science of Politics: *The Federalist* and American Political Science in the Progressive Era," in Charles R. Kesler, ed., *Saving the Revolution* (New York: The Free Press, 1987), 255.

33 Walter Lippmann, *Drift and Mastery* (New York: Mitchell Kennerley, 1914), 274–75.

34 American constitutionalism had made it possible to reconcile the "spirit of religion" and the "spirit of liberty." But such a reconciliation required the

separation of government and society, church and state. The acceptance of the idea of the rational state, on the other hand, required a new understanding of religion—one wholly secularized and democratized—that would be subordinated to the spirit of science. It required a new understanding of democracy, one in which the source of morality and legitimacy of the people is to be found in the evolving will of the intellectuals. The technical means to carry out that will is to be established in the bureaucratic apparatus of the administrative state. With the establishment of the modern research university, the expertise and method necessary to solve the problems of society could be generated. Science would be used in the service of compassion, or social welfare, thus uniting knowledge and power on behalf of humanity.

35 John Dewey, "Ethics and Physical Science," *Andover Review*, June 1887.

36 John Dewey, *The Ethics of Democracy* (Ann Arbor: University of Michigan, 1888), 28.

37 Ibid., 13–14.

38 Jesse Macy, one of the first presidents of the American Political Science Association, was typical of the early social scientists concerning the relationship of democracy, Christianity, and science. He noted: "The modern scientific spirit is simply the Christian spirit realized in a limited field of experience." The conjunction of science and religion, Macy argued, culminated in the view that scientific truth provided the foundation of modern democracy. "Science and democracy have come into the modern world at the same time. They are mutually related as cause and effect." Jesse Macy, *American Political Science Association Presidential Address*, 1916; *American Political Science Review* 11, no. 1 (February 1917).

39 Thus Herbert Croly, one of the most important Progressive intellectuals of the early twentieth century, insisted that "democracy must stand or fall on a platform of possible human perfectibility." This notion of perfectibility, derived from Rousseau, is attainable only when it becomes possible to reconcile the particular and the general will. Therefore, Croly, like Comte, measured the progress of man in terms of his willingness to serve his fellow man. "If it be true that democracy is based upon the assumption that every man shall serve his fellow-man, the organization of democracy should be gradually adapted to that assumption." Nonetheless, Croly was well aware that "the majority of men cannot be made disinterested for life by exhortation, by religious services, by any expenditure of subsidized works, or even by grave and manifest public need. They can be made permanently unselfish only by being helped to become disinterested in their individual purposes. . . . In the complete democracy a man must in some way be made to serve the nation in the very act of contributing to his own individual fulfillment. Not until his personal action is dictated by disinterested motives can there be any such harmony between private and public interests." Public duty and private interests can be reconciled in careers on behalf of service to the state and society. Herbert Croly, *The Promise of American Life* (Cambridge, MA: Harvard University Press, 1965), 418.

40 August Comte, *Catechism of Positivism*, trans. R. Congreve (London: Kegan Paul, 1852), 313.

41 See Gillis Harp, *Positivist Republic: Auguste Comte and the Reconstruction of American Liberalism, 1865–1920* (University Park: Pennsylvania State University Press, 1994).

42 George D. Herron, *The Christian Society* (Chicago: Fleming H. Revel, 1894), 32.

43 Not surprisingly, the great religious reawakening of the early twentieth century occurred wholly outside the established churches, many of which had accepted the authority of the positive philosophy. As Eldon Eisenach noted, "members of what later came to be called 'fundamentalist' churches were increasingly consigned to the cultural equivalent of resident alien status. But it was modernized evangelical theology and the new social sciences and not secular liberalism that drew up the expulsion orders." *The Lost Promise of Progressivism* (Lawrence: University Press of Kansas, 1994), 103.

44 When looking at the early Progressives, whether liberal and socialist like Henry Demarest Lloyd, Eugene Debs, and Lester Frank Ward, or laissez-faire conservatives such as William Graham Sumner and E. L. Godkin, they were in agreement in their opposition to the doctrine of natural right. Indeed, the status of natural right at this time is revealed in Merriam's description of Franklin H. Giddings as one of the few who attempted to uphold a theory of natural right. "Disclaiming any connection with the earlier forms of this theory, he understands by natural rights those which are natural in the scientific sense of the term," Merriam noted. "On this basis Giddings defines natural rights as 'socially necessary norms of right, enforced by natural selection in the sphere of social relations.'" *A History of American Political Theories*, 310–11. It is clear that by the time Giddings had written his book *Principles of Sociology* in 1896, the theoretical and political understanding of natural right had become completely unintelligible and therefore meaningless. Science and natural selection had come to dominate scholarship.

45 See footnote 23 concerning the first books written in the new discipline of sociology; they were written by Southerners in defense of slavery. After the Civil War, social scientists accepted race as a legitimate category for defending the inequality of blacks, but rejected slavery as an historical anachronism.

46 Merriam, *A History of American Political Theories*, 311–12.

47 Ibid., 312.

48 Croly, *The Promise of American Life*, 81.

49 Merriam, *A History of American Political Theories*, 297.

50 Ibid., 298.

51 Ibid., 298.

52 Ibid., 311–12.

53 Ibid., 312.

54 John William Burgess, *Reconstruction and the Constitution, 1866–1876* (New York: C. Scribner's Sons, 1902), viii–ix, 133.

55 Cited in Thomas F. Gossett, *Race: The History of an Idea in America* (New York: Oxford University Press, 1997), 284. Quotes are from James Ford Rhodes, *History of the United States from the Compromise of 1850 to the Final Restoration of Home Rule at the South in 1877*, 7 vols. (New York: Harper & Brothers, 1893, 1906).

56 W. A. Dunning, *Reconstruction: Political and Economic, 1865–1877* (New York: Harper & Row, 1907), 213.

57 Hannah Arendt, "Race-Thinking Before Racism" in *The Origins of Totalitarianism* (San Diego, CA: Harcourt, 1976), 159.

58 Leo Strauss, *Natural Right and History* (Chicago, University of Chicago Press, 1953), 7.

59 Ibid., 33.

60 Ibid., 7.

61 Leo Strauss, "Epilogue," in *Essays on the Scientific Study of Politics*, ed. Herbert
Storing (New York: Holt, Rinehart & Winston, 1962), 309.

62 Ibid. Strauss noted that "the Aristotelian distinction between theoretical and
practical sciences implies that human action has principles of its own which
are known independently of theoretical science (physics and metaphysics) and
therefore that the practical sciences do not depend on the theoretical sciences
or are not derivative from them. The principles of action are the natural ends
toward which man is by nature inclined and of which he has by nature some
awareness. This awareness is the necessary condition for his seeking and
finding appropriate means for his ends, or for his becoming practically wise
or prudent. Practical science, in contradistinction to practical wisdom itself,
sets forth coherently the principles of action and the general rules of prudence
('proverbial wisdom'). Practical science raises questions that are within
practical or political experience, or at any rate on the basis of such experience
reveal themselves to be the most important questions and that are not stated,
let alone answered, with sufficient clarity by practical wisdom itself. The sphere
governed by prudence is then in principle self-sufficient or closed."

63 Ibid., 310.

64 Leo Strauss, *On Tyranny*, ed. Victor Gourevitch and Michael S. Roth, cor. and
exp. ed. (Chicago: University of Chicago Press, 2013), 194.

65 Strauss, *Natural Right and History*, 314.

66 As Strauss noted, "One can say, and it is not misleading to say, that the Bible
and Greek philosophy agree in regard to what we may call, and we do call in
fact, morality. They agree, if I may say so, regarding the importance of morality;
regarding the content of morality, and regarding its ultimate insufficiency.
They differ as regards that *x* which supplements or completes morality, or,
which is only another way of putting it, they disagree as regards the basis of
morality." Quoted in "Progress or Return?" in *The Rebirth of Classical Political
Rationalism*, ed. Thomas L. Pangle (Chicago: University of Chicago Press,
1989), 246.

67 Ibid., 239.

68 Strauss, *Natural Right and History*, 29.

CHAPTER 14: WISDOM AND MODERATION: LEO STRAUSS'S ON TYRANNY;
MODERN THOUGHT AND ITS "UNMANLY CONTEMPT FOR POLITICS"

1 Presented at the Annual Meeting of the American Political Science
Association, Hilton Hotel, Chicago, Illinois, August 29, 2013.

2 Leo Strauss, *On Tyranny*, ed. Victor Gourevitch and Michael S. Roth, corrected
and expanded edition, including the Strauss-Kojève correspondence (Chicago:
University of Chicago Press, 2013), 22–23.

3 Leo Strauss, *Natural Right and History* (Chicago: University of Chicago Press,
1953), 161.

4 Leo Strauss, *Thoughts on Machiavelli* (Chicago: University of Chicago Press,
1968), 5.

5 Strauss, *On Tyranny*, 23.

6 Strauss, *Natural Right and History*, 31–32.

7 Ibid., 33.

8 Ibid., 32.

9 Ibid., 123–24.

10 Ibid., 141.

11 Strauss, *On Tyranny*, 194–95.

12 Ibid., 38.

13 Ibid., 27.

14 Strauss, *Natural Right and History*, 320.

15 Ibid., 320–21.

16 Leo Strauss, *Liberalism Ancient and Modern* (New York: Basic Books, 1968), 24.

17 Strauss, *Natural Right and History*, 318.

18 Ibid.

19 Strauss, *On Tyranny*, 207.

20 Ibid., 209.

21 Ibid., 210.

22 Ibid., 238.

23 Ibid., 211.

24 Ibid., 211–12.

25 Ibid., 212.

26 Kojève, to Strauss, September 19, 1950, 255.

27 Ibid., 209.

28 Strauss, *Natural Right and History*, 318.

CHAPTER 15: TRUMP AND THE FUTURE OF AMERICAN POLITICS

1 Ludwig von Mises, *Bureaucracy* (Indianapolis: Liberty Fund, 2007; originally published 1944), 101.

2 Walter Lippmann, *The Good Society* (New York: Little, Brown, 1937), ix.

3 Ibid., x.

4 Ibid., 380.

5 Ibid., x–xi.

6 Ibid., 374.

Index